ON MODERNISM

ON MODERNISM

The Prospects for Literature and Freedom

Louis Kampf

THE M.I.T. PRESS
Massachusetts Institute of Technology
Cambridge, Massachusetts, and London, England

To my parents

PREFACE

The critic's duty, William Empson has remarked, is to follow his nose. Surely one's own direction depends on one's sense of smell. The critical attitudes which control this book derive from a personal sense of current needs: not the needs of criticism, but those of life. Consequently I have felt little urge to quarrel with other critics; their apocalyptic interpretations of "the modern temper" (Why the definitive article?) I find not wrong, but irrelevant. The death of god, the rise of science, the appearance of mass culture — these clichés, though probably true enough, tell us little about the states of mind from which our feelings, thoughts, and actions proceed. Since my interests lie in the urgencies of the moment, I shall address myself to these states of mind.

Quotations are drawn, in all cases, not from the standard scholarly texts, but from editions readily available to the reader. Translations are used whenever available.

Finally, I have tried not to make this work an annotated bibliography. I refer to the scholarly and critical work of others only when it has strongly influenced my own thinking, or if I have directly borrowed a point. The hours one spends in a library should bear better fruit than a footnote.

Louis Kampf

Cambridge, Massachusetts
January 1967

CONTENTS

1

THE PERMANENCE OF MODERNISM

I DO NOT WISH TO DISCUSS the *nature* of modernism. What-ever the nature of the parent, we are all too sure of the diversity of its offspring. For if anything is to characterize our general sense of the present, it is surely the exhilaration, or depression, brought on by the dizzying variety of philoso-phies, social and political systems, and styles of art which constantly assault our intellects and feelings. I gladly leave the task of defining our age to some of our deeper philoso-phers, theologians, and social thinkers. What I should like to consider instead may not resolve our collective identity crisis, but it may help us locate the sources of some of our difficul-ties. Here is the question I shall pose: What elements in the past made possible the present diversity of artistic styles and the corresponding diversity of roles played by artists and in-tellectuals? I doubt whether an etiological determination will cure the disease; rather one's depression, or elation, about the current state of affairs is likely to increase the nearer we get to its source. Being modern, and naturally diseased, I cannot leave well enough alone; being an intellectual with some pride, I assume you will be only too happy to take the plunge with me.

For the official supervisors of our arts, one's favorable reaction to a happening is, I suppose, an index to one's modernity (or so it was twenty-four hours ago, in any case). I could begin with a theoretical dissertation on the nature of the happening, but since I have no clear understanding of its ontological status — whether it really exists as a genre — I shall have to concern myself with a single event, which may or may not be a happening. An account by a participant follows:

An enormous crowd. Loges, pit, balcony, chuck full. Deafening uproar of the "pastists" who wished to break up the concert at any price. For an hour the hipsters resisted passively. At the beginning of the fourth network of noise, an extraordinary thing happened: suddenly five hipsters — Boccioni, Carra, Amando Mazza, Piatti and I — were seen to come down from the stage. They crossed the orchestra and, in the full center of the circle, with punches, sticks, and walking-sticks attacked the pastists, drunk with stupidity and traditional rage. The battle lasted in the pit for half an hour, while Luigi Russolo imperturbably [sic] continued to direct his nineteen noisters on the stage.

Amazing accord of bloody faces and noisy discords, pellmell in an infernal hubbub. The battle over *Hernani* seems child's play in comparison with this mêlée.

All our riots hitherto had taken place in the streets, in the corridors of the theatres and after performances. For the first time the artists having played an hour on the stage were brusquely divided into two groups — one continuing to perform their art, while the other went down into the pit to attack a hostile and hissing public. Thus the escort of a caravan in the desert defends itself against the Touaregs. Thus the infantry, set out as sharpshooters, sometimes defends the construction of a military bridge.

Our knowledge of boxing and our enthusiasm for fighting enabled us to emerge from the struggle safe and sound, with two or three scratches. The pastists had *eleven wounded* who had to be taken to the first aid station.[1]

[1] Quoted in Nicolas Slonimsky, *Music Since 1900* (New York, 1938). Significantly, the "musicians" who took on the audience were plastic artists of some note. This account was pointed out to me by Arthur Berger, the benefit of whose discussions of music I have enjoyed for a number of years.

For the serious student of the arts, the real significance of this event is to be seen in the total obliteration — finally, after so many unsuccessful attempts — of any distinction between performer and audience, between stage and pit. As a result, the performance includes its own critical machinery: The artwork, the audience's reaction, and the performers' reaction to the audience's reaction are all fused into one grand democratic participatory action. Everybody gets into the act. It is enough to make Joan Littlewood green with envy.

The event just described might well be the latest Andy Warhol spectacular at the Museum of Modern Art, attended by a distinguished audience headed by Governor Rockefeller. The depressing truth is that the foregoing is an account written by F. T. Marinetti of a concert of futurist music which he and Luigi Russolo staged at the Teatro dal Verme in Milan on the 21st of April, 1914. I have only substituted the word "hipsters" for "futurists." The composition, entitled *4 networks of noises*, was performed by an orchestra of nineteen noise-instruments, and conducted by Russolo. If it were not for the seriousness of Marinetti's account one would obviously take the whole dreary business as a joke. Unfortunately, it all sounds too much like the politically inspired reaction to Luigi Nonno's opera *Intolleranza* at its premiere in Venice in 1961. Violence or total passivity, both inspired by motives irrelevant to the work of art itself, are the only conceivable reactions. No real criticism — resulting in *judgments* — seems at all possible; and since it seems impossible, there is of course no end to it. For by this time we have had collegiate conferences on the theory and practice of happenings, critical articles and books, graduate seminars, perhaps even a White House conference — all on happenings. Some future historian might describe the situation as follows: "A cloud of critics, of compilers, of commentators, darkened the face of learning, and the decline of genius was soon followed by the corruption of taste." [2] We shall probably have the good fortune to escape having a great ironist write our history and put us in our place, but when Gibbon made this comment in discussing the ill health of the arts under Hadrian and the Antonines, he meant it, for one thing, to be relevant to his own times. One need only think of the accomplishments of the goddess Dulness in Pope's *Dunciad* — "Thy hand, great Anarch! lets the curtain fall;/ And universal Darkness buries All." — to get a sense of how inevitable the parallel to the decline of Rome seemed to a humanist in the eighteenth century; how inevitable the darkness brought on by artistic disorder, endless critical tattle, and irrelevant scholarship. In turn, since we are the somewhat ungrateful heirs of the Enlightenment, Gibbon's comment applies to us. Who would argue about the fact that most of our contemporaries interested in the arts seem more concerned with the critical debates surrounding — occasionally swallowing — artistic events rather than the events themselves?

One of the principal reasons for the dominance of criticism, both now and during the years of Pope's and Gibbon's careers, is the disintegration of any firm notion of artistic form. Since this problem initially became unavoidable during the eighteenth century, one can readily understand why Gibbon's evaluation should seem so relevant for our own time. As Dr. Johnson did not know how to judge "The Comedy of Romance" (novel, to us), we do not know how to judge a happening. Often enough, neither the artist nor the spectator knows with any reasonable degree of certainty just what the shape of a thing is or what emotions it is trying

---

[2] Edward Gibbon, *The Decline and Fall of the Roman Empire*, Modern Library Edition (New York, n.d.). All quotations of Gibbon are from this volume.

to elicit. Since the object is, by definition, entirely original, just what are its standards and objectives? As a result, the object or event becomes an occasion for a peculiar, and in the event necessary, kind of critical activity: We generally do not discuss the value of the thing, but what it *is* and how we perceive it. How does one make a judgment of a happening without first considering what the foundations of that judgment are? Or first deciding whether the happening has really happened? Much the same situation obtains for many literary works which, unlike a happening, demand to be taken seriously. People in the past may have been puzzled by the artistic status of a novel, or the prose-poem, or Gide's *Journals,* but they were reasonably sure that they were perceiving, and consequently reacting to, a work of art. Alas, the very existence of their certainty, when coupled with the objective uncertainty of the literary genres involved, made a critical evaluation of one's response an almost unavoidable part of the experience. The experience of an odd literary form remains puzzling since we do not know precisely where to locate its source. As a result, we ask questions about it. The classical literary forms — epic, lyric, tragedy, and so forth — elicit their appropriate reactions, and we, or rather people in the past, have had few problems about the foundations of those reactions: In one way or another, it is assumed, they are located in the nature of the form, that is to say, in its capacity to elicit a specific emotional response — pity or fear in the case of tragedy, for example. Now the possibility of this classical notion — and it has become largely impossible for us — depends on some basic assumptions about the nature of knowledge. Can we assume, and readily distinguish, the existence of precise mental categories? Is there any clear correspondence between our mental categories and the structure of the external world? Can we readily perceive this correspondence and therefore have confidence in our judgments of the external world? I shall discuss the matter in greater detail further on, but for the moment it should be fairly clear that if we are to react to classical genres in an unproblematic way, the answer to each of these questions must be, Yes. Better yet, we should never be confronted with the necessity of asking ourselves these questions. For once they arise, the critical evaluation of our reactions follows, only to be followed by the attempt to discover the nature of what one has reacted to. The act of esthetic perception has turned into criticism, but a criticism almost entirely concerned with defining the object and our perception of it: in short, epistemology.

That the problem of knowledge has become involved in both the creation and appreciation of works of art — in a film like *Last Year In Marienbad* it seems to be the only subject matter — need not surprise us. There is hardly an area of knowledge which has not been significantly affected by a similar development over the past few centuries. I would hardly be exaggerating if I claimed that the very existence of our sciences and arts in their present shape is predicated on the problem of knowledge having become a problem. At least since Galileo, for example, physicists have found it necessary to be concerned with the theory of knowledge: a concern which reflects much more than the human penchant for idle philosophical speculation. Ernst Cassirer has put it this way: "It is always highly significant when a science, instead of directly and resolutely seeking its object, suddenly deserts this 'natural' attitude for another; when it feels compelled to inquire into the nature of its object and into its own concept, and into the very possibility of the science itself. At such turning points in research it is clear that reflection gains a wholly different status and must be conceded a much more important role in the upbuilding of science." [3] Reflections of an epistemological sort become an integral part of the science, just as the meditations on the possibility of artistic form become part of — no, create — Proust's great work.[4] Cassirer continues: "Everyone has to decide them [questions about the possibility of science] independently, and his general conclusions almost always bear the stamp of his own scientific principles as well as that of his concrete research." And just so in the arts: As Sterne's reflections on the possibility of fiction become part of the fabric of *Tristram Shandy*, the work becomes increasingly — to the point of idiosyncracy — an illustration of the author's artistic principles, rather than proceeding with the concrete business of telling a story. We have seen the more unpleasant artistic consequences of this situation in the narcissistic exhibition of the futurist noisters. In the sciences, we need go no further than the theoretical confusion of current particle physics.

All this implies, it seems to me, that modernism is, and has been for some years, a permanent state of mind. When we reflect on the foundations of the solutions to our problems, those problems renew themselves by means of the very solutions we have offered: speculations about reflection symmetry, which forms the basis of Eugene Wigner's parity principle, have led to the fall of parity; and with the fall of parity Wigner and other physicists have become uneasy about symmetry itself; [5] and was it not bourgeois drama's singular success in renewing the possibility of passion in the

[3] Ernst Cassirer, *The Problem of Knowledge: Philosophy, Science, and History Since Hegel*, trans. W. H. Waglam and C. W. Hendel (New Haven, 1950).

[4] Proust's essay on the relation of literature to biography, posthumously published as *Contre Sainte Beuve*, became part of the texture of *Remembrance of Things Past*.

[5] See Wigner's "Violations of Symmetry in Physics," *Scientific American*, Vol. 213 (1965).

theater which eventually led to its emotive sterility? As our arts come to reflect on themselves more and more, their real subject seems to be the theory of their own composition, and the concern for the nature of their own reality becomes quite obsessive. And with each new theory about reality, we need a new art. Another aspect of this development can be seen in the use our arts make of antiquity. For us, there is no such thing as classicism; in spite of our claims, we do not really go back to the Greeks or Romans. A medieval poet like Chaucer readily absorbed that part of the classical heritage available to him, and did so with very little self-consciousness. But surely this sort of thing has hardly been possible since the Middle Ages, nor was it quite possible, even then, for so methodologically self-conscious a poet as Dante. To use Lessing's insight about Winckelmann, if our work is not to be smothered by the mechanical copying of some ideal notion of classical form, we shall all have to be self-conscious *neo*classicists.[6] In this particular guise, we shall at least have the opportunity of being Racine rather than Garnier, Pope rather than Cowley. Each of us must shape the classics, if we are to use them at all, to the exigencies of our own notions about reality. This might give them life; Winckelmann's progeny, on the other hand, are typified by the brilliantly chiseled but cold and lifeless stone of Canova. Thus neoclassicism, in order to remain artistically viable, must always look for fresh ways of using the classical tradition, must always be new, and therefore modern.

That we are involved in a continuous process of destroying — rather than absorbing — the past is hardly news; nor is the fact that critical activity, whether literary, philosophical, or political, has played a prominent part in this

---

[6] On this point, I have found E. H. Gombrich's *Lessing, Proceedings of the British Academy*, XLIII (London, 1957), most helpful.

process. "Every day socialists are blamed for being good only at criticism, at the denunciation of evil, at denial." [7] But, as Alexander Herzen continues:

> Such a renunciation [of political and religious institutions] is not the caprice of a diseased imagination, not the cry of an individual insulted by society, but the death sentence of this society, the premonition of the end, the realization of the disease dragging the decrepit world to its doom and to resurrection in other forms. The contemporary state will fall before the protest of socialism, its strength is spent, what it could give it has given. Now it is living on its own flesh and blood, it is incapable of developing any further or of arresting development. It has no more to say or do and so it has concentrated all its energy on conservatism, on defence of its position.

Herzen has told us that the state — and think of the artistic parallels — will fall because it has become irrelevant to the needs of society, and has consequently given rise to the criticism voiced by socialism. Its own reaction — like the reaction of doctrinaire classicists in the arts — is to forego criticism and conserve its moribund forms. The alternate chosen by the socialist — or perhaps the modernist, or even neo-classicist — would be to use criticism in order to metamorphose the old into new forms, well knowing, one hopes, that this would involve a condition of permanent revolution, that is to say, the condition of modernism. It seems that T. S. Eliot's association of royalism, Anglicanism, and classicism was not as arbitrary as it once appeared.

Now the fact that Herzen expressed these sentiments about the events of 1848 should not lead us to the amused and condescending assumption that both he and some of our more apocalyptic contemporaries are being a bit silly. Who is to take seriously judgments which have been endlessly re-

---

[7] Alexander Herzen, *From the Other Shore* and *The Russian People and Socialism*, no trans. given (Cleveland and New York, 1963).

peated for more than a hundred years? Yet both Herzen and our contemporary critics are right. For, as we have seen, criticism and the destruction of foundations has become a permanent and logical part of our historical development. I do not mean this in the Hegelian sense of some transcendent spirit revealing itself in reason reflecting on reason. The matter is much simpler and less metaphysically slippery than that. Since a high degree of epistemological self-consciousness has become an unavoidable part of our intellectual life, we naturally — to repeat the point — have made reflection on foundations a large part of our physical and social sciences, not to speak of our arts. Consequently, change is often the result of conscious human activity based on logical reflection, rather than a random process. Furthermore, it is permanent: but its permanence should not lead us to the conclusion that it necessarily implies a general state of disorder — although this is certainly a possibility. The changes are, after all, based on the logic of each situation. Goethe, I believe, has something important to tell us on the subject:

> If we see at the outset the regularity of nature we are apt to think that it is necessarily so, and was so ordained from the very first, and hence that it is something fixed and static. But if we meet first with the varieties, the deformities, the monstrous misshapes, we realize that although the law is constant and eternal it is also living; that organisms can transform themselves into misshapen things not in defiance of the law, but in conformity with it, while at the same time, as if curbed with a bridle, they are forced to acknowledge its inevitable dominion.[8]

Goethe's reflections on botany's underlying theory of knowledge were brought on by this puzzlement and concern over the philosophical validity of Linnaeus' nonhistorical taxonomic approach. He sees that biological change has a logic which is to be discovered in *immanent* — rather than tran-

[8] Quoted by Cassirer.

scendent — laws. Goethe's notions and concerns had to be taken up by other workers in the field to enable biology to have an historical development. As long as it remained a static set of categories which were to be industriously filled out by future generations of researchers, it was clearly incapable of changing. But once the process of change is brought on by epistemological reflection, the history of biology develops according to the logic of its own problems. This sort of thing — and I do not wish to strain the parallel — has happened in the history of modern artistic forms. Once we have questioned the foundations of the classical notion of static and permanent literary categories, those categories will develop, or disappear, according to the logic of the questions we have asked about them. As a result, the history of these forms, including the monstrosities like happenings, should be, in some sense, lawful. Thus the development of modernism is to be understood in terms of the questions we have asked about the foundations of knowledge. For instance, we shall be able to understand how external forces affect modernism's changing forms only if we are reasonably clear on the logic which created the possibilities for change.

The artist's awareness that the history of his art has a logic has brought about an unusual, and problematic, attitude toward that history. He is historical, yet he feels no sense of progressive development in his particular art; there is no feeling of event following event, form fusing into form, with the artist's own work emerging at the end. Rather than seeing the past as a number of events developing in time, the tendency is to see those events concatenated in space. The work of most contemporary artists does not *develop* from the art of the past, since they are likely to have looked at history as a totality and from studying the logic of that totality picked whatever was necessary for their own artistic problems. This situation holds not only for our contemporaries, for it applies equally to the art, whether revolutionary or academic, of the nineteenth century. Most nineteenth-century artists look to the past, but they feel no sense of development from their immediate predecessors: they may look to Rembrandt, but they are not likely to look to Reynolds. A painter like Rubens, on the other hand, though highly original, draws on the work of both the Northern and Southern traditions which immediately preceded him. He does this as a matter of course, and his ability to do so allows him to combine Baroque theorizing about space with his own realistic tradition, thereby producing landscape which has the drama but lacks the excessive artifice of Baroque. And Rubens does so in a vigorous and unproblematic fashion. Compare this to the many architectural revivals which were a commonplace of the nineteenth century: Sir Charles Barry's neo-Renaissance Reform Club (1837) in London, for example, or Charles Garnier's neo-Baroque Opera (1861–1874) in Paris. Or consider Cézanne's comment on Émile Bernard: "When he draws he produces only old stuff, which suggests his dreaming about art and what he has seen in museums. . . . Even more, it reveals that philosophizing spirit which comes to him from too great a knowledge of the old masters whom he admires." [9] It is, of course, the museum which has quite literally corralled history inside a space and thereby made the notion of development in the fine arts an anomaly. And so with literature. Wordsworth's thematic and formal concerns emerge from the eighteenth-century conventions which he inherited; indeed, the originality of Wordsworth's poems in *Lyrical Ballads* is based on his attempt to deal with

[9] Quoted by Lionello Venturi in "Cézanne," *Encyclopedia of World Art* (New York, Toronto, London, 1960). I owe my knowledge of this quotation to Joseph Ablow, on whose vast and sensitive knowledge of the fine arts I have drawn throughout this work.

problems in poetics created by work like that of Gray and Cowper. The situation is much different for the next generation of Romantics. Shelley and Keats may be dealing with thematic material which descends directly from Wordsworth and Coleridge, but surely they rifle almost the entire history of poetry, including the Greeks, Dante, Spenser, and Milton, to discover the forms which will best answer their demands. To return to our own times, think of Pound and Eliot flattening history into one enormous two-dimensional space, a space whose logical properties are fixed by the necessities of their poetic needs.

To be aware of history is to be aware of its destructiveness. For those who wish to be rid of the past, who see it as a prison built by institutions and modes of feeling which have outlived their usefulness, two kinds of reaction are possible. One of these is typified by the remarks of Herzen I quoted earlier. This attitude begins with an awareness of the human suffering involved in the uprooting of traditional ways, yet it does not allow itself the narcissism of despair or nostalgia. In the destruction of the past, it sees the possibilities of the future; in the death of institutions, the possible transformation of human life itself. As Herzen said, the job of a politically aware human being in this situation is to criticize. If the criticism is to lead beyond self-indulgence, it must of course rest upon a set of humane values: not some dogmatic assertion about the nature of life in the future, but rather some fairly simple assumptions about what really matters in being human. Thus for Herzen, as we shall see later, even though there may be apparent changes in political direction, the goal of transforming the destructiveness of change into humane, and unsettled, possibilities always remains the same. If these humane values are missing, the alternative is bound to be a spiteful joy, a delight in destruction. In the arts, this reaction is transformed into an esthetic which can give birth to violent celebrations of the coming apocalypse: The esthetic of the action painter or pop artist simply constitutes a gloating destruction of the past, a destruction whose purpose is to create instant art history. Now this estheticizing of social and personal destructiveness is, it seems to me, the sole objective of a happening. Reflect on the following events which occurred at some recent "musical" performances: a cellist diving into a tank of water; a violinist breaking a rare violin; recording tape wound around members of the audience — but why go on? If it were all done with the energetic joy of Harpo Marx, we could join in the fun of jeering at what is pompous and self-important in music and in social habit. But in the presence of these nasty children we sit in terror, wondering whether anything in us has really given birth to all this, or whether our social instincts, our very sense of society, can sustain this kind of onslaught. For a happening, being a public act, is just as much a political event as Herzen's statement on the relevance of socialism. And since it seems to be taken seriously by many of our academies and critical organs, it is a political — *not an esthetic* — event to be reckoned with.

Superficially, Jack Gelber's play, *The Connection*, seems to be in league with the motives underlying happenings: It is destructive of dramatic form, institutions, social conventions, and psychological wholeness. Seen only in terms of its objective contents — without referring to the theatrical effect on the audience — the play, depressingly, seems to offer no way out of its suffocating self-destructiveness. But if we see the performance in this way, as I shall attempt to show, it will be our own doing, not the play's; the disease will be ours, not the author's. Even though *The Connection* seems to be completely restricted to its own realm and the world of politics is utterly irrelevant to its characters, the play's effect constitutes more of a political act than that of most plays which are self-consciously political. In this way it turns its apparent destructiveness to a subtle, and personally profound, social use. In attempting to do this, this theatrical event can serve, for the moment, as a paradigm for modernism in general, for both its problems and their possible resolutions.

As one enters the loft in which *The Connection* was first produced, a seedy looking group of men is aimlessly lounging or lying or walking around a stagelike platform at the front. They seem annoyed by our presence, and since we are made to feel like intruders, the momentary impulse is simply to leave. Perhaps, one feels, this is not a theater after all; somehow one has come to the wrong place. A neatly dressed and well-groomed man walks officiously to the platform or stage and manages to tell us, in spite of the many interruptions by the men lounging around, that we are about to see a play dealing with the problem of drug addiction. The men on the stage turn out to be real addicts who have been hired to act in the play. They are to portray — surprisingly — addicts. The playwright has sketched out their roles and has provided them with a skeletal plot. But the "play" is really a curious mixture of invented situation and of reality, for these junkies have come to the theater because they have been promised heroin as a reward; the plot is to just wait until the connection brings the stuff; the stage action is to consist of each "character" presenting to the audience a brief disquisition on his addiction. What we are to see, in short, is naturalistic documentary put inside the frame of an artificial experimental (to use Zola's term) situation. For the sake of the audience's enlightenment, the junkies, like rats pushing a lever in expectation of a food pellet, will go through their paces stimulated by the reward of heroin at the end of the act.

[17]

The action proceeds: We — both characters and audience — wait for the connection; there is jazz to be listened to; some talk; a few people arrive; but, on the whole, we wait — who knows for what?

If one stops to reflect on the formal elements of the play, the only conclusion to be drawn is that all form has disappeared. The whole performance gives one the sense of a hesitating and uncertain improvisation, and there is a total absence of what one might think of as traditional literary style. This is best illustrated by the fact that the playwright loses control over his actors:

JAYBIRD: *(the playwright)* You cats are actors?
COWBOY: *(the connection)* I'm not acting. You should have thought about that when you hired us.
JAYBIRD: I'm not angry. Just amused. All you do is talk, talk, talk. Is there no end to this babbling? This part was to be blood and guts drama. It's not for me that I plead with you. Think of the audience.[10]

But the difficulty lies precisely in the presence of the audience. As each junkie does his turn, addressing us with his personal sketch, the front he has put on for the audience disappears, and his real personality comes to the fore — perhaps for only a moment. The awareness of his indiscretion, though, leads the character to pull back, to deny that what has just occurred has any reality. Take, for example, the following exchange between the playwright, the connection, and the audience:

JAYBIRD: I do know that there isn't any hero in this play. I wrote a play with four heroes. Didn't I explain that part? You are all heroes. I mean in the theatrical sense. Cowboy, can't you act like a hero? It's the basis of Western drama, you know. Can't you make an heroic speech? You have not been upstaging it, at all.

[10] All quotations from the play are from *The Connection* (New York, London, 1960).

. . . Our hero. Cowboy, you can do for the show, Cowboy. We're all together. Say something.

COWBOY: It's too much risk going out and scoring every night. I mean I'm followed every night and I have to scheme a way of getting back here. I'm tired. Man, I've been moving my whole life. You think I enjoy leaving love behind? I haven't anything to say. Is that what you wanted, Author?

Whatever private sense of order Cowboy may have is, of course, dislocated by the playwright directing his speech and actions at the audience: The character tailors his reality to the exigencies of his arranged performance, and so he lapses from role into role — from the role he plays in life to the roles he plays for the audience, the playwright, and the other actors. In turn, our experience becomes badly disordered. The traditional drama's main task is to order experience, to make sense of the events taking place on the stage and thereby leave the audience with an awareness of life's orderliness, whether that order be comic or tragic. *The Connection*, instead, leaves us bewildered about the nature of order itself. What are we to make of the characters' inability to get off the stage, to conclude a live situation — or a dramatic one — logically? The following exchange takes place after one of the junkies has almost died onstage of an overdose of heroin:

JAYBIRD: I'm sick. We've lost it. We've lost it.

JIM: (*the producer*) What have we lost?

JAYBIRD: The end, you fool. The end.

JIM: We'll all die. That's the great idea for you. We just die.

SOLLY: (*one of the addicts*) Don't be silly. I can't. I'm out of it.

JIM: That's not the point. How do you propose to get off the stage logically? Ah, you see. Shakespeare, tragedy, that sort of thing has been making it for a long time. This is a time-tested formula. What more can you ask? I'll die too. Don't think I'm not willing to die.

[19]

> If it will bring in the revenue. I'll die of exhaustion
> carrying you off. You see? Perfect plot, eh, Jaybird.

The real events taking place on the stage have developed a structure separate from the one intended for the play. As a result, the action seems to have no underlying form which we can abstract and from which we can generalize about dramatic form. No doubt in spite of ourselves, because of the nagging sense of disorder we feel, we are forced to reflect not only on the nature of dramatic form but on the reality of what we have seen, on the relationship of the forms of life to the forms of art. Or are there no forms, after all? Has the whole matter of structures — of rational connections — become irrelevant for us? I shall pose this question again after a brief, and necessary, digression.

Whatever our doubts about *The Connection*'s right to be called a play, whatever our confusions, there can be no doubt about its emotional impact. No one who has ever experienced a performance of the play could conceivably question the reality of the event. It takes one over with a fierce and unrelenting vengeance. The first time I attended a performance, one of the characters pursued me into the men's room itself in order to beg for a handout. I had no doubt that I would be approached by a peddler any moment. Yet, in spite of this emotional power, the play has no permanence. Its strength lies precisely in its exploitation of momentary expressive effects. It can be read with some benefit, but the reading will carry little conviction; nor will a second viewing have anything like the effect of the first. Like life, which the event pretends to be, it cannot be repeated. But if there is this naturalistic documentary pretense, with its usual consequence of *artistic* impermanence, can we talk of the play's emotional impact in terms of naturalistic drama? Most traditional drama — and, for the moment, let us include the major plays of the Western tradition from Aeschylus to the appearance of Ibsen in that category — takes as its chief concern the systems of belief underlying its characters' actions. Its procedure is to examine either the characters or the values or both. The sources of these beliefs may be god, some transcendental ethic, or society. Whatever the source, traditional drama's task is to reconcile the spectator, emotionally and, perhaps, rationally, to the system of belief it has explored. Something of this sort, I believe, is generally implied by the somewhat difficult, and I think best discarded, notion of catharsis. If a play accomplishes this, it has performed a political act, for to reconcile the individual to the given system of belief is, of course, to reconcile him to his society and to an acceptance of the status quo. There are important exceptions to this in the tradition, like *King Lear:* But surely that we think of Shakespeare's play as being modern should help to make my point. Naturalist drama, on the other hand — and here I mean most plays in the tradition of Ibsen — takes as its chief concern the exploration of society. The analysis of character is used for the analysis of society. If the play's impact has convinced the spectator of the correctness and justice of the analysis, he should leave the theater convinced of the necessity for social, and perhaps political, change, and ready to act toward the implementation of this change. The politics of naturalist drama is against the status quo; it is socialist, or at the least, reformist.

The Connection, in spite of its pretense at documentary technique, makes an almost complete break with the emotional and political objectives of naturalism. In a naturalisic play, we accept the illusion created on the stage and take it for reality: Once we assume that the stage is a room with one wall missing, for instance, and that the players do not know they are being watched, we are likely to accept almost anything, as long as it maintains a decent level of verisimilitude. But in *The Connection*, we are unsure, since the play won't allow us to make the initial pretense. The person sitting next to a spectator might be an actor — or is he? And just how many people on the stage are actors? What is one to make of the loft the play was performed in? So much of the naturalistic illusion depends, after all, on one's sense of being in a theater, of watching a performance — albeit one pretending to be reality. The illusion is dissolved yet again by the playwright's manipulation of his characters in sight of the audience. Thus our realistic awareness of the playwright's attempt at forcing the characters into preconceived roles undercuts the possibilities of the naturalistic illusion. But our doubts about the characters, whether they are actors or actual junkies, create dramatic possibilities impossible for naturalism. At this point, allow me to remind you of Diderot's paradox of the actor: that to convey the illusion of reality the actor should cultivate artificial methods. He must not become the character he is portraying: *"S'il est lui quand il joue, comment cessera-t-il d'être lui?"* [11] In *The Connection*, the actors, because they are addicts, cannot maintain the artifice of role-playing; their extradramatic needs keep breaking through, and, as we have seen, take over the play. Reality keeps rudely displacing the illusionistic performance: It is method-acting with a vengeance. If it is real people and real emotions the playwright is toying with, his situation becomes anomalous, even dangerous, for he will be peeking in on reality, rather than creating a play. Indeed, the characters accuse him of — and hate him for — voyeurism.[12]

---

[11] *Oeuvres*, Bibliothèque de la Pléiade, ed. André Billy (Paris, 1951).
[12] I owe this insight to Robert Brustein's "Junk and Jazz," in his *Seasons of Discontent* (New York, 1965).

COWBOY: Sit down, Mother. Damn it! You can't find anything out about anything by flirting with people. What do you think we live in, a freak show?

And it is not only the playwright who stands accused but also we, the audience. The play is really a lengthy accusation addressed at the spectator's callous fascination with, and condescension to, the lower depths. If this is the case, the performance has turned from the problems of the stage (the documentary about addicts), from the problem of society, to the problems of the audience. Now plays have always done this sort of thing in some manner: The actions of Oedipus or Hamlet or Tartuffe should, if they are to perform their proper dramatic function, lead members of the audience to a consideration of themselves; and so with Sophocles, Shakespeare, and Molière who, I assume, used, peeked in on, and manipulated characters in order to explore their own personal concerns. One difference between the old and the new is that in traditional drama both audience and playwright generally did these things inside a context of public, more or less shared, beliefs and assumptions about life and art, thereby keeping the experience from being entirely private. The important difference about *The Connection* is that we, and the playwright, are privately attacked. The latter, in fact, gets hooked and begins to experience — he does not know what:

JAYBIRD: I don't know . . . I don't know what's happening to me.

And the audience, though it has not taken heroin, is hooked even worse — or perhaps, better. For we turn on ourselves, not society. The play demands that we transform *ourselves* with more than a small dose of passion. If we are to make connections with the world outside ourselves — with human beings who seem utterly strange, with society itself, which might seem even stranger — must we not transform ourselves first? Must we not be hooked? Consider the following statements taken from a somewhat melodramatic, though moving, interview given by Judith Malina, who directed *The Connection*'s original production, and her husband, Julian Beck, who took care of its design. The interview was given in Munich, where the couple had taken their dramatic company, The Living Theater, after it had been hounded out of the United States by the Treasury Department. Beck, on his company's purpose:

> To break down the walls — and to stress the sanctity of life. . . . We never wanted to make anything that people "liked" or that people "agreed with." The things that people have always liked, well, we're not so sure about them. . . . Some say, "We're not ready for it." They say that we can't do away with police, armies, wars. That we can't do what we want. I say we can — and we can do it now.

Miss Malina, on the same subject as her husband:

> We want to change people. We're not going to cozzen them into believing that the situation they're in is nice and pretty and good, and that they should stay there. . . . We want people to see who they are — and change! We want to help people free themselves of going to a job they hate. Of hating life. . . . I demand of each man everything! I want total love. I want no governments. I want no armies, no police, no warfare. I want no money. I want love as our standard! [13]

These words should pacify whatever doubts one might have about *The Connection*'s attitude to destruction, for they are another version of Herzen's statement which I quoted earlier, a version of the anarchist attitude — rather than socialist or reformist — to society and institutions. The work of the past is to be destroyed, but this is only to break out of the

[13] Quoted from an interview printed in *The New York Times*, Entertainment Section (November 7, 1965).

past's cage, a prelude for the possibility of building the future on the basis of a human emotion which is private and real, which is grounded in the actuality of human contact. And in spite of the Becks' seeming naïveté, their production of *The Connection* made this human contact a dramatic actuality.

One of the consequences of this procedure is that the notion of literary form becomes almost entirely irrelevant. Another traditional notion which is necessarily discarded is the business of *imitating* reality, since the reality which matters is created in the individual spectator's relationship with the play. Rather than have us empathize with its characters, the play draws us into — makes us a part of — its action, and attempts to coerce us into a perhaps uncomfortable union. If this union should obtain, it would dissolve the nagging critical and epistemological concerns which were part of our initial reaction to the performance, and would thus succeed in at least partially destroying the historical necessity for criticism which I discussed earlier. The spectator's connection is, after all, with reality, of which he forms a significant part; it is not as if he were watching a work of art. *The Connection's* lack of symbolic texture is intended to keep us away from the formal assumptions of literature, to keep us from reacting to a work of art.

Odd things happen to our esthetic reactions, as a result. If we are sophisticated spectators, having a decent knowledge of the tradition and some measure of intelligence, we generally perceive a work of art while staying outside its frame. In a play — though a poem, story, painting, or piece of sculpture will do — we connect with events inside the frame by making them reflect on ourselves. If the play has the capacity to do this, we believe in its reality, and we return to the frame to make judgments about the events and people in it

— this in spite, probably because, of our knowledge that the incidents have been invented. On the other hand, if the play does not elicit something akin to this reaction, its contents are likely to seem all too unreal. The unsophisticated spectator — like those, to take extreme cases, in *The Knight of the Burning Pestle,* or the occasional lady who pummels one of the characters on stage because he has mistreated his stage mother — does not make the play reflect on himself. As a result, if he is to connect with events in the play, the pretense of reality is not enough for him. Being a clod, he takes the playwright's creation for reality, and proceeds to break the frame itself. Consequently, the work of art — the very concept of art itself — has been destroyed, and both the poor actor and the playwright are left unprotected by their frame. Let me return to our sophisticated spectator, for the moment, in order to understand another aspect of this procedure. When he feels like relaxing for an evening, he might go to watch a melodrama. He will be absorbed by the action on the stage; in fact, he is likely to say that the play has taken him outside himself. Melodrama — or anything like it — in spite of its capacity to absorb us, the sophisticates, does not lead us to reflect on ourselves. And so we never connect with the frame at all: The experience has not really been esthetic. Now *The Connection* and, in different ways, the plays of Pirandello and Brecht, will not allow us to react in accordance to this traditional procedure.[14] Furthermore, the very existence of these modern plays, even though they constitute an obvious development from naturalistic theater's concern over reality, makes our appropriate experience of older drama problematic. Our dramatic rules and our ways

[14] Some of the foregoing remarks derive from discussions with Norman N. Holland concerning his forthcoming work, *The Dynamics of Literary Response.* I am not at all sure whether Mr. Holland would agree with any of them.

of reacting to the stage are not permanent categories, nor do they remain unaffected by new dramatic procedures. Unlike some scholars who would like us to react to Ibsen as Ibsen's contemporaries did and to Shakespeare as Shakespeare's, we all know this, and our — and the artist's — knowledge of impermanence is typical of the modern arts. We are all uncertain about our artistic frames: The artist can exploit this and create something as profoundly moving and morally significant as *The Connection*, or he can fall victim to it and unloose an event as empty and nasty as a happening.

I have tried to show that *The Connection's* real subject is the matter of making connections; to make them even at the price of obliterating the divisions, or frames, which create, and allow the continued existence of, our artistic categories. What are the connections to be made? Not only for this play but for modernism in general, as we shall see.

A. There are the attempts of the pathetically isolated characters to connect to the world outside the junkies' pad; to connect to the daytime world of social institutions from their night world of private relationships. For the characters this is to be accomplished only through heroin, whether their desire leads to the connection or to the police. As the actors are told by Jim, the producer: "Our other actors are off in the real world procuring heroin." "Actors?" protests one of the characters, "All right, junkies," answers Jim.

B. There is the matter of connecting to oneself; or simply connecting all the apparently random events which are our lives, and deriving from them, or seeing at their core, something which relates those events, and gives us our sense of who we are. We are told by Solly, one of the characters: "The man is you. You are the man. You are your own connection. It starts and stops here."

C. Is there a central, all-encompassing authority we all

connect to? Do things hang together because there is some central force, some principle which relates them in systematic fashion? The characters discuss whether there is, in fact, an international dope ring. If there is, one of the characters tells us, "then somebody must be the head of it."

D. The play touches on the connection of the language we use to the concepts we are attempting to express and use for the sake of making judgments. Gelber here employs the hipster's language, especially its richness of puns expressing opposite moral evaluations. The junkie's word for the greatest good, heroin, is "shit." On the other hand, the word still carries all its usual unpleasant connotations.

E. The dramatic problem of connecting to the audience constitutes an attempt to make the spectator break out of his private reality, to prevent him from making the world his own dream. The characters in *The Connection* spend most of the play trying to connect with someone — including the audience — outside themselves. Most importantly, since the attempt assumes a reality outside our senses, this poses the question of what our reality is, how we know it, and how we create it. If, indeed, we create it, do we create anything which goes beyond our own biological and psychic needs?

To erupt into reality, and thereby create our connections, becomes the task of the work of art. It sounds somewhat less modest than the traditional imitation of reality to delight and teach. Of course, numberless works of the past have dealt with the problem of reality. *The Connection*, rather than dealing with the problem, attempts to enact it. This puts an almost unbearable burden on the work of art, for to enact reality is a permanent task: No human act, unlike an abstract literary form, can ever pretend to finality. Instead of using the frame which tradition has established, of exploiting the state of mind and knowledge we bring to a work of art, the work of art must destroy these, and somehow mold us into the capacity for perceiving its own method — or perceiving just what it *is*. This task often demands a radical shift in form, or an equally radical way of using the old forms. For we now expect the work of art — and here lies both its modernity and that modernity's permanence — to create a *situation* in which we create our own values, make our own connections, and shape our own forms, whereas traditionally the work of art — since it is an ordered object rather than a situation — was valued precisely because of its capacity to do these things for us. The connoisseur of modernism cannot stand back and judge something which is complete, for the work draws him — irresistibly, if it works — into its frame, and he can only judge what value it has by allowing himself to be hooked and then determining just what in the experience is real, just what has had its effect. *The Connection* strikes at our assumptions about the nature of reality. And so it stands as our paradigm, because each of the works of modernism, rather than doing the job of reconciliation, courts conflict, and attempts to challenge not our values but the very foundations of those values. This situation obtains not only in our arts. Doubts about the foundations of our knowledge have had their effect in all human endeavors, and as more people have become aware of those doubts, philosophical problems, formerly the privileged obsession of an elite, have become matters of general, even mass, concern, of personal psychology, of community and society, and of political action. The speculative freedom engendered by this situation, its self-perpetuating and self-enlarging permanence, can lead to intellectual despair and to viciousness in expressing that despair; it can lead to a desire for order at almost any cost, or a systematized disorderliness which borders on madness. On the other hand, the challenge to our foundations, as

I have said before, can lead to a freedom which creates order spontaneously, which constantly renews our capacity for feeling, that is, our capacity to connect. Of one thing we can be sure, the doubts, and the freedom, have created something which will not readily allow itself to be stopped.

2

SKEPTICAL DOUBTS

IT IS ONE OF THE COMMON assumptions of our intellectual history that our fashionable modern disease, doubt, skepticism, the failure to connect — call it what you will, for the moment — has its source in Descartes. By the time Dryden was composing *Religio Laici* (and more vehemently so a generation later, at the end of the seventeenth century, when Swift was at work on *A Tale of a Tub*), Descartes had become the villain of those conservative forces which insisted that religious belief had to be based on a simple, and to them obvious, act of faith. For Dryden and Swift, abstract reason was dangerously irrelevant in dealing with the foundations of our beliefs, and its use could lead only to, at best, confusing metaphysical speculation, at worst, a corrosive skepticism. This distrust of reason, and of Descartes in the bargain, is to be found not only among the conservative elements in the seventeenth and eighteenth centuries; it is, in fact, a theme often repeated by the heroes of the Enlightenment. D'Alembert's rather touching attempt to reconcile the achievement of Descartes with his own prejudices against reason is a performance one sees repeated in the work of Voltaire, Diderot, and numerous others. In one of the most important and representative essays written in the eighteenth century, the *Pre-*

liminary Discourse to the Encyclopedia of Diderot, he tells us:

Let us always respect Descartes, but let us readily abandon opinions which he himself would have combatted a century later. . . . The genius that he manifested in seeking out a new, albeit false, route in the darkest night was unique with him.[1]

The irony of having his work considered the source of confusion and uncertainty would, I suspect, not have escaped Descartes. For, if nothing else, Descartes' major objectives were the attainment of intellectual clarity and certainty. His significance for us, we generally assume, lies in his attempt to rest the sciences on firm and unambiguous foundations. Yet in order to proceed with this master task, Descartes had to declare his doubt about all received knowledge, about the whole work of the past. It is this doubting Descartes, I think, whose legacy we have really inherited, who touches our most sensitive nerves. The following from the first page of the *Meditations on First Philosophy* will make the point:

I have realized that if I wished to have any firm and constant knowledge in the sciences, I would have to undertake, once and for all, to set aside all the opinions which I had previously accepted among my beliefs and start again from the very beginning. . . . I will therefore make a serious and unimpeded effort to destroy generally all my former opinions.[2]

This done, the task is to reconstruct our knowledge on rational principles. Descartes begins by asserting that the reasoning process itself is certain and invariable:

Arithmetic, geometry, and the other sciences of this nature, which treat only of very simple and general things without con-

[1] Jean d'Alembert, *Preliminary Discourse to the Encyclopedia of Diderot,* trans. R. N. Schwab and W. E. Rex (Indianapolis, New York, 1963). All quotations of d'Alembert are from this volume.
[2] René Descartes, *Meditations on First Philosophy,* trans. L. J. Lafleur (Indianapolis, New York, 1960). All quotations of Descartes are from this volume.

cerning themselves as to whether they occur in nature or not, contain some element of certainty and sureness. For whether I am awake or whether I am asleep, two and three together will always make the number five, and the square will never have more than four sides; and it does not seem possible that truths so clear and so apparent can ever be suspected of any falsity or uncertainty.

We are left with the problem of relating these certainties of reason with the world outside ourselves. For Descartes, the difficulty disappears, in part at least, in his conclusion that perceiving and thinking are related — perhaps identical — processes:

It is this, properly considered, which in my nature is called perceiving, and that, again speaking precisely, is nothing else but thinking.

It was Descartes' great insight (an insight his critics did not understand, and which it has taken our philosophy and psychology, indeed our arts, centuries to recover, if, in fact, they have done so) that the physical act of perception cannot be separated from the judgments of thought.[3] Descartes' following example should make the matter clear:

Thus, for example, I find in myself two completely different ideas of the sun: the one has its origin in the senses, and must be placed in the class of those that, as I said before, came from without, according to which it seems to me extremely small; the other is derived from astronomical considerations — that is, from certain innate ideas — or at least is formed by myself in whatever way it may be, according to which it seems to me many times greater than the whole earth. Certainly, these two ideas of the sun cannot both be similar to the same sun existing outside of me, and reason makes me believe that the one which comes directly from its appearance is that which least resembles it.

[3] In these reflections on the nature of innate ideas, I owe a great deal to the philosophical approach of both Noam Chomsky and Jerrold Katz. See especially the former's *Aspects of the Theory of Syntax* (Cambridge, Mass., 1965) and the latter's *The Philosophy of Language* (New York, 1966).

Still, how do we make the jump outside ourselves, if indeed our knowledge is dependent on our innate ideas? The solution lies in Descartes' acceptance of the old scholastic notion "that everything which is true is something, as truth is the same as being": The very inner consistency of the ideas (their truth) implies that they must correspond to something which exists. We shall see, in a later chapter, that this conclusion is not at all obvious to many modern artists — think of Mallarmé or Mondrian to whom the notion of internal consistency is the only esthetic reality, a consistency which has no relevance to the world outside the object of art.

The theological version, as I choose to call it, of Descartes' argument on the reality of our knowledge is, of course, the more famous one. Descartes no doubt reverted to it because his argument just given was not likely to make much of a psychological dent in anyone who took Descartes' suggestion about total doubt seriously. In brief, and avoiding the painful details, the argument runs something like this: The fact that I doubt convinces me that I exist; if I exist, I can prove there is a god; if there is a god, he is a good god; if he is, indeed, a good god, he would not fool me into believing in something which does not exist; therefore, my knowledge of the external world must be reliable. Now all this depends on our capacity to accept the notorious ontological argument for the existence of god. Here is Descartes' version:

This idea, I say, of a supremely perfect and infinite being, is entirely true; for even though one might imagine that such a being does not exist, nevertheless one cannot imagine that the idea of it does not represent anything real, as I have just said of the idea of cold.

God's existence is thus derivable from the clear and distinct innate idea of a perfect infinite being. It is difficult to understand how Descartes could convince himself of any of this twaddle. I can only suppose that anyone who, from the beginning, strongly believes in the existence of god is capable of accepting almost anything which he feels will give the belief a rational foundation. Obviously, the sense of mental gymnastics which one is bound to carry away from the foregoing was not likely to convince many of the skeptical thinkers or artists of the generations following Descartes. Unfortunately, they were all too likely to miss Descartes' importance and to see him as the apologist for the church and a barbarous scholasticism. In short, Descartes' awareness of a problem, and his attempt to solve it, posed difficulties which had not been readily apparent before: He had not established the certainty of our knowledge, as he supposed; rather he created greater doubt than had been known before.

The whole tradition of empiricism, both its accomplishments and shortcomings, has been an attempt to counter, or simply deal with, Descartes' arguments concerning innate ideas. I should like here to discuss Hume, not only because he is the most brilliant of Descartes' critics but because he so pointedly leaves us with the problems which constituted the artistic and moral concerns of *The Connection*. The problems, as I said earlier, have become permanent, and one can see them equally in Locke, Hume, and Russell, or in the shape of Gelber's play. I should warn the reader that the repeated use of the word "connection," to which he will be forced to submit, is none of my doing — not much, in any case. Hume employs the word endlessly; and if I were William Empson I should, no doubt, pursue the subject strenuously.

An Inquiry Concerning Human Understanding is one of Hume's several attempts to deal with the Cartesian doubt and to determine the proper foundations of our knowledge. Hume tells us:

CHAPTER TWO

The Cartesian doubt, therefore, were it ever possible to be attained by any human creature (as it plainly is not), would be entirely incurable, and no reasoning could ever bring us to a state of assurance and conviction on any subject.[4]

On any subject! Here, of course, is the main point of *my* inquiry: That doubts about the foundations of knowledge have had a decisive influence on — no, have forced in entirely new directions — the forms of our arts, sciences, and modes of action. And no amount of reasoning, in whatever directions, is likely to still our doubts. Hume's comment on Descartes' "theological version" is much to the point:

To have recourse to the veracity of the Supreme Being in order to prove the veracity of our senses is surely making a very unexpected circuit. If his veracity were at all concerned in this matter, our senses would be entirely infallible, because it is not possible that he can ever deceive. Not to mention that, if the external world be once called in question, we shall be at a loss to find arguments by which we may prove the existence of that Being or any of his attributes.

Hume, in order to reassure us of the validity of our knowledge, strikes at what to him is the root of the Cartesian confusion; but it is a blow, which, we shall see, had best not been struck in that particular manner:

Descartes maintained that thought was the essence of the mind — not this thought or that thought, but thought in general. This seems to be absolutely unintelligible, since everything that exists is particular; and therefore it must be our several particular perceptions that compose the mind. I say *compose* the mind, not *belong* to it.

In splitting Descartes' coupling of thought and perception, Hume apparently rids us of all problems relating to mental

[4] David Hume, *An Inquiry Concerning Human Understanding*, ed. C. W. Hendel (New York, 1955). Except when I have indicated otherwise, all quotations of Hume are from this volume. Concerning Hume, I have learned much from, though often disagreeing with, Antony Flew's *Hume's Philosophy of Belief* (New York, 1961).

[38]

activity and innate ideas. Further, since there seems to be no
thought in general, we need not concern ourselves with the
relationship of the laws of thought, or logic, to the — I hesitate to call it activity — operations of the mind. For the latter simply receives what is given to it, and it does so quite
naturally, as the stomach would receive food. Thus Hume
seems to rid us of the Cartesian doubt by basing our knowledge of the external world on a natural physical operation
which would seem to be much more fundamental and intuitively graspable than the operations of reason or the belief in
god. The difficulties created by this solution lie in wait for
Hume, and he will have to face them; and so will those who
attempt to base their reasoning and practice on pure experience, whether this be in history, politics, or the arts.

To be rid, once and for all, of all doubts, misapprehen-
sions, and worrisome questions about the foundations of
knowledge! It is an objective with which few would wish to
quarrel. But to attain this end, a good many corners will have
to be cut, many questions left to themselves — or to the
obstreperous philosopher who refuses to accept the proper
limitations of science. What then is the first step in stilling
the Cartesian doubt? Here is Hume's suggestion:

And if we can go no further than this mental geography, or
delineation of the distinct parts and powers of the mind, it is at
least a satisfaction to go so far.

But as Hume proceeds to warn us, humble as the task of
"mental geography" may appear, as removed as its task of
charting the operations of the mind may seem from anything
so grandiose as providing us with a firm basis for the reliability of our knowledge, we may be in for a few surprises. But
more on mental geography:

The only method of freeing learning at once from these abstruse
questions is to inquire seriously into the nature of human under-

standing and show, from an exact analysis of its powers and capacity, that it is by no means fitted for such remote and abstruse subjects. We must submit to this fatigue in order to live at ease ever after, and must cultivate true metaphysics with some care in order to destroy the false and adulterated.

The capacities of the mind are more or less evident, and Hume takes them for granted. It is the knowledge of its limitations, though, which is to set us eternally at peace. Yet in turning the problem of knowledge into the philosophy of mind, Hume gives it a dangerous twist; for to direct the quest for objective certainty inward is to steer it into notoriously ambiguous, even emotional, territory. Hume, after all, does not look at the mind as an object whose structure might be discernible; rather it is a collection of perceptions, or perhaps sense data, to use our contemporary jargon. As a result, the investigation will not allow us to formulate objective laws about the mind's way of knowing. Instead we shall have a decription (at best, general principles) of the relationships possible for perceptions: in short, mental geography. But, one must ask at this point, what relevance have these internal relationships to our knowledge of the external world?

According to Hume, all our "ideas" — and this expression, like "perception," also seems to correspond to sense datum — all our ideas, no matter their apparent originality, are based not just on experience but quite literally on "impressions."

We may prosecute this inquiry to what length we please: where we shall always find that every idea which we examine is copied from a similar impression.

Apparently mental activity consists of our looking into a viewer in which an ever-changing collection of pictures, placed there by impressions, is to be seen.[5] These ideas have *meaning* if they are translatable into impressions:

[5] The novelist Robbe-Grillet's views on perception are quite similar, as will be shown in a later chapter.

When we entertain, therefore, any suspicion that a philosophical term is employed without any meaning or idea (as is but too frequent), we need but inquire, *from what impression is that supposed idea derived?*

Now Hume has taken the liberty of making the significant jump from logic to psychology, for "meaning" and "idea" are apparently interchangeable. The implication seems to be that only sense data are meaningful, and these are based, of course, on impressions. There is an element of sleight of hand in all this, for Hume means us to accept the notion that everything which is meaningful, a linguistic and logical category, must correspond to something in the external world. But Hume is, momentarily, really trying to convince himself, to still his own Cartesian doubt, for as his argument proceeds, he honestly faces more and more of its difficulties. For the moment, we could simply ask him the unkind question of why ideas are based on impressions? Avoiding that difficulty, let us allow Hume his naturalistic assumption of the mind's capacity to perceive anything outside itself, that is, to transform impressions into ideas. This still leaves us with some very serious uncertainties. Do all ideas correspond to impressions? They are, apparently, at least based on impressions. But if so, in what way? Which ideas are based on anything actually existing outside ourselves and which are imaginative combinations of ideas based on impressions? Hume's answer is that those ideas we feel most strongly correspond to something in the external world and are therefore to be believed. It should be obvious that we often feel things we know not to exist most strongly. In any case, by making a manner of feeling the basis of belief, Hume has again internalized the problem: There are no objective standards for our trust in the objective reality of any idea; we must simply, perhaps not so simply, feel that it is based on an impression. I would have the reader keep this in mind, for the notion is of primary importance to an understanding of what happens in the modern arts, in modern approaches to politics, both before and after Hume.

There are still further doubts bequeathed us if we allow Hume his assumption that ideas are based on impressions. For one, the matter of connections. Since ideas are not generated and shaped by an organizing mental faculty, but rather come into being as distinct or atomic units produced by impressions, how in fact do they connect? Someone might ask (annoyingly) whether they connect at all. Hume, rather sensibly, insists that ideas do of course connect and do so in the following manner:

> To me there appear to be only three principles of connection among ideas, namely, *Resemblance, Contiguity* in time or place, and *Cause* or *Effect.*
> That these principles serve to connect ideas will not, I believe, be much doubted. A picture naturally leads our thoughts to the original. The mention of one apartment in a building naturally introduces an inquiry or discourse concerning the others; and if we think of a wound, we can scarcely forbear reflecting on the pain which follows it.

But Hume is guilty of the same sleight of hand he had perpetrated earlier. He has begun with the matter of associating ideas but somehow ends with the conclusion that these ideas lead us to their originals in the external world. Furthermore, is he really talking about the mechanics of connecting distinct pictures or ideas? Are not some of the associations verbal and products of meaning — that is, of semantic laws rather than psychological ones? In any case, the principles of association, since they are not a product of reason, but rather of feeling, or something like it, hardly seem to stand on very firm ground.

We are now ready for the heart of Hume's argument: What has come before is merely the prelude to the final stilling of our Cartesian doubts. For Hume the basic principle of association is, of course, causality. In pursuing the investigation of cause and effect, Hume was forced into speculations which, I suspect, did not entirely please him, and whose results were somewhat unexpected. He begins with an attempt to distinguish the kinds of knowledge to which we lay claim:

All the objects of human reason or inquiry may naturally be divided into two kinds, to wit, "Relations of Ideas," and "Matters of Fact." Of the first kind are the sciences of Geometry, Algebra, and Arithmetic, and, in short, every affirmation which is either intuitively or demonstratively certain. . . . Matters of fact, which are the second objects of human reason, are not ascertained in the same manner, nor is our evidence of their truth, however great, of a like nature with the foregoing. The contrary of every matter of fact is still possible, because it can never imply a contradiction and is conceived by the mind with the same facility and distinctness as if ever so conformable to reality.

Hume's distinction between these two kinds of knowledge, which he would have be absolute, at first seems to be psychological and based on two different mental faculties, only one of which relates to the external world. We must remember, however, that Hume would rather not have us talk about mental faculties since the mind is really a collection of ideas. If so, what is the relationship between the ideas which constitute these two categories of knowledge? Hume would insist, of course, that the ideas of geometry, for instance, are ultimately based on impressions, and therefore do not indicate the presence of a special mental faculty — that is, an innate idea. But this should clearly indicate that Hume's distinction between Matters of Fact and Relations of Ideas is *logical*, not psychological, for its only basis is the principle of noncontradiction. And so we are still left with the same question: How are our ideas (our knowledge), of whatever category, related to the external world?

Immanuel Kant saw clearly that Hume was really confusing two sets of distinctions and that this led to some of the difficulties I have just pointed to. For one thing, there is the question of the relationship between the principles of our understanding and the external world. For another, there is the more problematic relationship between these principles of our understanding — that is, psychological laws — and the transcendental principles of our logic: to use Kant's expression, "Are synthetic a priori possible?" But for Hume these distinctions must be reducible to impressions, and therefore, very much in spite of himself, he must return to the most basic kind of Cartesian doubt and question our most basic inductive procedures. As he says:

What is the nature of that evidence which assures us of any real existence and matter of fact beyond the present testimony of our senses or the records of our memory.

The answer, one hopes, will be reassuring; though by this time, I assume, we have all become a bit wary. But the answer:

All reasonings concerning matter of fact seem to be founded on the relation of *cause* and *effect*. By means of that relation alone we can go beyond the evidence of our memory and senses.

But what is the source of this relation, the source of all our connections? Hume's answer may prove to be somewhat problematic:

I shall venture to affirm, as a general proposition which admits of no exception, that the knowledge of this relation is not, in any instance, attained by reasonings *a priori*, but arises entirely from experience, when we find that any particular objects are constantly conjoined with each other.

If the knowledge of causality is derived from experience, several difficulties come readily to mind. The most obvious one is that it was precisely the distrust of experience which had led Descartes to his doubt; and so to make it the source of

[44]

our most fundamental principle of knowledge is not likely to be very reassuring. A more subtle difficulty is seen by Hume himself:

We have said that all arguments concerning existence are founded on the relation of cause and effect, that our knowledge of that relation is derived entirely from experience, and that all our experimental conclusions proceed upon the supposition that the future will be conformable to the past. To endeavor, therefore, the proof of this last supposition by probable arguments, or arguments regarding existence, must be evidently going in a circle and taking that for granted which is the very point in question.

As his argument proceeds, Hume makes the point much more strongly, the doubts become more prominent, and it strikes me that the cool and detached philosophical argument turns into a very personal struggle in which Hume is trying to save, both for himself and for us, the primacy of experience as a foundation for ordered knowledge. But here is the argument just quoted as elaborated a page or so further on:

For all inferences from experience suppose, as their foundation, that the future will resemble the past and that similar powers will be conjoined with similar sensible qualities. *If there be any suspicion that the course of nature may change,* and that the past may be *no rule for the future, all experience becomes useless and can give rise to no inference or conclusion.* It is impossible, therefore, that any arguments from experience can prove this resemblance of the past to the future, since all these arguments are founded on the supposition of that resemblance. [My italics.]

Hume, it seems, is depending on our intuitive certainty about induction. Indeed, who among Hume's contemporaries, after the apparent success of Newton, would venture to think differently? Had not Newton's equations and the laws of motion made the predictions of astronomy, both backward and forward, a logical certainty? But of course

[45]

Hume, rather than reemphasizing the confidence of his contemporaries, gives voice to the skeptical doubt. For only a few pages before concluding that all experience becomes useless without the assumed certainty of the principle of induction, Hume had asserted that in reasoning about matters of fact there could be no logical certainty, that the opposite of any event could, in fact, occur.

Let us take Hume a step further — or rather backward. If all our ideas, to be meaningful, must be based on impressions — that is, experience — just where does induction, which is the basis of all inferences from experience, come from? Here is Hume's solution for this unpleasant doubt:

All inferences from experience, therefore, are effects of custom, not of reasoning.

In order to stay outside the confines of his own logical circle, Hume has turned his solution of our skeptical doubt into a learning theory: We acquire our knowledge of causality through custom, through habitually seeing the same events in succession. Unfortunately, we have been left to puzzle over the same problem. If our learning anything from custom is dependent on the causal principle, just how are we to learn causality from custom? It hardly matters how often we see two events occurring successively; if we do not have the capacity to connect them, no connection will be made; and least of all are we likely to infer the causal principle from them. As Hume's argument proceeds, he is quite aware that his learning theory has not allowed us to escape from the circle; he finally takes the following way out:

This belief [in causality] is the necessary result of placing the mind in such circumstances. It is an operation of the soul, when we are so situated, as unavoidable as to feel the passion of love, when we receive benefits; or hatred, when we meet with injuries. All these operations are a species of natural instincts, which no reasoning or process of the thought and understanding is able either to produce or to prevent.

But if the knowledge of the causal principle is a species of instinct, it is, in effect, an innate idea: An instinct could hardly be learned from an impression; nor does an instinct have anything to do with necessity. If causality is as necessary as "the passion of love," it rests, alas, on very uncertain and entirely subjective ground. Since an instinct is not reducible to impressions, we can ask no meaningful questions about it; the problem is thus logically insoluble, and we must necessarily leave it shrouded in mystery; here is the end of all possible questioning, and we should find ourselves at peace. Unfortunately, insoluble mysteries tend to attract the greatest number of questions: Hardly anyone asks questions when there are none to be asked. But in fact, Hume need not have goaded us in his particular way. For if causality is a species of instinct, one can reasonably search for its operations inside the organism. Hume is trapped by his empiricism — that is, by the very means he has used to still the Cartesian doubt; the means which have led him back to Descartes force him to posit an innate idea.

If we are to accept Hume's solution and call causality a species of instinct (that is, an innate idea), just how are we to connect our ideas to the external world? Unhappily we are faced, once more, with the Cartesian doubt. Hume, dutifully, tries to face up to it:

Here, then, is a kind of pre-established harmony between the course of nature and the succession of our ideas; and though the powers and forces by which the former is governed be wholly unknown to us, yet our thoughts and conceptions have still, we find, gone on in the same train with the other works of nature. Custom is that principle by which this correspondence has been effected. . . . Nature . . . has implanted in us an instinct which carries forward the thought in a correspondent course to that which she has established among external objects.

We have not really gone anywhere: The problems related to custom have not disappeared; instinct is still something internal; and, at best, we have been provided with mental geography — no more, and perhaps less. Hume, as usual, eventually comes around to the skeptical implications of his argument, even if only to reject the skepticism:

All events seem entirely loose and separate. One event follows another, but we never can observe any tie between them. They seem *conjoined*, but never *connected*. But as we can have no idea of anything which never appeared to our outward sense or inward sentiment, the necessary conclusion *seems* to be that we have no idea of connection or power at all, and that these words are absolutely without any meaning when employed either in philosophical reasonings or common life.

Further, Hume considers that this situation might obtain in the relation of will to action: The connection between his willing to move his arm and the arm's motion is mysterious, and one seems to know only that the events occur in succession. We are clearly driven to the following conclusion:

When we say, therefore, that one object is connected with another, we mean only that they have acquired a connection in our thought and gave rise to this inference by which they become proofs of each other's existence — a conclusion which is somewhat extraordinary, but which seems founded on sufficient evidence.

An extraordinary conclusion, indeed, for someone who is trying to renew our confidence in the relation of our ideas to the external world. The more hidden possibilities of skepticism Hume uncovers, the more he needs to assure us that the connections we make are founded on sufficient evidence. We do live; we perform the tasks needed to carry on; and we could hardly hope to do so without making connections, without taking causality for granted. Yet we doubt, and in trying to convince ourselves that there are no problems, we invariably discover new ones.

What is the connection of mind to the world? And what has mind to do with the rules of logic? The self-evident success of science in the century preceding Hume's had made these questions more pressing than ever. Just how, one had to ask, is science possible? What connections do Newton's equations have to reality and why are they capable of generating accurate predictions? And what, if any, foundations do differential equations have in reality? The very structure of Newton's science — his use of the principles of mechanics and of the calculus — creates the problems, and, in fact, he is forced to give them critical consideration in the *Principia*. Since Hume's time, the attempt to answer these questions has, in fact, forced us to ask any number of new questions. Do Newton's equations, for instance, provide us with a causal nexus; or do they simply symbolize a system of functional dependence? And just what is the meaning of causality at a distance? Kant's great work (which we refer to as *critical* philosophy) was the first significant attempt to deal with the success of science in a unified way. To reconstruct metaphysics, however, he had to ask, and wonder, how science was possible. But the example of Kant illustrates for us how often philosophy — especially in its important tasks — has become the epistemology of the sciences; sciences which we, unlike the celebrators of Newton in the eighteenth century, understand to be in constant flux. And so the Kantian search for foundations is still the main part of our philosophy; the critical effort remains permanent.

Allow me to return one last time to the question of Hume's skepticism. I find it moving — at times, perhaps, comical — to watch Hume uncover greater and greater difficulties, while supposedly trying to still my, and his, Cartesian doubt. Why does he insist on putting both of us into a state of almost incurable perplexity? Perhaps the following contains a clue:

Why should not the acknowledgment of a real distinction between vice and virtue be reconcilable to all speculative systems of
philosophy, as well as that of a real distinction between personal
beauty and deformity? Both these distinctions are founded in the
natural sentiments of the human mind; and these sentiments are
not to be controlled or altered by any philosophical theory or
speculation whatsoever.

As we can see, Hume is attempting to illustrate that the various kinds of judgments human beings make, especially those
in ethics and esthetics, are grounded in human nature; their
source is naturalistic rather than religious; and their meta-
physic is to be understood in terms of experience rather than
the formulations of reason. In pursuing this scientific naturalism (a pursuit I much admire), Hume has led us into
strange and uncharted paths; in fact, he has tried to map the
mental geography of a country whose topography undergoes
constant change. For once we are aware that there is a problem of connections, that the Cartesian doubt is philosophically incorrigible, we shall probably put our best energies into
the making of connections, into looking for them in new
ways, or into creating them out of our most personal needs.
And this, as Hume has indicated, will have its effect in all
human endeavors, especially in ethics, politics, and art. We
shall keep trying to connect, to still the doubt; or, perhaps,
finally give ourselves up to the alleged delights of randomness.

THE DRIVE TO SURRENDER OURSELVES to disorder (indeed to
cherish it as official policy, as a positive good) has attained
prominence only in the recent past. In the seventeenth and
eighteenth centuries, problems posed by the theory of
knowledge were taken up with the urgency and the high de-

gree of seriousness demanded by the task. The job of criticism became one of reconstruction, of establishing new connections; in fact, one can readily reverse the foregoing order: The job of reconstruction made criticism a major necessity. Any effort of this sort is likely to concentrate its energies on the nature of our moral judgments, and, indeed, there were numerous attempts to construct moral systems on a naturalistic foundation. Much of the impetus behind these efforts derived from the increasing knowledge of foreign cultures: It became obvious that some foreign notions about morality failed to agree with ours; and since our convictions, if we were naturalists, rested on somewhat shaky foundations, it began to appear less than self-evident that these strange foreigners were necessarily wrong. Instead of posing as the stern judge of moral perverseness, the moral philosopher became an incipient cultural anthropologist; and since he was likely to share the neoclassic belief in the uniformity of human nature, his tendency was to look for the general laws underlying the varieties of moral judgment. The desire to look at others with a measure of critical detachment resulted in a reversal of the process: The critical detachment was turned on one's own moral assumptions. This can be seen most readily in such popular fictional accounts of European customs as Montesquieu's *The Persian Letters* and Goldsmith's *Letters From a Citizen of the World*. Since both works purported to be collections of letters written by foreigners, their very different moral orientations put the prevailing European beliefs and customs in an ironic light. The possibility of irony was created by the uncertainty surrounding the foundations of moral judgments: It was difficult to tell whether the foreigners or the Europeans they looked at with astonishment were to be laughed at. Irony, even if based on certainties, tends to create doubts, and the doubts tend to create a skeptical openness. Bayle's *Dictionary* is not ironic simply to escape the censor, for there is to be found a real ambiguity about the possibilities of belief in almost everything he writes. The latest scholarly consensus seems to indicate that the articles about religion, which were once taken to be ironic, are the statements of a sincere believer. One possible reaction for the skeptic, and it was a fairly common one in the seventeenth and eighteenth centuries, is to declare one's faith in a higher authority — the church or the monarch, for example — since neither reason nor experience can provide a proper foundation for belief; one's very skepticism leads to the necessity for authority. It is hardly accidental that the rise of skepticism brings with it the absolute monarch, literary academies with authority, and, at first, the dogmatic assertion of literary rules — all these best exemplified by the France of Louis XIV. Racine's passionate defense of literary rules and his faith in the dogmas of Jansenism are really aspects of the moral skepticism which, I believe, lends his tragedies their unrelenting intensity. The highly rational arguments about morality must ring out with a passion, for there is nothing but that passion to back them.

As part of his critique of causality and the foundations of knowledge, Hume made some observations about the foundations of moral judgment. His remarks, though incidental, derive from the implications of his epistemological researches: That faculty by which we discern truth and falsehood, and that

by which we perceive vice and virtue, had long been confounded with each other; and all morality was supposed to be built on eternal and immutable relations which, to every intelligent mind, were equally invariable as any proposition concerning quantity or number. But a late philosopher has taught us, by the most convincing arguments, that morality is nothing in the abstract nature of things.

[52]

Like causality, morals cannot be based on reason. In the ambiguous fashion typical of so much writing on morals in the eighteenth century, Hume has a "Friend" say:

All the philosophy, therefore, in the world, and all the religion, which is nothing but a species of philosophy, will never be able to carry us beyond the usual cause of experience or give us measures of conduct and behavior different from those which are furnished by reflections on common life.

So much for both religion and reason as foundations for morals. If Hume is to continue his fight for naturalism, morals will apparently have to be derived from experience — or so his Friend claims. But if morals are to be based on experience, they will be, as Hume has all too well taught us, on very uncertain ground; for they will be based on causality — that is, a species of instinct, something which is ultimately internal and, perhaps, private. Yet the search for a moral system which will derive its maxims from experience is something still very much with us.

The Enlightenment's ultimate concern, one tends to forget, was for the reconstruction of morals; quite expectedly, most of the thinkers we associate with the period tried to derive a system of morals from experience. The object was to make the study of morals, somehow, part of the general scientific effort. The most common approach involved a version of the Baconian pursuit: One collects all the information on the customs of all the known civilizations; from a judicious comparative study of this information one can readily tell what is different, what similar; finally, the moral universals are derived almost automatically from the similarities. Voltaire concludes his *Essay on the Manner and Spirit of Nations* with a comparison of Eastern and Western customs. Among his conclusions we find the following:

Religion teaches the same principles of morality to all nations, without exception; the ceremonies of the Asiatics are ridiculous, their belief absurd, but their precepts are just.[6]

Voltaire does not mean to imply that European religious beliefs are any less ridiculous than those of Asia; what does matter is that morality is independent of religious belief and therefore natural; furthermore, it is uniform, and the uniformity is readily perceived if one disregards custom and, in good neoclassic fashion, searches out general nature.

The Enlightenment's most grandiose attempt to make the Baconian pursuit relevant to morality lay in the alleged purpose of Diderot's great *Encyclopedia*. I shall return to this subject in a different context, but for the moment, consider the following from Diderot's encyclopedia article entitled "The Encyclopedia." The object of the scientific effort, we are told, is to make us

. . . understand the general course of natural events and take each thing only for what it is, and — consequently — inspire in men a taste for science, an abhorrence of lies, a hatred of vice and a love of virtue; for whatever does not have happiness and virtue as its final goal is worth nothing.[7]

This is rather typical Diderot, since he is in the habit of almost hysterically identifying truth with virtue, falseness with vice. But the very passion with which Diderot asserts the identification in his formal essays helps to reveal its glibness, the passion being a substitute for considered reasoning. If virtue is to be derived from our possession of true knowledge, just what is the process by which we learn the moral law from experience? It is a problem which d'Alembert poses for Diderot in *D'Alembert's Dream*, a fictional dialogue which,

[6] *The Portable Voltaire*, ed. B. R. Redman, trans. not given (New York, 1949).

[7] Denis Diderot, *Rameau's Nephew and Other Works*, trans. J. Barzun and R. H. Bowen (Indianapolis, New York, Kansas City, 1964). All subsequent quotations of Diderot are from this volume.

unlike Diderot's formal philosophical work, does not indulge itself with moral rhetoric. Diderot, after burning the only manuscript of the work (so he thought) at Julie de L'Espinasse's (d'Alembert's mistress) request, eventually allowed a newly discovered copy to be published in Grimm's *Correspondance Littéraire*. Significantly, this newsletter was only privately circulated: Diderot never permitted his moral certainties the luxury of being assailed when writing for the general public. Here is his answer to d'Alembert:

> But it's perfectly obvious that we don't draw any conclusions at all — they are always drawn by nature itself. We do nothing but describe the connections among phenomena, connections that are either necessary or contingent. These phenomena are known through experience. In mathematics and physics the connections are necessary; in morality and politics they are contingent or probable, as they are in the other branches of speculative knowledge.

Diderot, when speaking in his own voice, is still not willing to admit the implications of his naturalistic position. Hume, after all, had demonstrated rather clearly that we cannot assume that connections are drawn by nature itself; that our only knowledge of connections is internal; that the operation involves, ultimately, a species of instinct. It was difficult for Diderot to accept the implications of this notion for morality, for it tended to undermine the connection of truth and virtue, an apparent commonplace for the *philosophes*. It is left to one of the other characters in the dialogue, the physician Bordeu, to pursue, with little mercy, the implications of Diderot's position. For Bordeu, all connections are made by the brain's mechanical operations and therefore have no objective reality; as a result, we cannot really derive morals from facts. For Hume this line of thought indicated that morality must be based on some instinct; to Bordeu it only reveals that all moral distinctions are unreal. And Bordeu does not hesitate to accept the implications of this conclusion, for unlike the moralist Diderot, he considers himself to be a pure scientist. The principles of virtue, he tells us, cannot be studied since they do not exist; the language of morals is simply a convenient symbolization for a number of our instinctual desires; on the basis of these desires we make what we generally call moral judgments. Thus virtue is derived neither from abstract principle, nor from nature, but lies within us, in our drives, the chief of which are pleasure and its attendant corollary, utility. It should be clear that this notion makes any sort of general maxim — any connection between my moral judgment and those of others — nearly impossible, for my pleasure will not necessarily be the pleasure of another. In fact, the notion allows Bordeu to suggest the crudest kind of enforced eugenics:

Because of our chicken-heartedness, our skittishness, our laws and our prejudices, precious few experiments have ever been made. Hence we do not know what copulations might be totally unfruitful or what different ways there may be of combining the pleasant with the useful. We don't know what sort of species we might expect to produce as the result of varied and sustained experimentation.

Bordeu continues to suggest that goats should be bred with men, and his motives for this experiment do, indeed, involve a desire to combine "the pleasant with the useful." "The mixture," he tells us, "would give us a vigorous, intelligent, tireless, and swift-footed race of animals of which we could make excellent domestic servants." Diderot is using Bordeu as a dramatic character, supposedly as a scandalous foil for his own position; but he is well aware that Bordeu's suggestions consist only of notions implied by his own philosophical position. This tells us why Diderot is so fond of using dialogue as a literary form. As in Bayle's use of irony, it is not simply to confound the censor. Nor should Diderot's use of the form — and Hume's — be mistaken for Plato's. In the

Socratic dialogues, the rest of the cast generally serves as a foil for Socrates, and there is no doubt in anyone's mind as to who is the wise man, who the fool. But when Diderot's and Hume's opponents tell us that the moral law is illusory, they make a real point, for they simply exploit the possibilities for ambiguity created by a theory of knowledge based on experience: Hume and Diderot have created their own opponents. Diderot himself is torn between his felt convictions and his commitment to science: Man is a mechanical configuration, yet morality is real. Diderot's dealings with his daughter are revealing: He assiduously exposes her to many areas of knowledge and experience — he even takes her for a walk in the red light district, yet he does not trust the knowledge of fact to take care of her moral education, and he is careful to school her on the proper modes of behavior. All this time he makes sure that the girl remains unacquainted with his own immodest behavior: that he keeps a mistress and is quite unabashed about being involved in other extramarital affairs. One might remember that Rousseau's sad quarrel with Diderot — his best friend — was really over the issue of morality, for Rousseau, unlike many others, clearly saw the implications of Diderot's philosophical position for morals.

In his writings on morals, Hume, of course, rejects the position represented by Bordeu. He tells us:

Those who have denied the reality of moral distinctions may be ranked among the disingenuous disputants; nor is it conceivable that any human creature could ever seriously believe that all characters and actions were alike entitled to the affection and regard of everyone. . . . Let a man's insensibility be ever so great, he must often be touched with the images of *right* and *wrong*; and let his prejudices be ever so obstinate, he must observe that others are susceptible of like impressions.[8]

[8] David Hume, *An Inquiry Concerning the Principles of Morals*, ed. C. W. Hendel (Indianapolis, New York, 1957). The quotations of Hume following in this section are from this volume.

Moral *activity*, even though its foundations may be problematical, is a fact. Moreover, it is not simply a mask for some other kind of internal activity, for it is based on real feelings. But Hume does not pursue this particular line of investigation — not for the moment, in any case. His impulse is to participate in the Enlightenment's search for a naturalistic morals, although he may ultimately reject the logical possibility of this search. After all, was it not Hume who told us that all knowledge had to be derived from experience? But here he is on the nature of moral science:

> The very nature of language guides us almost infallibly in forming a judgment of this nature; and as every tongue possesses one set of words which are taken in a good sense, and another in the opposite, the least acquaintance with the idiom suffices, without any reasoning, to direct us in collecting and arranging the estimable or blamable qualities of men. The only object of reasoning is to discover the circumstances on both sides which are common to these qualities — to observe that particular in which the estimable qualities agree, on the one hand, and the blamable, on the other; and thence to reach the foundation of ethics and find those universal principles from which all censure or approbation is ultimately derived.

The moral law, in short, is to be derived from our study of human behavior, rather than from abstract principles. What qualities, we ask, do men consider estimable, what blamable, and proceed from there, basing our reasoning on these seemingly incontestable facts. Now the notions of "estimable" and "blamable," if they are to go beyond private instinct, must be based on the acceptance of some social norm. For Hume this norm lies in the utility of an action. But, we need to ask, useful to what end? An action, after all, cannot be useful in the abstract. Hume deals with the question as follows:

> Utility is only a tendency to a certain end; and were the end totally indifferent to us, we should feel the same indifference to-

ward the means. It is requisite a *sentiment* should here display itself in order to give a preference to the useful above the pernicious tendencies. This sentiment can be no other than a feeling for the happiness of mankind, and a resentment of their misery, since these are the different ends which virtue and vice have a tendency to promote. Here, therefore, *reason* instructs us in the several tendencies of actions, and *humanity* makes a distinction in favor of those which are useful and beneficial.

Utility, then, must be based on some ultimate, some absolute which Hume calls — rather vaguely — humanity. This feeling for the happiness of mankind may be based on our hatred of pain and our love of pleasure, but we are not sure. In short, morals, like causality, must be based on a species of instinct: An instinct not being based on an impression, we cannot, as Hume has told us, reasonably talk about it.

What then is there to be said about the principles of morals? For one thing, we can discuss the function of utility as a norm. Just how does utility become converted into virtue? Hume has an answer:

It must still be allowed that every quality of the mind which is *useful* or *agreeable* to the person himself or to others communicates a pleasure to the spectator, engages his esteem, and is admitted under the honorable denomination of virtue or merit.

The individual making moral judgments is a *spectator watching the stage of humanity*: Some of the performances prove to be agreeable, others less so. In any case, his judgment depends on his reaction to the drama society presents; that reaction, in turn, is based on the esthetic of utility. The notion has the apparent virtue of combining psychological and social factors, yet it does have its difficulties. Ideas as to what constitutes usefulness may, after all, change; and as Hume has pointed out, the things which give us pleasure change from society to society, from age to age. Since Hume has placed us in the role of spectators making judgments, we are forced into making a critical effort: It becomes necessary for us to decide just what gives us pleasure, just what touches our emotions. What an odd turn this argument has taken, for we began with the objective of reassuring ourselves about the unproblematic nature of our moral judgments. After all, the precise nature of the events which touch the appropriate emotions in us may, in fact, be uncertain. Hume, in illustrating that the maxims for conduct are not permanently grounded in reason or god or natural law, has created the possibility for ambiguity. Unless we have the classicist's or the religious fanatic's dogmatic conviction in the unchanging nature of human character and society, any moral judgment — if it is to have a naturalistic foundation, if it is to be grounded in experience — will have to depend on the individual's emotional reaction to an event. As we shall see (and have already seen in *The Connection*), pressure arising from this situation will exert a considerable influence on the moral uses of art and the forms through which these uses will be made effective. Looking to Hume's time, for the moment, it is just this uncertainty about the individual emotional reaction which made irony so potent a weapon in the eighteenth century. The usual received, and officially embalmed, notion about irony is that it can be effective only if there is general agreement between the ironist and his reader; this agreement is based, supposedly, on a society firmly sharing a common set of values. But why be ironic if your reader agrees with you in any case? And would it not be somewhat boring, even dreary, to read something which simply confirms what we know? Defoe, after all, wound up in the stocks for an ironic attack on the religious establishment: I assume he did not land in that unhappy position because someone agreed with him. An even better example would be the reception of Swift's *Against the Abolishing of Christianity in England*, a pamphlet he wrote to defend the Test Act and the Church of England. Swift, not surprisingly, found himself almost universally reviled for an attack on Christianity. Yet it is the possibility of this wrong reaction which lends irony its intense literary and moral possibilities. The eighteenth century produced great irony not because the majority of readers shared common assumptions about a majority of human concerns but precisely because those assumptions had stopped being common. Touch a great ironist — Dryden, Swift, or Gibbon — and you touch a skeptic, whether he be of the religious establishment (Dryden, Swift), or against it (Gibbon). It is Hume's kind of approach to the foundation of morals — the attempt to affirm the reality of moral judgment by grounding it in experience — which gives rise to the uncertainty and, consequently, the openness which allow irony its effect as a literary mode. There are other possible, and perhaps more important, consequences. If our reactions to events are determined by our notions of utility, are we not capable, in turn, of manufacturing experiences which will impress the desired notions of utility on the unsuspecting? Can't we even attempt — with a reasonable hope for success — to transform the very psychological sources of pain or pleasure? Hume tells us that no civilized human being would deem asceticism useful. Yet who would deny that some religions have managed to convince a vast number of apparently civilized people that fasting and sexual continence do, indeed, have their uses. And the success of the church, as Gibbon will show us later, lay precisely in its sharing of Hume's insight into rational argument's incapacity to convert men to belief. If the acquisition of moral maxims depends on the emotions which actions on the human stage elicit from the spectator, the church and the state have been availed of an extremely powerful, though potentially dangerous and unpredictable, weapon. These institutions can choose what they deem useful (that is, moral) and stage the proper emotional situation which will make the desirable maxims real. Let me put the argument somewhat simple-mindedly, so that we can see the source of this notion in Hume's epistemology: The word "good" is derived from impressions; if so, we can reproduce the impressions which gave rise to this idea of moral approbation. In producing these impressions and staging these events, church and state are likely to be artful — both in the good and the pejorative sense of the word. They are, in fact, likely to use art and have often done so with great success. In turn, the use of the arts for the creation of morals— rather than the arts imitating received moral ideas — makes something very different of the work of art. We have seen an extreme and recent example of this process in *The Connection*. But more of this further on.

Hume has still left us with some nagging philosophical puzzles. If moral judgments are a matter of the individual spectator being pleased or displeased, just how is one man's pleasure to be connected with another's? How are we to derive *general* rather than private moral laws? Hume answers as follows:

Whatever conduct gains my approbation, by touching my humanity, procures also the applause of all mankind by affecting the same principle in them.

Hume, in step with the Enlightenment, assumes that human nature is uniform and accepts the reality of a universal principle. But this assumption leads back to the doubt created by causality seen as a species of instinct. It internalizes the whole problem by assuming that its source is to be found in an innate idea. We are certain of one thing: We do make moral distinctions, and these may, possibly, have their source in an instinct. But as for certainty about general laws — hardly. Hume, in order to reassure us, keeps insisting that there is a great and clear distinction between the actions we approve and disapprove of. But as he points out, approval or disapproval often enough depend on a *social* norm; to use Hume's example, the ancient Greeks, oddly enough, approved of sexual habits somewhat different from ours. But let us take an instance which offers even greater difficulties and challenges Hume's assumption in a much more fundamental way. What if a given society has no single set of social norms? Or if the norms are fudged and ambiguous? How, in these instances, are we to draw clear distinctions between actions of which everyone either approves or disapproves? Hume, for example, makes the claim that the companionable qualities are generally approved of, and therefore constitute a virtue. This may have been wholly valid when applied to a group of Scottish gentlemen, but Hume's contemporary (for a brief period, his friend), Rousseau, insisted, and attempted to illustrate by the manner in which he lived, that the qualities of cheery friendliness, of superficial good-fellowship, were hypocritical masks for a society afraid of displaying its honest feelings. Or, to take a similar instance, Hume dismisses the unusual maxims by which Diogenes and Pascal conducted their lives, for they were arrived at through philosophical speculation. Hume explains:

They are in a different element from the rest of mankind, and the natural principles of their mind play not with the same regularity as if left to themselves.

Again, Hume assumes that if "natural principles of mind" are "left to themselves," there will be regularity and uniformity. If we are to accept this, we must dismiss Hume's whole epistemological structure, for it is possible only if we assume the existence of innate ideas. The obvious point is that both Diogenes and Pascal, precisely because they gave their minds free play, chose to ignore the social norms (and

[63]

their universal acceptance is absolutely necessary for Hume's moral reasoning) and pursued their individual inclinations in the choice of maxims for behavior. But are we so very sure that they were wrong and their societies right? What if I should be pleased by the example of Pascal and decide that it is useful? I may, as a result, fail to connect with anyone else in my society, yet I might be leading the moral life, the others the immoral. Finally, what if one of our social norms happens to be the admonition to be uncommon? Do not we, after all, make it a habit to tell our students to be nonconformist?

This open situation — where the maxims of morality seem to have no objectivity and are ultimately located in the privacy of personal sentiment, where there seems to be no reasonable connection between the moral judgments of individuals, where a belief in a universal moral law seems, in fact, to be based on an act of faith in the uniformity of man's nature — this situation does, after all, create the possibility, the freedom, for public acts and political policies which will attempt to create connections and thereby establish moral maxims. Both *The Connection* and Alexander Herzen's statement (quoted earlier) are attempts to perform this task, and both were made possible by the open, and confused, situation which had developed over a period of many years. The attempt is also implicit in the intellectual objectives of something like Diderot's *Encyclopedia* or in the work of the many societies for the reformation of manners or propagation of virtue which flourished during the eighteenth century. The task of discovering moral maxims might direct us to the study of history: There are the raw facts which are open to interpretation; from these we might derive moral universals and to these we hope to connect by the judgments we make, by the relevance which we perceive past events to have for our own moral lives. Are these not the objectives which Voltaire and (we shall see later) Gibbon set themselves in their histories? The task might be performed by literature, especially drama: The development of bourgeois tragedy in the eighteenth century was an attempt to do just this. Finally, politics might attempt to carry the burden of connecting our separate maxims on morality. It can do so in at least two important ways. First, by simply empowering the state to determine just what is moral. This morality may be enforced despotically or through a leader who by dint of personal example creates a moral tone which gains universal acceptance. Dictators who wish to be the leaders of moral nations have had — at least since Cromwell, and later Robespierre — to lead moral and exemplary lives; it was entirely superfluous for Louis XIV to do so. Second, politics can form moral connections by creating and adhering to a theory which is grounded in *human needs* — rather than rationality, the natural law, or authority — and which, like Rousseau's *The Social Contract*, assumes that there is no separation between the objectives of government and the aims of morality.

THE IDEA THAT POLITICS — the art of dealing with human beings through the agency of the state — ought to provide us with moral connections, should hardly strike us with the ring of modernity. The ritualized reference to Plato's views on morality and the republic might serve as a useful reminder of the notion's venerability. It is the fashion among conservative political scientists to lament the decline of amoral diplomacy, and the substitution, in international relations, of moral issues for political geography. Metternich's machinations at the Congress of Vienna, we are told, are much preferable to the moral fulminations of Hitler. I am hardly convinced that we have substituted morality for the rational pursuit of the national interest; or whether that pursuit ought to be referred to as rational. Neither the Yalta Agreement nor the Truman Doctrine impress me as monuments to righteousness, and it is difficult for me to think of Churchill, Stalin, Roosevelt, and Truman as embodiments of our, or any, moral law. The matter is hardly as simple and obvious as many conservatives would have it. The papacy, for instance, has gone through long periods during which it rarely used its institutional strengths or exercised its religious influence to provide Christendom with moral connections; rather, its main interest was in diplomacy and power politics. But, on the other hand, do not many of our notions of the morality of politics and the state derive from Christian institutions and beliefs? Calvinism, the Puritans, and many evangelical sects take the state to be the embodiment of god's moral law on earth. Think of Dimmesdale's Election Sermon in Hawthorne's *The Scarlet Letter:* "The relation between the Deity and the communities of mankind." The relation ought to be moral: The members of the community should feel connected because they are saints. But think also of Dimmesdale, the preacher of God's moral word, being sinful and therefore feeling totally cut off, entirely removed from the possibility of human (that is, moral) contact. More important for our purpose is that Dimmesdale feels guilt to the exclusion of all other emotions. For by exploiting this emotion, by using a psychological device, the evangelical sects hoped to reestablish our moral connections, both to god and to each other. Moral maxims, defunct for having lost their intimate connection with religious institutions, were to be reconstructed and given universality on the basis of an emotion — guilt. Thus the propagation of guilt became a major task for the church and the many protestant sects. The possible success of their propaganda depended on a variety of factors: The sect might derive its moral authority from its control of the state; or, not having political power, from the attractions, whatever their nature, of its revolutionary stance. But most important — and think of Weber's discussion of the psychological origin of the spirit of capitalism — is the appeal's being made to our most private feelings: not to rationality, not to the general good, not to the honor of an abstract republic, but to the reality of one's very personal pain or joy. And the instruments of this appeal, whether the state's or the revolution's, are, of course, political.

What if the religious impetus should not be available? In its absence, how is politics to provide us with moral maxims which go beyond personal belief? The possibility of unifying our moral judgments becomes smaller and smaller as our freedom increases, as the social situation becomes more open. As a result, we are faced with an often stultifying irony: The more we need to make moral connections, the less capable we become of making them; the greater the freedom to choose, the smaller the reliability of one's choice. We might be tempted to give up our freedom, but as Rousseau tells us in *The Social Contract*, the choice not to choose creates its own difficulties:

To renounce our liberty is to renounce our quality of man, and with it all the rights and duties of humanity. No adequate compensation can possibly be made for a sacrifice so complete. Such a renunciation is incompatible with the nature of man; whose actions, when once he is deprived of his free will, must be destitute of all morality.[9]

[9] Jean-Jacques Rousseau, *The Social Contract*, ed. C. Frankel, trans. not given (New York, 1957). Except when I have indicated otherwise, all quotations of Rousseau are from this volume.

If history places us in an era blessed, or cursed, with a general consciousness of liberty, the arbitrary use of force becomes a human impossibility, whether we exert the force against ourselves or whether someone is doing the forcing for us. To force me irrationally into an act I reject is not only to degrade me, it is to degrade whoever does the forcing; it is, most dangerously, to degrade the concept of humanity itself. For to change our consciousness of liberty involves a change in our consciousness of what we are; and without liberty we shall perhaps think of ourselves as mechanisms, animals, brutes, abstractions — any number of things, but hardly human beings. I shall try to clarify my amplification of Rousseau's notion by returning, momentarily, to the matter of religious belief. Imagine a believing Christian of the twelfth century who might feel convinced that there are no real political choices available to him. Ultimately, he believes, all authority comes from god, and is administered by the church or some other institution. This deprivation of freedom does not give him a sense of his own inhumanity, for there is no political concept of personal liberty available to him, nor are there social, political, and economic institutions to embody these concepts. In fact, the notion of giving up one's will to god's might well be part of what he considers to be his humanity: *In la sua volontade e nostra pace*. But to deprive a man who feels the possibility of openness, of choice, of his liberty marks the beginning of his dehumanization. Liberty is the presupposition, in short, of our modernity.

If the actions of the state are to have moral content, rather than deriving from its capacity to use force against the individual, those actions will have to be the expression of some mutually agreed on notion of justice. If this condition is met, the state's necessary limitation of our freedom will not appear unjust, nor will it seem to be the result of mere caprice. The codification of justice is the job of political theory — or political science, as we like to call it. It is a task which involves the rationalization of the use of force. Formerly, the appointed task of political science was to reconcile the state to god or to reason; but for us, these masks of reason will hardly serve to reconcile us to the loss of liberty, and the state's use of force will have to be rationalized in terms of an ideology, or, more potently, in terms of ourselves — our feelings and understanding. Since Hume has shown us that justice is a superstition, it is, at least, difficult to justify the state's usurpation of freedom on the grounds of that very justice. Superstitions tend not to be taken very seriously when offered as the foundation for moral action. Further, justice is surely not to be derived from the principles of reason. Can we then accept social convention as the foundation of justice? Here is Hume's comment:

It has been asserted by some that justice arises from *human conventions* and proceeds from the voluntary choice, consent, or combination of mankind. If by *convention* be here meant a *promise* (which is the most usual sense of the word), nothing can be more absurd than this position. The observance of promises is itself one of the most considerable parts of justice; and we are not surely bound to keep our word because we have given our word to keep it. [*An Inquiry Concerning the Principles of Morals*]

Quite clearly, the notion of a social contract as the foundation for justice has been destroyed; men will not act morally, in accordance with a commonly accepted code, simply because they have agreed to do so; indeed, there must be an agreed on notion of justice (that is, a kind of social connection) if the idea of a social contract is even to be conceived: There is no possible transition from the raw use of power in the state of nature to the shared moral assumptions, the just actions, of the social contract. Then where are we to look for the foundations of justice? Hume — and here he is typical of political thought in the Enlightenment — would trace its origin to its utility. But we must remember that Hume has taught us that utility is based on a species of instinct and therefore comes from within the individual. Thus justice, if it is to be derived from reason, from natural law, or from god, has as its ultimate source not society but the very nature of the individual citizen. If we are not to force justice on this citizen, we will have to *convince* him, whatever the means, that justice is, after all, useful.

Only the perverse would argue against the social necessity of justice: It must be present if we are to have any sort of workable and human political organization; in fact, it must be anterior to it. The consciousness of liberty, we have seen, makes the individual's reconciliation to justice a serious problem — not merely as an issue for philosophy but for the possibility of social and political morality. It is here that Rousseau, with his bent for emphasizing above all else the reality of human feelings, is of supreme importance. The ultimate demand which justice is capable of making, Rousseau points out, is to ask the individual to willingly go to the scaffold for his violation of the moral law. Here are his reasons:

The end of the social treaty is the preservation of the contracting parties. Whoever wants to enjoy the end must will the means, and some risks, and even some dangers, are inseparable from these means. The man who would preserve his life at the expense of the lives of others ought in turn to expose his own for their protection when it is necessary. The citizen is not a judge of the peril to which the law may expose him; and when the prince says to him, "It is expedient for the State that thou shouldst die," he ought to die, because it is only on that condition that he has enjoyed his security up to that moment, and because his life is not to be considered simply as the boon of nature, but as a conditional gift from the State.

Do we, in fact, ever sign this sort of contract voluntarily? The sovereign might bully us into it; as for the "State" — how are we to sign a contract with that entity? Rousseau, we must remind ourselves, is not trying to establish the reality of an abstract social contract and base the state's (occasionally cruel) justice on it. It is an irreducible fact of our lives that we are born into the state; its capacity to administer justice is the condition of our freedom, indeed, of our humanity; yet our lives are the state's property. Just how are we to reconcile ourselves to this?

Man is born free, and yet we see him everywhere in chains.

That theory of knowledge of which Hume is the exemplary representative, but to be found in one form or another in much of the major writing of the Enlightenment, has helped to create a situation where problems of public policy — of justice, of social and political connections — have become matters which must be dealt with in terms of personal psychology. We have been taught that our political principles and moral maxims are not to be derived from the concept "man," that we must base our reasonings on experience. But experience does not tell us what the shape of politics ought to be — only that we do, in fact, need politics. Once we find ourselves incapable of accepting rational or traditional foundations, the matter of giving politics form becomes very much like the problem of structure in the arts; politics must deal with the breakdown of the frame erected by its traditional institutions and their ideologies, much as *The Connection* will ultimately have to deal with the disappearance of the frame erected by traditional and rationalized theatrical forms. Instead of the forms naturally connecting with the psychological assumptions of a society (or audience) and the individuals in it, we shall have to determine and puzzle over just how the methods we create to establish

[71]

connections will fit the psychological possibilities of the moment. Indeed, much of our effort will go into determining just what those possibilities are: We shall all — artists, intellectuals, politicians — become propagandists, and therefore, necessarily, social psychologists.

Man is born free, and yet we see him everywhere in chains.

Rousseau's famous statement illustrates his finest insight into the nature of modern politics; for what he illustrates, in typically melodramatic fashion, is the conflict of psychological need and formal necessity created by the state. Political theory, if it is to respond to the needs of the state, must illustrate (more: it must make people believe) that the state's formal and restricting necessities are based on humanity's desire for freedom. Rousseau's statement, though we cannot readily explain its precise implications, strikes a sympathetic string in all of us. Its pathos gets to the heart of the matter, for it recognizes — and somehow we have really known these things all along — that social and political forms are not to be derived from principle, regardless of how strong our belief in that principle is; that the very fact of our rationality creates the disease of our social and political contradictions; that, as a result, the forms of our institutions may be unfixed and may shape themselves in response to the rational and irrational demands of the human environment; in short, that politics will have to reconcile apparent opposites. To recognize the necessity for both freedom and chains is also to recognize the possibility that political organizations might develop in opposite directions: toward democracy or dictatorship. But the ambiguity which Rousseau recognized in all political forms shows us that democracy and dictatorship may exist together; in fact, they may be different versions of the same impulse. Think of *The Social Contract*'s variety of implications for Robespierre, the Jacobin liberator who tried to create the dictatorship, enforced by violence, of the liberated.

To retain his humanity, Rousseau has told us, man must make moral choices; to make moral choices, he must be free. Yet man's freedom is dependent on the restrictions imposed by society, for the possibility of meaningful choice depends on the existence of those social norms which assure us that our moral maxims represent more than private desires. The state attempts to institutionalize these norms by giving them the official status of law. But just how does the state go about establishing its norms? And how, in turn, is the authority of those norms to be established? Here is Rousseau on the subject:

Since no man has any natural authority over his fellows, and since force produces no right to any, all justifiable authority among men must be established on the basis of conventions.

Let us forget, for the moment, the difficulties concerning the origins of conventions discussed earlier. If we accept the fiction of a convention which legitimizes authority, just how do we make this convention real to the citizen? What is to make him believe that it is relevant to his own life? The problem is of the greatest importance to Rousseau:

It is this that has, in all ages, obliged the founders of nations to have recourse to the intervention of Heaven and to attribute to the gods what has proceeded from their own wisdom, that the people might submit to the laws of the State as to those of nature and, recognizing that the same power which formed man created the city, obey freely, and contentedly endure that restraint so necessary to the public happiness.

If we cannot accept the authority of god, what fiction will convince us that we are obeying freely? How are we to accept the laws imposed even by a democracy or a popular leader? Rousseau's answer is the notion of the general will. The notion's ambiguity — it can be used as a justification for practically any sort of government — is notorious; it is often confusing and vague; yet something like it seems to be absolutely necessary for a politics which is based on morality, a politics which does not depend on absolute authority. It is doubly necessary where the ties of tradition have been broken, where the old forms seem to be incapable of binding or convincing anyone. The general will is to connect our private maxims with those of others; this will result in general laws which will be legitimized in the following manner:

> In order, therefore, to prevent the social compact from becoming an empty formula, it tacitly comprehends the engagement, which alone can give effect to the others — that whoever refuses to obey the general will shall be compelled to it by the whole body: this in fact only forces him to be free; for this is the condition which, by giving each citizen to his country, guarantees his absolute personal independence, a condition which gives motion and effect to the political machine. This alone renders all civil engagements justifiable, and without it they would be absurd, tyrannical, and subject to the most enormous abuses.

Rousseau almost seems to ask people to lie to themselves, to engage in a game of double-think. In reality, Rousseau recognizes that if we are to feel any identification with the work of the state, we will have to feel at one with it; and this will invariably force us to live with paradoxes, not lies. For we are both individuals and members of an organism. Unlike Hobbes and other proponents of power politics, Rousseau, when using the analogy of the organism, does not ignore the individuals which compose it, for he wants them to retain their quality of humanity. The organic wholeness of the state is not based on its own nature but on the nature of human feelings, on men's moral being, on their desire for liberty. To effect the sense of wholeness, then, we are forced to use anything readily available which has a genuine source in human feeling. For us, and for most Europeans and Americans in the past two centuries, the most readily available means of expressing the general will is likely to be some form of representative government. But as Rousseau sees, representative government will have to legitimize itself to everyone (not just those it immediately represents) if it is to be whole, if it is to provide us with connections which both bind and free. The mechanics of legitimation are as follows:

Except in this original contract, a majority of votes is sufficient to bind all the others. This is a consequence of the contract itself. But it may be asked how a man can be free and yet forced to conform to the will of others. How are the opposers free when they are in submission to laws to which they have never consented?

I answer that the question is not fairly stated. The citizen consents to all the laws, to those which are passed in spite of his opposition, and even to those which sentence him to punishment if he violates any one of them. The constant will of all the members of the State is the general will; it is by that they are citizens and free. . . . When, therefore, the motion which I opposed carries, it only proves to me that I was mistaken, and that what I believed to be the general will was not so. If my particular opinion had prevailed, I should have done what I was not willing to do, and, consequently, I should not have been in a state of freedom.

Now this whole rationalization will be acceptable only if it profoundly convinces us of its truth, and it can do so only by an appeal to our emotions. The feelings to be affected might be part of our nature, they might derive from tradition, or they might be inculcated by the state's propaganda — of which propaganda Rousseau's rationalization might form a part. In any case, some idea which elicits an emotional response will have to be available, whether it is a desire for representative government, for moral liberty as against natural, or whatever. If the emotion be absent, the connections tying the individual to the state are bound to break, thus denying the state the opportunity of creating the possibility for moral choice. Rousseau understood that the relevant feelings — the desires for both individual and communal choice — were to be found in all human beings; that the state, if it was to be more than an arbitrary mechanism, had to shape its institutional forms in conformity to these feelings; that rather than formulating abstract structures or conserving empty institutions, it had to conform to the general will. This accounts for the conservative strain in Rousseau, for he believes that if reconstruction is not to take place in a human vacuum it must be based on available institutions. It also accounts for Rousseau's belief in a *state*, rather than a universal, religion: He is not against individual religious liberty, but he does see the necessity for wholeness, for a connection between our public forms and our most private yearnings. And religious feeling is real: If properly used by the state it will be an instrument of unification, of moral wholeness, rather than division. Man's chains will create the conditions for his inner freedom.

Rousseau's, and others', unavoidable emphasis on psychological effect could lead to results as strange as the French Revolution's Religion of the Supreme Being and to the unintentional black humor of the ceremonies at Notre Dame — ceremonies not so different in purpose from those performed by the cardinal in Genêt's *The Balcony*. Indeed, if we are to think of the state religion as a stage performance which breaks through its frame in order to assault the spectator's (citizen's) feelings, we can understand Rousseau's almost fanatic position on the immorality of the theater. What lies behind his *Letter to d'Alembert on Spectacles* is the belief that state and church are our proper stages for moral unification, that the theater (that is, an instrument of propaganda), in drawing on the reservoir of human feeling, can only act as a divisive, and therefore immoral, force.

What role is the legislator — the artist of politics — to play in all this? For one thing, he will be confronted with the problem of employing, or creating, useful fictions; he will have to become a psychologist and decide which fictions have a real foundation in human feelings. But the task of the legislator in the modern state, Rousseau tells us, will be much bigger, much more ambitious:

Those who dare to undertake the institution of a people must feel themselves capable, as it were, of changing human nature, of transforming each individual, who by himself is a perfect and solitary whole, into a part of a much greater whole, from which he in some measure receives his being and his life; of altering the constitution of man for the purpose of strengthening it; of substituting a moral and partial existence instead of the physical and independent existence which we have all received from nature.

The prospect sounds frightening, and Rousseau's program has more than a faint resemblance to the spirit of 1984, to some of our cruder notions of human engineering. Yet the demands Rousseau makes of the legislator are based on a humane understanding of the individual's situation opposite the modern state. If we are to keep humanity from splintering into innumerable isolated units — a clear possibility once the framework of traditional institutions has become irrelevant to human feelings — we cannot depend on nature or natural law to take its own course; since nature has been freed by the new epistemology and our consciousness of freedom, since its alleged rules have become unbelievable, we shall have to shape nature ourselves. If there is to be liberty, rather than total disorder or absolute dictatorship, the conditions for liberty will have to be recreated to fit a new pattern.

Much the same situation is to be seen in the arts once the

classical rules lose their ready acceptance, once the spectator asserts his freedom to make judgments on his own. The artist must create new connections with his audience; he will have to develop unities based on existing possibilities for feeling if he is not to lock himself in the cage of his private world, if he is not to indulge the equally disastrous atavisms of random disorder and total mechanical organization. Useful fictions will have to be created: The artist will find it necessary to convince us, by whatever available means, that his work is real. Perhaps he will have to go further and become a legislator; not in the realm of ideas, as Shelley would have it, but in the realm of our artistic perceptions, our sense of unity. In short, he will have to *create* — not simply draw on — our modes of feeling. In order to do this, he will have to create his own role. The idea of the artist as imitator of nature will have no more relevance to modern possibilities than the idea of the legislator expressing either the divine will or the dictates of natural law. And so the artist becomes more and more the critic of foundations; indeed, the builder of, as well as propagandist for, new ones; he may be led to epistemology or to social criticism; his expressive form could range from the pure creativity of fantasy to the realism of history; whatever his path, its direction is far from clear. Rousseau himself tried to enact many of these roles. Surely it is of great significance that the search for one's proper social role first becomes an important literary theme in the eighteenth century. It is difficult to think of anything like Johnson's *Rasselas* or Voltaire's *Zadig* being written at any other time. The subject of the individual's search for a social role has since become a staple for the novel; in fact, it is almost inseparable from its history. But the significance of Johnson's and Voltaire's attitude is that they look on the idea of freely choosing one's social role as an evil leading to unhappiness and disorder. In short, they both saw that to *enact* a role in society (rather than stepping into the one which tradition has waiting for us and thus not performing a role at all) not only creates the possibility of personal unhappiness but tends to break traditional social connections. But in spite of the understandable feelings represented by this conservative attitude, perhaps in spite of ourselves, history has made us a gift of freedom and saddled us with the necessity for choice. Rousseau saw this clearly, and his reward was, of course, an almost total separation from his society. For once we are forced to play roles, each succeeding one is likely to be found wanting and to provide little more than a prelude or incentive for the succeeding one. Thus Rousseau attempts to transform the nature of musical notation, the nature of politics, the nature of literature; he alternately commits himself to being a diplomat, composer, critic, social scientist, moral reformer, novelist, autobiographer; and by the way he lived he tried to transform accepted social customs or possibly to destroy them altogether. The necessity of choice forced Rousseau to live with his own paradoxes: It led him to a profound desire for order, and to the yearning for total freedom and independence; there is his longing for human contact and fellowship, yet also his paranoiac insistence on being left alone. And all this is so often expressed in the language of violence by direct appeals to the public, one appeal often being in clear contradiction to an earlier one. Only in his political theory was Rousseau capable of using his conflicting emotions and, by giving these emotions the form of rational discourse, transforming them into an ideology whose aim was the unification of mankind. But *The Social Contract* rests on Rousseau's consciousness of his own and society's paradoxes.

This awareness and the melancholy words with which he tries to seduce us make him one of our first modern men:

Man is born free, and yet we see him everywhere in chains.

THE CONSCIOUSNESS OF LIBERTY, that open consideration of our moral, artistic, and political maxims, is partially based on our awareness of history: To look at the past with some sense of its own nature, its own character, is to become aware of its many possibilities, of the directions history might have taken. It is a commonplace that our feelings about the past tell us something about the present. Now our sense of there being a history — that is, a past which we have to reconstruct, rather than a clear and simple sequence of separate events which leads up to the present and to the future — is one particular aspect of modernism's necessity for criticism; or perhaps, one of its causes. Since we do not feel ourselves developing logically from the sequence of events immediately prior to us, a chronicle of those separate events cannot reasonably give us a convincing account of the past. It has too often been said that the distinguishing mark of modern historical writing is its emphasis on fact. The reverse is closer to the truth: Only as the exclusive emphasis on fact begins to lose its importance will real historical concerns be ready to appear. For only then do we become capable of dealing with the nature of development itself, rather than casually assuming that the listing of a succession of events implies a developmental sequence. Once history stops being a simple recital of political facts, its most urgent concern is likely to be with causality. For history will have to *construct* a narrative, and thereby connect events which had once stood alone, which had provided their own connection. Hume, while discussing the association of ideas [in *An Inquiry Concerning Human Understanding*], suggests how these connections are to be made:

To return to the comparison of history and epic poetry, we may conclude from the foregoing reasonings that as a certain unity is requisite in all productions, it cannot be wanting to history more than to any other; that in history the connection among the several events which unites them into one body is the relation of cause and effect, the same which takes place in epic poetry.

Hume, it is clear, sees historical writing not as a recital of events but as an intellectual and imaginative effort on the part of the historian dealing with those events. The connections he needs to make might force him, as they did Montesquieu and Voltaire, to consider aspects of man's life in society other than the political. After all these years, does not the question of just what knowledge is relevant to historical narrative still form a lively bone of contention? Does not today's historian need to make the critical decision whether such semirespectable fields as social anthropology and psychoanalysis will really provide him with historical knowledge; whether they will connect the events of the past; whether they are events in themselves? In any case, the historian (and his reader) now bears the burden of making the proper connections. And we shall need to do more than connect those events among themselves. Since *we* are making the connections, we shall have to consider the relation of the present to the past: How else are we to get a proper perspective on our causal associations? Furthermore, the reader, since he is relying on the historian's connections, will have to question that historian's relation to the events described — indeed, the historian should do so himself. There is no way out of it, we shall have to write and rewrite our histories.

For Edward Gibbon, the connective link between events in *The History of the Decline and Fall of the Roman Em-*

pire is provided, naturally enough, by the search for the causes of that decline and fall. Gibbon's motive for this search — what connects him to his material and lends it shape — lies in his intellectual attitudes, in his Humean skepticism. He sees his work as the epic (and recall Hume's association of the epic and history) of the decline and fall of humane rationality, of that civilized urbanity which had reached its summit during the age of the Antonines. This attitude, in turn, connects Gibbon's work to his own times, for he is writing the epic of the Enlightenment, the age in which rational intellect had to combat the dark cloud of ignorance, much as it did during the decline of the Roman empire.[10] Being the epic of the Enlightenment, the work must, of course, be an ironic mock-epic. For the skeptic, the necessary critical function reveals only decline and fall; the reconstruction which will emerge after the destruction of the present is the work of the future, and of this no epics can be written, only utopias. *The Dunciad*, with its mocking vision of doom, rather than Voltaire's *La Henriade*, is the epic of the eighteenth century. For the latter is a conscious lie; it is not about the heroism of the past or present; it is, indeed, a utopia, a plan for an enlightened future.

An intellectual of the Enlightenment cannot look at the history of Christianity, even if he is a believer, as an early chronicler might have done. For one thing, someone like Hume will be constantly aware that what we see and hear may be a function of our historical moment, that the conditions of the moment may allow us to see some events but not others. Thus we — the historian, the present age, the reader — by our awareness of these subtle determinants, become as much a part of any modern account of the past, as that past

---

[10] The notion of *The Decline and Fall* as an epic was suggested to me by Harold L. Bond's *The Literary Art of Edward Gibbon* (Oxford, 1960).

itself. Gibbon points this out when he discusses the chronicles written by many of the Gnostic sects:

Each of these sects could boast of its bishops and congregations, of its doctors and martyrs, and, instead of the four gospels adopted by the church, the heretics produced a multitude of histories, in which the actions and discourses of Christ and of his apostles were adapted to their respective tenets.

That each sect apparently composed its sacred accounts in order to justify itself teaches Gibbon, first of all, that religion has a history. If the Church had to choose four official gospels, then that choice itself might have a history — it might, in fact, be connected to other events. Worst of all, the Church, like the sects, might have made its choice for the purpose of self-justification. The assumption that the four gospels were adopted simply because god willed it becomes highly suspect or, at least, problematic. Indeed, the gospels have entered the realm of history. Second of all, and of greater importance to us, the historical practice of the sects teaches Gibbon that religious history ought to have the same standards as any other history; more strongly, it shows him that we should bring to religious history the same canons for belief which we use in dealing with our own personal pasts. But this last notion, which would seem to be trivial and somewhat obvious, does present us with difficulties — not only for religious history, but for history in general.

I shall look at some of these difficulties as they concern Gibbon, our first modern historian. It strikes me that Gibbon, rather than Voltaire, is the first major historian who gives us some sense of being our contemporary. The reason for this is of the greatest importance: Gibbon's modernity stems from the feeling he creates that history, rather than being a straightforward narrative of events, is composed of a series of problems each of which must be looked at with a good deal of philosophical subtlety. But let us examine Gibbon's procedure in the following passage; it is almost at the very end of his famous Chapter XV, the chapter which deals with the causes of mass conversion during the early years of the Christian faith:

But how shall we excuse the supine inattention of the Pagan and philosophic world to those evidences which were presented by the hand of Omnipotence, not to their reason, but to their senses? During the age of Christ, of his apostles, and of their first disciples, the doctrine which they preached was confirmed by innumerable prodigies. The lame walked, the blind saw, the sick were healed, the dead were raised, daemons were expelled, and the laws of Nature were frequently suspended for the benefit of the church. But the sages of Greece and Rome turned aside from the awful spectacle, and pursuing the ordinary occupations of life and study, appeared unconscious of any alterations in the moral or physical government of the world. Under the reign of Tiberius, the whole earth, or at least a celebrated province of the Roman empire, was involved in a praeternatural darkness of three hours. Even this miraculous event, which ought to have excited the wonder, the curiosity, and the devotion of mankind, passed without notice in an age of science and history.

Gibbon's real subject, it should be clear, is the nature of historical evidence: His epistemological concerns have become, necessarily, part of the fabric of his narrative. The cutting irony of his remarks should be readily apparent to any of us modern unbelievers — or even to believers of a skeptical frame of mind. Now Gibbon's irony is not simply a means of beating the censor; it is an almost unavoidable consequence of his difficulties with the theory of knowledge. Gibbon draws the reader into his description: We have to interpret the meanings of the events along with him; we must decide which way the irony cuts. This collaboration is not based on any system of mutually shared beliefs; it depends, rather, on our mutual doubts, our doubts about the judgments we make of others' experience.

Hume, in trying to resolve his Cartesian doubts concerning the possibility of knowledge, has told us that historical knowledge must at some point be based on experience:

We learn the events of former ages from history, but then we must peruse the volume in which this instruction is contained, and thence carry up our inferences from one testimony to another, till we arrive at the eyewitnesses and spectators of these distant events.

Only the testimony of someone who has experienced an event can make that event believable. But a Christian's experience may include the witnessing of miracles. The problem lies in just what and whose statements we believe to be connected to *actual events*; not whether those statements are based on someone's experience. We must ultimately make a judgment of the validity of the eyewitness' experience. Hume, unfortunately, tells us at one point in his argument that the chief principle by which we connect statements with events, causality, being a mental operation based on a species of instinct, is as incomprehensible in relation to ordinary events as it is to prodigies of nature. Hume's (extremely convincing) argument, by internalizing the problem of knowledge, has deprived us of any legitimate argument for challenging the connection between the believer's experience (his impression) and the actual event. As a result, we are left to deal with the miraculous — to the unbeliever, the incredible — only in terms of irony. The believer may take the report of a miracle at face value; the skeptic is likely to know better.

Gibbon's treatment of the evidence for miracles, indeed his general approach to historical sources. rests on Hume's speculations and conclusions about these subjects in his philosophical writings. The insistence on the naturalistic approach to all problems, on bringing the laws of secular history to bear on religious history, and the search for natural causes to explain the general acceptance of miracles — all these are equally the concern of the philosopher and the historian. The motives Hume posits for the acceptance of miracles, in Section X of *An Inquiry Concerning Human Understanding,* are almost identical to those Gibbon attributes to the early Christians in his Chapter XV. Finally, there is Hume's own irony in dealing with the miraculous:

There is another book in three volumes (called *Recueil des Miracles de l'Abbé Paris*) giving an account of many of these miracles, and accompanied with prefatory discourses, which are very well written. There runs, however, through the whole of these a ridiculous comparison between the miracles of our Saviour and those of the Abbé, wherein it is asserted that the evidence for the latter is equal to that of the former, as if the testimony of men could ever be put in the balance with that of God himself, who conducted the pen of the inspired writers. If these writers indeed were to be considered merely as human testimony, the French author is very moderate in his comparison, since he might, with some appearance of reason, pretend that the Jansenist miracles much surpass the other in evidence and authority.

We ought to look at this footnote of Hume's in the context of his argument; for Hume's irony depends on his having clearly demonstrated that the evidence for Christ's miracles is as unacceptable as those for the Abbé's, that if we accept the evidence for the earlier prodigies we should, a fortiori, accept that for the more recent ones. Hume's basic argument is easily summarized: It is that an observer's report, if it is to be acceptable and believed, must correspond to the general course of our experience. What then are we, people living now, to make of miracles if we have never experienced any? Here are Hume's thoughts:

A miracle is a violation of the laws of nature; and as a firm and unalterable experience has established these laws, the proof against a miracle, from the very nature of the fact, is as entire as any argument from experience can possibly be imagined. . . . The plain consequence is (and it is a general maxim worthy of our attention) that no testimony is sufficient to establish a miracle unless the testimony be of such a kind that its falsehood would be more miraculous than the fact which it endeavors to establish.

Hume's point is, in short, that if we believe nature to be lawful, there is no logical basis for accepting any evidence for miracles; we would not believe one if we saw it with our own eyes. For Hume's contemporaries, and for us, there is no reasonable way of avoiding these conclusions: We are, in our empirical sense of evidence, products of the Enlightenment and therefore weigh the evidence of the past, including earlier historical accounts, in accordance with the laws of nature. Along with Hume, we are likely to make comments of the following sort:

It forms a strong presumption against all supernatural and miraculous relations that they are observed chiefly to abound among ignorant and barbarous nations. . . . When we peruse the first histories of all nations, we are apt to imagine ourselves transported into some new world where the whole frame of nature is disjointed, and every element performs its operations in a different manner from what it does at present.

Here is a wholly modern attitude toward the writing of history, an attitude which is constantly aware that historical knowledge is dependent on the epistemology of the knower and that epistemologies change with the passage of time. Hume asks the most basic, and therefore most difficult, questions about the *foundations* of historical knowledge. These questions are posed simply on the basis of his researches in "mental geography"; and if we are familiar with these, we know that Hume will inevitably reach the conclusion that our perception of history — the connections we make, the causes we impute — may often depend on our personal feelings, on the psychological states which our time has made possible for us.

This modern attitude toward the philosophy of history is the dominant theme of Gibbon's practice as an historian. Here is Gibbon wondering about belief in the resurrection:

At such a period, when faith could boast of so many wonderful victories over death, it seems difficult to account for the scepticism of those philosophers who still rejected and derided the doctrine of the resurrection.

Gibbon leaves us — indeed, makes us deal with — the problem of whom one believes, the Christian doctors or the pagan philosophers. To do this we must decide what our standards for evidence are; how else are we to come to terms with Gibbon's meaning? It is obvious that some people at some time believed in miracles. If the Christian believer accepts the early miracles, why should he not accept recent ones? One way of dealing with the problem, Gibbon points out, is to assume that god withdrew his special dispensation from a sinful world, and, as a result, the occurrence of miracles came to an end. But this assumption, Gibbon illustrates, leads to some serious difficulties:

And yet, since every friend to revelation is persuaded of the reality, and every reasonable man is convinced of the cessation, of miraculous powers, it is evident that there must have been *some period* in which they were either suddenly or gradually withdrawn from the Christian church. Whatever area is chosen for that purpose, the death of the apostles, the conversion of the Roman empire, or the extinction of the Arian heresy, the insensibility of the Christians who lived at that time will equally afford a just matter of surprise. They still supported their pretensions after they had lost their power.

At whatever time we place the disappearance of the miraculous, there will still be a number of superstitious souls who experience miracles. Why should we reject the evidence of their senses? Gibbon, after posing the question and embarrassing us with the impossibility of an answer, decides to drop it altogether. He changes his approach to the problem, and bypasses it in Humean fashion. He will not question the evidence for miraculous events, since, as Hume has taught us, there is no sure way of connecting evidence to event — miraculous or ordinary — in any case; instead, he will change the ground of the question to the psychology of belief, and ask why people accepted the reality of Christian miracles. Just a few of his devastating imputations follow:

Whatever opinion may be entertained of the miracles of the primitive church since the time of the apostles, this unresisting softness of temper, so conspicuous among the believers of the second and third centuries, proved of some accidental benefit to the cause of truth and religion. . . . The primitive Christians perpetually trod on mystic ground, and their minds were exercised by the habits of believing the most extraordinary events. They felt, or they fancied, that on every side they were incessantly assaulted by daemons, comforted by visions, instructed by prophecy, and surprisingly delivered from danger, sickness, and from death itself, by the supplications of the church. The real or imaginary prodigies of which they so frequently conceived themselves to be the objects, the instruments, or the spectators, very happily disposed them to adopt, with the same ease, but with far greater justice, the authentic wonders of evangelic history.

Gibbon has tried to illustrate, with deadly success, that the belief in miracles is based entirely on one's psychological predisposition to believe. Chapter XV of Gibbon's work is, almost in its entirety, an illustration of this proposition earlier formulated by Hume. We learn that the success of Christianity — that is, the acceptance of its miracles — depended wholly on a combination of accidental circumstances properly exploited by the Church. The truth or falsity, the rationality or absurdity of Christianity's doctrines had little, if anything, to do with it.

The psychological predispostions for belief were readily

available to the early Church. For us, matters are likely to be different. We are bound to exploit our knowledge that belief is grounded in the psychology of individual human beings; we might be tempted to induce those predispositions necessary for the desired belief by the clever use of propaganda — as, indeed, the Jesuits and a number of evangelical sects often did. For a man of the Enlightenment, this psychological predisposition might be shaped by the history he knows, in the view he takes of the past, and by the manner in which he consciously appropriates historical epochs. The writing of secular history becomes a substitute for hagiography. Its purpose is ideological and propagandistic; its real concern, the present and the future. Think of the underlying reasons for Voltaire's portrayal of the age of Louis XIV; and think of Gibbon's purpose in stressing the rationality and politeness of the age of Augustus. One of the possibilities of Gibbon's work is that it will succeed, by drawing the reader into its mode of apprehension, in creating a psychological predisposition which will eventually produce an enlightened attitude toward men and society which will reject the gathering forces of darkness, the irrationality, and "the cloud of critics." This attitude demands Gibbon's irony: To absorb it in reading *The Decline and Fall* is to affirm one's capacity for doubt, one's capacity to remain sane. For our perception of Gibbon's irony not only connects us with his work and with the past; much more importantly, it makes it possible for us to deal with the oppositions created by our own, and Gibbon's, theory of knowledge.

3

ARTISTIC SPACE

HUME'S URGENT ATTEMPT TO DISPEL his Cartesian doubt by grounding the foundations of knowledge in common experience has tended to internalize the problem of epistemology. He has, unwittingly, cast a substantial doubt on the possibility of any theory of knowledge (a set of objective standards) which is independent of the individual knower. Whatever the laws of association which connect our experiences of the external world — resemblance, contiguity, or causality — they must eventually refer to ourselves; for we learn these laws through the agency of the causal principle itself, which, as Hume has illustrated, must be an irreducible element of our constitutions, an innate idea. Thus there is no clear line, no space, between ourselves and the external world, for the only thing which connects us with it is cause and effect — something private, a species of instinct. We have already seen the effect this notion had on moral theory, political ideas, and on our way of looking at the past and that the effectiveness of any of these pursuits becomes dependent on our sentiments, our personal predispositions, and how these are manipulated. What are the implications of all this for the arts? Hume, in a digression from his epistemological concerns, has told us that the appeal made to taste by a work of art — or to moral sentiment by an action — must be immediate; it must be made to our humanity, not to a set of abstract principles. A work, or an action, which we judge by coolly standing back, might elicit our rational approval but will not really convince us, for it will have no concrete effect. Hume is interested in the affective qualities of art, because like any good neoclassicist he is concerned with art as a moral instrument; with both its capacity to delight and teach. But if the work of art is to be made, and judged, in terms of its affect, its capacity to convince our emotions, we find ourselves confronted by the same difficulties we experienced in our attempt to derive universal moral maxims from experience. Just how are we to know whether a given work of art, or a human act, will have the same effect, will convince, or elicit the same judgment from one individual as another? Hume, of course, assumes that the laws governing our reactions are universal, since they are based on some social norm like utility. A savage, he tells us, has only his own pleasures in mind; a civilized man will, instead, have some notion of public utility. The philosophic difficulties aside — and I have discussed them earlier — can we really assume that the "civilized" man will care a hang about public utility, or, if caring, that one man's ideas about utility will be another's? Thus if we are to convince anyone, we are likely to do so in an extremely personal manner; perhaps in terms of the very foundations of our knowledge — as we have, in fact, seen in *The Connection*. It is just this sense of an extremely personal method of attack, especially when it is not related to a common and basic epistemological concern, which makes one feel the lack of expansiveness in even the best modern poetry. It is the difficulty of connecting one's necessarily private response with anything else in the external world that makes the experience of so lovely a poem as Stevens' "The

Candle A Saint" so narrowing, so evanescent, and so temporary.

The difficulties which emerge from both Hume's theory of
knowledge and the general attitudes it represents are likely to
go beyond anything Hume might have suspected. Let us accept, for the moment, Hume's assumption that a work of art
is to inculcate moral feelings by appealing, ultimately, to our
instincts, or at least one species of instinct — causality. It will
not be long before we realize that a *particular* moral, one
which supposedly represents a social norm — for instance,
that apprentices should listen to their masters, behave themselves, and work hard — will not readily insinuate itself into
the hearts of even those apprentices who wept copiously at a
performance of Lillo's *The London Merchant.* I use the example of Lillo because for the eighteenth century, to major
figures like Diderot and Lessing, his plays illustrated the emotional and didactic possibilities of realistic bourgeois drama.
Once we realize that the didactic possibilities, taken in this
narrow sense, are rather slim, what are our reactions likely to
be? If we do not believe in Lillo's message to start with, we
might simply take the play as a melodrama, and have a good
weep; or we might take it as self-parody (rather than irony,
which is based on mutual doubt) and have a laugh at its expense. As a result, we make it possible for the notion of
morality to be exiled from our concept of art altogether. The
artist's objective might be simply to move people, to shock or
titillate without purpose, solely for the sake of affect. On the
other hand, the artist who has the capacity to understand the
problems with which history has saddled — rather challenged — him, and who can see their relevance to basic
human concerns, will find himself turning to the deeper
levels of emotional insight demanded of him, to more profound considerations of the sources of morality, or perhaps to

[95]

the fundamental questions of how we know and how we connect. Instead of indulging himself with the simple-minded reactions of *The Rehearsal, The London Merchant,* or *Ubu Roi,* the playwright will be forced into the moral difficulties and uncertainties — and these might, after all, be both convincing and edifying — of *The Beggar's Opera, Woyzeck,* and *The Connection.*

It should not be wholly surprising that many artists anticipated the philosophers in sensing the subtle shifts in the theory of knowledge, in being alive to the gradual obliteration of the space between ourselves and the external world. For any awareness on the part of the beholder that there is no clear line between him and the external world, that a work of art, for instance, does not have an impenetrable frame around it, will destroy, or at least change, his anticipations, his very perception, of that work of art. As a result, the validity of forms with objective rules — rules which exist independent of the beholder — will be called into question, for they will have no psychological reality and therefore no capacity to move. Any competent artist is obviously sensitive to the anticipations of his audience. He is bound to know, by the very demands of his art, when the beholder's grasp of traditional forms has become doubtful, when these forms have stopped representing the shape of reality. He will also sense when the situation, the attitude toward knowledge, demands more than a modification of the old forms and requires, instead, a direct appeal to the emotions. Perhaps artists of the past have been quick to sense this sort of thing because their principal work was performed in the service of religion; in fact, they have always provided the most immediate contact between the church and its flock by lending this contact physical reality in the form of buildings, statues, and paintings. Thus artists have been the church's chief propagandists, and in order to retain their effectiveness need to anticipate the official apologists in sensing the possibilities and necessities of the moment. This becomes clear when we consider that artists were instructed by an edict of the Council of Trent, in 1563, to abandon their traditional forms and help propagate the faith by a direct appeal to the emotions. The Council of Trent had only given its official stamp of approval to something many artists had sensed and practiced (when the opportunity lent itself) for years. Michaelangelo, after all, died in 1564; and his work, I assume, did have its effects. But consider something much more basic, something which involves the manner in which the beholder's eye perceives the canvas. The single most important development in drawing the spectator into the canvas was the discovery of two-point perspective near the end of the fifteenth century. The technique destroyed the picture plane and created a world with depth, a world which goes beyond the canvas. Think of the contrast between the one-point perspective of Raphael's High Renaissance "School of Athens" — our perception of its figures at the front, on the picture's plane — and any early painting of Tintoretto's.

I have already discussed the difficulties a direct appeal to the emotions is likely to create for the notions of form and unity. These hardships — and the possibilities they reveal — can be seen in the breakdown and stratification of rhetoric during the sixteenth century, its conversion from a meaningful and integrated element in moral and artistic discourse to an empty formalistic shell. The Middle Ages and the High Renaissance were, it is not too fanciful to claim, ages of rhetoric. The common acceptance among the learned of normative rules which regulated communication is both a cause and reflection of the tendency to approach almost everything in terms of a logical and unified structure. This, in turn, gives any theory or work of art an independent, objective status, separate from the knower or the beholder. Rhetoric was concerned with effect rather than affect — the latter was taken for granted — and the laws regulating effect, it was assumed, were objective and permanent. These procedures are dependent on the assumption that the mind, if not its products, has a structure which is more or less fixed and permanent; that its structure corresponds to the form of our logic; and that this logic can be naturally converted into ordinary discourse by rhetoric. Since the maxims of morality are supposedly derived from a general system, or even from a concept of nature, which has a logical structure, true rhetoric (unlike the false, practiced by the Sophists in Plato's *Phaedrus*, which can be used for anything) becomes a part of the science of morality and that science's most important connection with the practical world. In fulfilling these functions, rhetoric unites the demands of logical structure and those of public effect.

All this is beautifully illustrated in the *Metalogicon*, an exemplary and marvelously clear treatise on rhetoric and related subjects, written in the twelfth century by John of Salisbury. In Book I, John defends the trivium, for he claims that logic, grammar — which includes literature — and rhetoric are united both in having a common source and in their attempt to attain a common objective. He attacks a straw man, Cornificus, for his claim that rhetoric is irrelevant to wisdom, and that the natural art of persuasion has no rules. Reason, John tells us, perceives the system of rules in nature and these rules should be taught because they correspond to reality. But here are John's own words; they are worth one's attention:

One who would eliminate the teaching of eloquence from philosophical studies, begrudges Mercury his possession of Philology, and wrests from Philology's arms her beloved Mercury. Although he may seem to attack eloquence alone, he undermines and up-roots all liberal studies, assails the whole structure of philosophy, tears to shreds humanity's social contract, and destroys the means of brotherly charity and reciprocal interchange of services, Deprived of their gift of speech, men would degenerate to the condition of brute animals. . . . It may thus be seen that our "Cornificus," ignorant and malevolent foe of studies pertaining to eloquence, attacks not merely one, or even a few persons, but all civilization and political organization.[1]

Professor Kristeller's exhaustive studies of Renaissance humanism have taught us that Renaissance rhetoric largely adopted and developed the system which it received from the Middle Ages.[2] Consequently, the intimate link between Renaissance moral philosophy and rhetoric is hardly unex-pected. At first, the humanist in Italy was no more, or less, than a teacher of rhetoric. The *studia humanitatis* included rhetoric, grammar, and moral philosophy. Humanism, in short, was not a philosophy but a program of rhetorical and grammatical studies; a program which, because the subjects of rhetoric and grammar were considered to be basic and grounded in the structure of the mind and of nature, eventu-ally became linked to the teaching of morals. It is a link, as we have seen, which was never entirely secure. Even John of Salisbury, whom we might call a humanist of the twelfth-century Renaissance, did, after all, have to defend its validity. Whatever the weaknesses of the link, the High Renaissance accepted rhetoric as the natural system of logical communi-cation, that is, communication which had the property of unified form; a property which was a part of people's com-mon expectations, and which assured the rhetorician of his intended effect. Renaissance logic was the theory of commu-

[1] John of Salisbury, *Metalogicon*, trans. D. D. McGarry (Berkeley and Los Angeles, 1955).
[2] See especially the essays collected in *Studies in Renaissance Thought and Letters* (Rome, 1956).

nication in the world of learning: It was necessary for the proper knowledge of scholarly truth. Rhetoric, on the other hand, was the theory of communication between the learned and the lay public. Both logic and rhetoric were considered necessities for a complete theory of communication.[3]

Just what conditions make rhetoric possible? What assumptions about human nature make it real? The procedure of rhetoric can be valid only in terms of some notion which grants the mind a logical structure which corresponds to the structure of the external world. There is both a Port Royal *Grammar* and a Port Royal *Logic*. The *Logic* is, significantly, a development of the rhetorical categories of the *Grammar*. This derivation was assumed to be perfectly natural since both the *Grammar* and the *Logic* were based on Descartes' philosophy of mind, on his assumption that the mind has a logical structure of innate ideas which corresponds to the structure of the external world. Language and its theory, grammar, are representations of these innate ideas, and therefore our logic, if it is to be relevant to human discourse, must be based on the rules of grammar. According to the scholars of Port Royal, both logic and grammar — which included rhetoric — are necessary for the propagation of the true faith; they assume that the individual can be both reached and convinced by their *Logic* and the rhetorical means provided by the *Grammar*. But all this, it must be remembered, is based on the validity of Descartes' argument, on it having stilled his own, and others', doubts. For once we deny the mind its logical structure, we have shut off the possibility of its being moved by the force of logic. In order to convince, we shall have to assault the mind directly; our appeals will be to experience rather than logic; we shall have

---

[3] I owe this last point to Wilbur S. Howell's *Logic and Rhetoric in England, 1500–1700* (Princeton, 1956).

to provide impressions rather than reasonable arguments. Ultimately, rhetoric will need to be metamorphosed into drama. In the eighteenth century, David Hume was to formalize the practical problems of morals and art into philosophy; he began, as I have pointed out, with problems of knowledge which artists had sensed as early as the end of the fifteenth century. Here is his formalization:

It is evident that belief consists not in the peculiar nature or order of ideas; but in the *manner* of their conception and in their *feeling* to the mind.

At some time during the sixteenth century — say the end of the High Renaissance, a designation vague enough to be useful — both drama and the art of narrative find themselves burdened with a rhetoric which has become little more than an ornamental superstructure. This rhetoric corresponds to no apparent reality in its chosen subject matter. In fact, it is independent of it; nor can its forms be traced to the structure of the spectator's mind. The works produced by this rhetoric can be responded to only by the spectator's self-conscious and somewhat precious adoption of a predisposition toward its rules. This may involve both an artificial historical leap and an attempt to adopt, and act out, the rules which were relevant to some situation in the past. Whatever the shape of the rhetoric, it is not likely to convince anyone who is not already a convert; the strength of its appeal will depend on the attitudes struck by the members of a coterie. If looking for a contemporary analogue, we need go no further than the childishness, the precious antiquarianism of what we call camp style. Turning once more to the sixteenth century, some developments in its drama will make the point. Consider, for instance, the antiquarian drama cultivated by the members of the Countess of Pembroke's circle and best represented by Samuel Daniel's *Cleopatra*. While its empty rhetoric was titillating the affected and pedantic taste of a few courtiers, the richest period in English drama, with its novel language of the emotions, was entering its greatest phase. Or take the fanciful demands on one's cultivation made by any pastoral drama, even one as good, and in its way realistic, as Tasso's *Aminta*. Both drama and prose fiction try to rid themselves of their rhetorical baggage by adopting some notion of realism; the presentation of real life, it is supposed, will make a direct appeal to the emotions. But this leaves the writer with a problem we have encountered before: The emphasis on realism and affect tends to destroy the formal properties of any work of art. How are the lifelike elements in a drama, for example, supposed to connect? Just what in the realistic sequence of events is supposed to leave the spectator with something more than a disconnected set of vague feelings? The dramatic unities, supposedly derived from Aristotle's *Poetics* but really invented by Italian commentators like Minturno and Castelvetro, constituted the major attempt of the Renaissance to deal with these questions; an attempt, as we shall have occasion to see, which succeeded in hanging a critical millstone around the neck of dramatists for two centuries or more. The fact was soon forgotten, but at first the unities were intended to lend the drama a measure of verisimilitude: There was to be but one set for the play, since a stage is not likely to hold two different places at the same time — especially if they happen to be at some remove from each other; and the elapsed time was to correspond, give or take a few hours, to the fictional time of the play. As for the unity of action — the rule of having a single, rationally developed plot — it was to provide the connection for the events in the play and for the various emotions aroused in the spectator. Yet no real justification was ever advanced for these rules, neither on the basis of realism nor on the grounds of the mind's structure. The rule makers simply assumed that the unity of action was a predisposition so deeply engrained in any spectator by his artistic culture that any drama had to adhere to its command in order to meet the demands of realism. They were quite wrong, of course.

Whatever the reasons, and they are not overly complicated, as we approach the end of the Middle Ages the natural association of the various arts, their dependence on one another, begins to break down. Only rarely will one find a medieval piece of sculpture which was meant to stand separate from a building or monument. The Middle Ages had no real notion of autonomy in the visual arts: They were not considered to be independently "fine." The idea of an artistic production which is independent and integral is something we owe largely to the Renaissance. Sculpture begins to stand free of its niche, and we witness perhaps not the invention of easel painting but certainly its first significant use. As sculpture and painting become independent arts, they develop their own set of rules, a rhetoric independent of their setting. But once we ask these independent works to appeal directly to the emotions, their rhetoric is likely to break down. Before its liberation, the work's shape and its intended effect was largely determined by its setting — for instance, it being in a church. The shared and accepted religious philosophy which dictated the shape of the church also determined the worshiper's mode of perception, as it did the form of the decoration, sculpture, and painting which he beheld. Thus as we enter a Gothic church, many of its decorative details may appear disparate; but they clearly did not to the medieval craftsman or worshiper who saw them in terms of the church's total rhetoric. Now if the independent works of art all created their separate affects, just how is a building, like a church, to make a unified impression on the individual? And failing in this, how is it to connect with the worshiper in terms of its intended function? What, after all, is to keep the church from being a rather jumbled, though delightful, museum?

At this point, the reader, no doubt, needs to be assured that the direct appeal to the emotions was as real an issue for the arts of the sixteenth and seventeenth centuries as it is for ours. This is to be seen in many of the religious and artistic enterprises of the Counter Reformation. The edict of the Council of Trent ordered that,

By means of the stories of the mysteries of our Redemption portrayed by paintings or other representations, the people be instructed and confirmed in the habit of remembering, and continually revolving in mind the articles of faith.[4]

This pronouncement led the way for a minor flood of literature calling for realistic art as a proper vehicle of moral instruction, realism having the capacity to make a direct appeal to the emotions. The saints who had been idealized by Renaissance and Mannerist painters were to be given dirty feet: if their effect was to be immediate, they had to appear real.

The obvious relevance of the Counter Reformation to the arts (and the subject has generated much scholarly heat) is most evident in the artistic accomplishments, perhaps more important in the beliefs, of the Jesuits. A surprising number of the latter were artists, playwrights, or poets; furthermore, the Society commissioned a great deal of work, generally done to specification. The Jesuits believed that man could bring some influence to bear on the shaping of his destiny; if grace is to do its work, men will have to come to its aid and

[4] Quoted in Rudolf Wittkower, *Art and Architecture in Italy: 1600 to 1750* (Baltimore, 1958). I cannot overemphasize how much I owe to this marvelous book: It taught me how to *see* the baroque marvels of Rome; indeed, most of this chapter could not have been written without its guidance.

do their share. Art can obviously play an important role in bringing men to collaborate with the worldly manifestations of grace, in actualizing spirituality through the mundane. St. Ignatius' *Spiritual Exercises* indicate how this is to be accomplished. The exercitant, to prepare his soul for its confrontation with the world, must make the spiritual abstractions of Christianity real to his own emotions. The dogmas of the church are to become vivid by an assault on all his senses: He must feel the pain of Christ's passion; he must be seared by the flames of hell; nor is he to be spared the sight of suffering sinners, and the smell of their burning flesh. The exercitant must obliterate the space between the privacy of his own being (his personal instincts and desires) and the abstract, though objective, existence of Christian dogma. Only thus will the tenets of dogma become real; and only in this fashion — not by rational argument — will the exercitant's faith be made secure in face of the temptations and arguments of reason. The contrast of this unsentimental education to the ordinary academic instruction in scholastic dogma is akin to that between the formalism of a sermon by Bossuet and the frightening immediacy of one by Edwards; one aims for rational assent, the other for conversion. Only after the exercitant has internalized Christian dogma, after he has made the universal Christian drama a part of himself, is he ready to return to the stage of the world. It is something like the experience of the spectator at a naturalistic drama, a matter I discussed earlier. You may remember that this spectator is prepared for action in the world only after he has internalized the drama's action, after he has made it real in terms of his private concerns; only then will he be ready spiritually to confront the world on the stage and, if the conversion has been effective, *actually* confront the world outside the theater.

It is not entirely clear just how much direct effect the

Spiritual Exercises had on artistic practice. The matter is not really important, and therefore will continue to be a subject for endless scholarly debate. Of relevance to our immediate concerns is the well-known tangibility of Bernini's and his contemporaries' work, for it is part of the artistic attempt to match the emotional feats as the *Exercises.* Consider the effect created by Bernini in his *Aeneas, Anchises and Ascanius,* of the contrast between the dry, wrinkled flesh of Anchises pressed against the firm body of Aeneas. We behold real flesh, the sorrow is made tangible and reaches from inside the stone to our deepest feelings. The tangibility is used to attain an immediate effect; it attempts to breathe life, the possibility of drama, into the dead marble. And it is dramatic affect which artists of the Baroque will use to regain that unity of effect lost with the deflation of the old rhetoric. The Baroque created theatrical settings for halls, staircases, chapels — almost anything. It accomplished this by unifying all the elements of a structure with its decorations: Architecture fuses into sculpture; sculpture, in turn, becomes painting; and they are all thrust into the beholder's space — this for the one purpose of becoming an immediate, concrete cause of a spiritual and esthetic effect. For the total effect creates an illusion which is actually perceived by the spectator's eye; unless he fights what he sees, he will be helplessly drawn into the drama's world. The unity of the effect is, ultimately, as much in the spectator's feelings, in the species of instinct which connects his impressions, as it is in the objects which he beholds. This is why, Professor Wittkower points out, Roman architects and planners of the seventeenth century did not like the formalism of open vistas. Instead, he tells us, they

. . . preferred the enclosed court-like piazza to a wide perspective and exploited fully the psychological moment of dazzling fascination which is always experienced at the unexpected physical closeness of monumental architecture.

The possibilities of the approach are marvelously illustrated in a late Baroque example, Filippo Raguzzini's Piazza S. Ignazio in Rome. The piazza provides the setting, significantly, for the Jesuit church of S. Ignazio; a church whose nave is dominated by Father Pozzo's *quadratura* fresco on its ceiling — an illusionary allegory of the missionary works of the Jesuits — which makes the worshiper practically fly out of the church. The piazza itself is quite literally a theater. The life on it has consequently become a drama. But in this theater (in this real world), we are both spectator and actor. For the dwellings which face the church — from whose windows laundry may be hanging or mothers screaming for their children to come home — may serve, depending on our position, as wings on a stage, thereby converting the church porch into the theater's orchestra, or as boxes and balconies, thereby turning the piazza into the orchestra and the church porch into the stage. The effect is something like the one created by Frank Lloyd Wright's ambulatory, or ramp, at the Guggenheim Museum: The casual stroller — no one really looks at paintings — is both the beholder of and actor in a vast, constantly evolving, and perhaps living action. But there is a crucial difference between the Baroque piazza and the contemporary . . . I hesitate to call it museum. Wright's ambulatory was built solely for effect; if any other purpose was intended, it was surely to have the living spectacle divert the participant's attention from the contents of the museum — the incidental works of art. The shifting illusions of the Piazza S. Ignazio, on the other hand, are meant to create a unity between ourselves and the external world. We are united with the life of the piazza and the materials of art, for these have become part of each other while yet retaining their individual integrity. The creation of these effects derives from, and directs us to, the idea which controls and motivates the form of the piazza: the connection, inside the church, between the world of matter and the spiritual life. The connection is experienced whether we are about to enter, or have just emerged; it depends on our being drawn into the space around us; on the artistic work — and the shape created for reality itself — capturing us with an irresistible immediacy. In short, the task is to create the possibility for belief by going beyond (and I use Hume's phrase) an "order of ideas" to experience itself; experience which, since it is secretly shared with us by art, is to be the cause of the properly ordered effect — the intended system of belief.

What of the building itself? If it is to draw us from the piazza, it too will have to create an immediacy of effect, for it can no longer rely on the worshiper's ready acceptance of the spiritual reality inside its walls. It surely cannot depend, for example, on the efficacy of the scholasticism which, Professor Panofsky assures us, produced Gothic architecture and, I assume, the worshiper's appropriate response to it. Simply recall that much of protestantism's appeal was based on the privacy and emotionality of salvation, the primacy of the Bible, and the devaluation of the church. The church will need, quite literally, to become the house of god; it must become the theater on whose stage the real presence is to materialize. These demands were met by the typical church structure developed by architects of the Baroque. Vignola's Gesú, the mother church of the Jesuits built in Rome between 1568 and 1584, became, of course, the model for innumerable Baroque churches all over Europe. Its broad nave and short transept draw all attention toward the center of the church: toward the altar, the pulpit, and the large cupola. The play of light allowed by the cupola is of such importance that Vignola was led to introduce some modifications in the vault which allowed him to frame the light with the largest amount of darkness possible. The effect created by this real light bears the burden of symbolizing — rather, concretely being — the holy spirit during the celebration of mass; further, it actualizes the connection between the spirit's presence in the church and the external world. The holy spirit cannot be made into an object, of course. It must be experienced in the total drama for which the church is the setting. It is this setting which lends reality to the formal rhetoric of the mass. And the whole scene is punctuated, drawn together, and given life by the constantly changing yet dominant play of light — a light which bathes everything with the glow of reality.

This use of light to obliterate spatial distinctions is most beautifully — no, overwhelmingly — illustrated by Bernini's Cathedra in the apse of St. Peter's in Rome. I can hardly go into much detail about this complex work. But perhaps detail would be irrelevant in any case, since the effect of the Cathedra, in spite of the shifting spatial arrangements, is so simple, so immediate. The composition's task is to make the historical establishment of the Church real; to make it — the work of time — a physical fact at the moment of the beholder's contemplation. As the spectator draws (or is drawn) near, he finds himself in a space which he shares with the past, present, and future; he is in the midst of saints and angels whose physical location is uncertain; he is incapable of distinguishing image from reality, history from the present moment. St. Peter's throne — the earthly symbol of the holy spirit's eternal rule — floats, unsupported, in the absolute center of the composition. Yet our eyes are finally drawn to a point above it, to the real light originating from a window in the center of the angelic glory, a light which filters through the transparent image of the holy dove. And it is this light which really shapes how we perceive and experience the Cathedra, for it provides the illumination which binds into a unified effect, which gives meaning to, the play of colors and spaces created by the multicolored marble, the bronze and stucco of the figures and decoration. But I shall have occasion to return to the significance of light a bit further on.

The objective of these dramatic procedures is not, of course, simply to create a dramatic performance. In many ways churches have always done this, to the point of actually staging plays. No, the objective is rather to create a dramatic situation which is life itself, which connects with the real world, and which attempts to attain affect by drawing the spectator into its orbit. Ultimately, the dramatic procedures developed for these purposes are likely to develop their own static rhetoric; a rhetoric whose mechanical use will destroy the possibility for affect. Turning to actual theatrical performance, think of the fate of Garrick's style of acting. Diderot praised it for its direct appeal to the emotions, and Dr. Johnson expressed his admiration for its natural manner. Yet later generations rejected the style for its rant, for its artificiality, for its quality of rhetoric. The progress from affect to rhetoric has quickened today: Think of how little time was needed for method acting to degenerate into a transparent set of mannerisms; of how we tend to laugh at what had seemed utterly real just a few years ago. It is this quickened critical procedure, this seemingly irreversible urge to analyze the nature of our responses, which makes the apparent absence of acting-style a necessity for *The Connection*. After all, it was a naïve attempt to ensure verisimilitude which led, ironically, to the dogmatism of the dramatic rules; rules exerting sufficient authority to command the critical attention of Racine and Dryden, though neither felt convinced of their dramatic necessity. Racine, of course, accepted his chains; Dryden did so only very occasionally. Yet whatever difficulties they created for the playwright, rules of some sort were clearly necessary. For once the direct appeal to the emotions turns from its task of creating a unified effect to an empty rhetoric, once the verisimilitude of a play is used simply to elicit a number of disparate momentary responses, there is nothing to hold the production together, nothing to give its emotions a purposeful direction, except an imposed abstract form, a set of dramatic rules. The same difficulties elicit the response of the Classical Revival in German architecture of the eighteenth century. After the German Baroque had degenerated into a riot of effects, the Classical Revival attempted to impose an abstract symmetry on architecture. It tried to legislate a sense of unity which was in no way a response to the problems of the Baroque, which was not based on the possibilities of affect, and which, finally, reestablished the space between the beholder, or dweller, and his object of perception. In refusing to deal with the problematic legacy of the Baroque, the Classical Revival broke all continuity with the past, and tried to establish a moribund antiquarianism. There is no connection between Pöppelmann's Zwinger in Dresden and Gilly's design for a National Theater in Berlin; nor is there really much relation between Gilly's design, marvelous as it is, and the architecture of ancient Greece. For the Classical Revival was, typically, largely the creation of a scholar, Winckelmann; a scholar who, Lessing was ready to point out, happened to be misinformed about the art of antiquity.

It was Lessing who attempted, in the *Laocoon*, to reverse this trend toward classicizing. The attempt also dominated his career in the theater. Both he and Diderot, whom Lessing often followed, made the struggle a central theme of their dramatic criticism; it provided the impetus for their own plays as well. The popularity in France and Germany of Voltaire's classical tragedies — tragedies which allowed highly trained coteries the pedantic titillation of identifying rhetorical and dramatic rules or recognizing classical references — this popularity was vigorously opposed by Diderot and Lessing. They used British domestic tragedy, especially Lillo's *The London Merchant*, as a counterpoise to French classicizing. The pathos of bourgeois drama is, of course, meant to elicit tears which are shed spontaneously in response to the realistic situation onstage. But eighteenth-century attempts at realistic tragedy were generally artless and failed to attain any unified effect. The whole genre created problems which were not really solved until Ibsen taught us how to deepen the psychology of the realistic theater and how to conduct the released emotions toward a social purpose. Diderot and Lessing attempted to use the emotive possibilities of bourgeois realism by placing them inside the frame of the dramatic rules, a frame based on the psychology of Aristotle's *Poetics*. Recall that morality was Diderot's master concern; further, also recall his belief that all moral maxims are somehow derived from experience. Diderot's concern with the drama as an emotive instrument and his obsession with the creation of realistic illusions are based on his wish to create experiences which will lay the foundation for moral teaching. Thus the arts must quite literally create experiences which are emotionally real to the spectator but which must be forced into a shape which gives them moral purpose. Diderot, like almost everyone else in the eighteenth century, ultimately formulates the business of bringing reality into the work of art in terms of Aristotle's notion of imitation. Here it is applied to music by Rameau, the nonfiction hero (or villain) of Diderot's fiction, *Rameau's Nephew*:

A melody is a vocal or instrumental imitation using the sounds of a scale, invented by art — or inspired by nature, as you prefer [that is, Diderot]; it imitates either physical noises or the accents of passion. You can see that by changing a few words in this definition it would exactly fit painting, eloquence, sculpture or poetry.

Since Rameau is mainly concerned with the state of his stomach, the question of morality creates no problems for his definition of a work of art. But notice, if it were not for the qualification of "sounds of a *scale*," this definition would make a fine justification for *musique concrète*. Rameau proceeds to tell us that a sung melody must strive toward declamation if it is to seem real. Now we can look at this as an anticipation of Wagner or Debussy, because in all cases declamation — the attempt to introduce the real speaking voice — is regulated and given emotive direction by some underlying rule. But take away the scale from Rameau's definition, and you are left with the imitation of "either physical noises or the accents of passion" — which would anticipate neither Wagner nor Debussy, but the grunts and groans of John Cage's vocal productions.

Music has its scale. What is to provide the formalism in literature? If reality is to be used for a moral purpose, it must, obviously enough, seem real; and as Diderot has recognized in his *Paradox of the Actor*, artifice is necessary to convey the illusion of reality. Diderot's difficulties are best illustrated in his *Entretien sur Le Fils Naturel*. This dialogue was translated by Lessing into German, who readily acknowledged the great debt he owed it. It begins with Diderot running into Dorval, a man famous for his total dedication to morality. Dorval tells Diderot of his father's anxiety for the morality of his children: The world is wicked, and if one is not to succumb to its temptations, the image of goodness must be made vivid constantly to one's senses. The father intends to bring this about by having the members of the family reenact in the living room a memorable event from their own lives. The performance is to be repeated from generation to generation, thus guaranteeing the perpetuation of the father's moral teaching. The first performance, Dorval tells Diderot, is to be in a week. Alas, there is a hitch: The father has died before the premiere, and a friend wearing his clothes will need to imitate him. Dorval ends the interview by inviting Diderot to the performance under the proviso he remain hidden. Diderot, of course, attends. The performance goes on according to the script until the friend imitating the father makes his entrance. He imitates the father so well that the whole family breaks into an orgy of tears and, as a result, is incapable of carrying on. Diderot leaves extremely disappointed, for he does not know how the event was to end, and therefore is incapable of understanding its moral import. While walking home, he begins to suspect that perhaps the whole thing, including the false end, was a fictional drama and that he had been taken in. He rejects this, eventually gets a script for the whole event, and then proceeds to have a lengthy, and rather tiresome, discussion about it with Dorval. I am sure no one needs to be told what the discussion was about. But there is a final turn of the screw. The script which is the subject of discussion happens to be identical with *Le Fils Naturel*, a bourgeois drama supposedly written by Diderot. At this point, think once more of *The Connection*. Diderot's elaborate game, it should be obvious, contains more than the seed of those dramatic procedures which will grow into Gelber's play.

We are confronted here with a curious reticence — and Diderot was seldom a reticent man. Why did he refuse to pursue his insights to their logical conclusion? Why the failure to fuse the space, to meld the realities, of stage and audience? The answer lies, of course, in Diderot's moralism. If *The Connection*'s procedures are to be used didactically, the moral objective, as I pointed out, must be anarchism, a total transformation of the self, rather than the inculcation of a social norm. And it is the latter which Diderot and his disciple Lessing want of the theater. Lessing, in fact, defines dramatic genius as the capacity to make moral maxims vividly real for the spectator; dramatic genius reveals that the good is also beautiful. To accomplish this a frame which organizes raw experience to that purpose must be constructed. The classical rules are out of the question: Lessing cannot accept anything mechanical, for it would destroy the possibility of emotive effect. Indeed, Voltaire and the French classical tragedians are Lessing's favorite whipping boys. Realism is a necessary prerequisite if the playwright is to elicit an emotional response from his audience. Lessing therefore attempts, in his *Hamburgische Dramaturgie*, to justify domestic tragedy in terms of Aristotle's *Poetics*. For Lessing, the key notions in that much abused document are pity and fear. The spectator's pity for the character on stage elicits the emotion of fear. So far Lessing is no more than traditional in his interpretation. But take note of his comments on the notion of fear. It is, Lessing tells us,

by no means the fear which is aroused in us for another person by the misfortune about to befall him, but it is the fear which arises for ourselves, through our similarity to the suffering person; it is the fear that we ourselves may become this pitied object.[5]

[5] This and the following quotations of Lessing are from the *Hamburgische Dramaturgie* and were translated by H. B. Garland in his *Lessing: The Founder of Modern German Literature* (Cambridge, Eng., 1937).

For the spectator to feel this terror a connection must be established between him and the object of pity on the stage. To accomplish this, Lessing concludes, the tragic hero must be like the people in the audience; if he is to elicit the proper emotion he cannot be an ancient Greek king but will have to be a member of the middle class. The updating of the *Poetics* becomes the justification of domestic tragedy! But how does this get us to Lessing's basic interest in the drama — moral edification? Here too the answer will be found in Aristotle. For the purpose of rousing the emotion of fear is to effect catharsis, by which Lessing means, oddly enough, "the transformation of the passions into virtuous qualities." To each his own Aristotle. Lessing has converted the psychological device of catharsis into an ethical idea; virtue may, after all, be derived from our ordinary experience and the emotions to which experience gives rise. The necessity for a unfied and controlled moral effect has led Lessing away from the implications of Diderot's theorizing. Lessing settles not only for less than the possibilities of *The Connection,* he does not even explore the social and political implications of realistic drama. He is satisfied to leave the spectator with his private moral concerns rather than turning him toward society. Lessing is, after all, an establishment dramatist, though a liberal one. And here lies the reason for the elaborate attempt to justify bourgeois realism by the notion of catharsis. For catharsis, as we have seen, reconciles the spectator to the social norm; it settles him into acceptance of the status quo.

These ideas lead Lessing, a man of more than ordinary talent, to the propagandistic simple-mindedness of his famous bourgeois tragedy, *Miss Sara Sampson.* It was the basic epistemological assumption of the Baroque — the necessity for conversion to be effected by the experience of reality — which led to Lessing's use of realistic drama for propaganda; but the assumption contained implications which ranged far beyond his rather mild and humane concerns. The rousing of the emotions, the almost literal capture of the individual, all the artistic practices so successfully executed by the Baroque can, after all, become the weapons of political propaganda — moral or immoral. Consider Louis XIV's use of monumental art and architecture to literally impress the image of absolute power, of glory, on a population which paid for this privilege with its taxes. Bernini himself spent days watching Louis in action, sketching him in various positions that he might produce his great portrait bust of the Sun King. The bust turned out, interestingly enough, to look much like Alexander the Great, the type of royal glory. Finally, think of the propagandistic influence of the French Academies for painting and architecture in the eighteenth century. The Academies were created for the purpose of training civil servants who would paint, sculpt, and build for the greater glory of the state and monarch. The idea of art as political propaganda, familiar enough to antiquity, was rediscovered by Enlightened France. The rediscovery was made possible, and necessary, by some of the artistic and political consequences of the doubts concerning the foundation of knowledge. Rousseau, as I pointed out, showed the Enlightenment that the possibility of accepting chains, of reconciling oneself to political authority, had to be based on a real emotion — what Rousseau called the general will. What better way to impress this acceptance, to connect the subject to the sovereign, than to use the possibilities for affect created by the Baroque. Or, on the other hand, as Robespierre might have suggested, why not take advantage of the individual's very necessity to feel emotionally committed to the state? Why not use art's possibility for affect to sunder the individual's chains? It has, after all, been suggested that liberty was the invention of the arts.

As we know, for the frame of the arts to be broken in this

particular way, for connections to be made, or dissolved, in the interests of political power is to court dangerously the destruction of the notion of a fine art altogether. This may be necessary, for all I know, for the world to survive. Yet it hardly augurs a world one would much want to live in. Surely we are familiar with the possible directions of a political art strenuously dedicated to the perpetuation of an ordered society. We have our choices of Socialist Realism — rather those blessed with its products have hardly any choice about it; or worse, because freely produced and freely accepted, of the moral realism represented by the machine which produces paintings by someone like Norman Rockwell: a realism which, in its way, obliterates the space between the spectator and the work of art. He, the beholder, is the person in the painting. Why else would he look at it? But the space is not broken for the sake of emotional impact; nor is it broken for the sake of criticism or conversion. What could be further removed from the possibilities, the risks, of *The Connection?* No, the sole purpose is to tranquillize, to lead to the acceptance of some idealized notion of one's own life as a norm.

The same psychological assumption which generated the innovations of the Baroque made of its art a viable instrument for political propaganda. The Counter Reformation did, after all, conceive of art as a weapon in the service of the Church. Yet was not the objective of the Counter Reformation to transcend the Church as an institution? To appeal to the Christian's private emotions? The appeal of the best Baroque art is, of course, private. It attempts to initiate a personal religious experience rather than impressing us with the authority of the Church as an institution. We may be drawn, initially, to St. Peter's by our distant view of the dome, a view which has been impressed on everyone's mind as the symbol of the universal Church; but as soon as we are

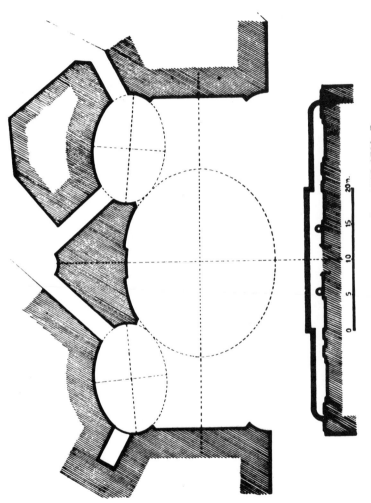

Filippo Raguzzini. Piazza S. Ignazio—plan. 1727–1728. Rome.

Caravaggio. Ecstasy of St. Francis. No later than 1597. The Wadsworth Atheneum, Hartford, Connecticut (Photo: E. Irving Blomstrann, New Britain, Connecticut)

Bernini. *Saint Teresa in Ecstasy* (Cornaro Chapel). 1644–1652.
Santa Maria della Vittoria, Rome.

Rembrandt. *The Night Watch*. 1642. Amsterdam.

thrust into Bernini's square and surrounded by his col-
onnade, it is our private emotions which are being played on.
The space between ourselves and the monuments representing the institution begins to be broken. A fine contrast between this procedure and that of political propaganda may
be drawn from that prototype of fascist planning, Mussolini's
monumental approach to the square. It makes the emotion
Bernini intended almost impossible to experience, for the
purpose of the approach is to remind us of the reconciliation
of two sources of worldly authority, the Church and the
State. But if we avoid this monstrosity and enter the square
from the side, we shall eventually, by a sequence of impressions which makes the process seem inevitable, be drawn to
that irresistible climax, the Cathedra. And here personal experience is everything; the institution has been removed
from consciousness. The privacy of the experience is punctuated by the natural light which is responsible for creating the
most important effect. This light dissolves us into the surrounding physical presence; light — not an institutional figure out of the Church's past nor a symbolic object which
may be analyzed in traditional terms — creates the spiritual
reality. In the Cathedra, it is the religious context which enables the light to summon forth the religious meaning of our
personal reaction. The context may be taken for granted and,
on the whole, suppressed from consciousness; yet light does
have numberless Christian connotations though these may
be conveniently vague. But let us consider the changes in the
use of light as its meanings become secularized. One direction taken by artists has been noted already: Light can become the worldly manifestation of the monarch's source of
power; it can symbolize the glory of the Sun King in both the
heavenly and political realms. But generally the method of
Baroque art is too intimate for the mass effects required by

political propaganda. Only the arrival of the mass media will enable us to affect large numbers by means of secular ideas. (Hence Rousseau's assumption that a national religion is necessary for the modern state.) But light can travel in directions other than political propaganda.

The painter who most clearly anticipates, perhaps creates, the practices of the Baroque is Caravaggio. His particular genius was to lend an intimacy of overwhelming power to the religious experience. Caravaggio accomplishes this by drawing us into the canvas in a manner which is possible for neither two-point perspective nor even Tintoretto's most seductive work. In his *Supper at Emmaus,* for example, Christ's foreshortened arm breaks out of the picture's plane and invades the beholder's space. As a result, Caravaggio has not only drawn us into the frame, he has created the illusion of bringing the painting to us. In addition, the logical disposition of the figures is sacrificed for the sake of emotional impact. Caravaggio's very technique is designed to elicit the largest amount of contact between painter and viewer: He drops the classical method of preparing his paints and of drawing his figures on the canvas. The canvas becomes, instead, a place to experiment with color and design; and this is clearly visible to the beholder. As a result, Caravaggio has largely obliterated the distance created by the finished quality of a High Renaissance painting, for we become involved with the very struggle for expression which we see on the canvas. Lest we jump to the conclusion that Caravaggio is really a modern expressionist, we should remember that he accomplishes his task in terms of his received traditions. He ultimately depends on Christian iconography for his subjects, and he expresses these by means of compositional devices based on those of Tintoretto and Titian. But, of course, his departures from the tradition are much more important. Caravaggio psychologizes the subjects of iconography by giving them an emotional content based on the affective potentialities of realism. What is the ultimate effect which a painting of a religious subject can hope to attain by realistic means? If the subject is a saint's moment of mystic union, it is to draw the beholder into an actual participation in this union. To accomplish this, the saint cannot be idealized; he must be recognizably human if the beholder is to identify with the reality of the mystical event.

The great problem for Caravaggio's realism — and for the Baroque in general — was how to translate religious vision, a private experience, into a tangible representation. Before the seventeenth century, painters quite literally picture spiritual metaphors: Take, as an example, the glow from a saint's heart. In the *Ecstasy of St. Francis,* Caravaggio has the task of translating the supreme moment into images which are intensely human. The painting attains its overwhelming effect by realistically portraying St. Francis in a trance. We are forced to deduce the spiritual and psychological event from the facial expression and the physical detail. Only the light reveals the mystery. But it is a *natural* light breaking from the evening sky, not a miraculous light streaming from heaven or from the saint's heart. Caravaggio has transformed a natural phenomenon into a symbol of an inner religious experience: a transformation which his personal vision of light allowed him to make. The process is similar to Wordsworth's repeated use of water. Consider the significance of the river Wye in "Tintern Abbey." Among other things, this quite real stream reminds us of the continuity of past, present, and future; it is a visible sign of both our mysterious and small beginnings and our ultimate, perhaps massive, union with many other streams in the open sea.[6] But there are impor-

---

[6] I have learned a great deal about Wordsworth and, further on, Hopkins from Geoffrey H. Hartman's *The Unmediated Vision* (New Haven, 1954).

tant differences between the poet and painter. Wordsworth's natural symbolism is highly personal; he expects us to feel our way into its meanings because our capacities for experiencing a specific natural scene, the river Wye, are similar to his. Caravaggio, on the other hand, still depends on our acquaintance with the traditional Christian meanings associated with light, however vague they may be. It is, finally, the Christian context which allows the beholder to connect with the realistic portrayal which had initially drawn him into the painting. But the effect depends, of course, on Caravaggio's having translated the Christian symbolism into a language which is private and psychological, rather than into an institutional rhetoric.

Bernini, in spite of his profound devotion to the religious themes of his major sculpture, carries the symbolic use of light a step closer to its secular destiny. In the Cathedra of St. Peter's, as I mentioned, he uses *actual* light rather than light realistically represented. In this case, the symbolic import of the light filtering through the dove is, on the whole, clear. But Bernini puts natural light to a much more ambiguous and problematic use in what is perhaps the most sensuous and elaborately illusionistic composition ever created by an artist: the famous, perhaps notorious, Cornaro chapel in the Roman church of S. Maria della Vittoria. Bernini's task is to make us *participate* in Saint Teresa's mystical union with Christ. For both this miracle and Teresa's suspension in midair can be accepted by us only if we become a part of the composition's sensuous and spiritual activity; that is, if it insinuates itself into our field of perception and causes the whole event to become our private vision. Baroque painting was, of course, confronted with this problem in the representation of saints. Illusionist painters often solved it by showing the saint, rather than in an attitude of devotion, actually soaring off to heaven in the company of angels. A fine example of the technique may be seen in Canuti's and Haffner's fresco, *Apotheosis of St. Dominic,* in the Roman church of SS. Domenico e Sisto. The assumption which shaped the whole theatrical scene is that the vision — made real by the illusionism — is in our minds.

How does Bernini make us part of his composition? As we face the Cornaro chapel, our eyes are firmly drawn to a spot somewhere behind the altar where we behold the delicately sculpted Teresa prone in midair, her mouth open in a gasp. A seraph is in the act of plunging the arrow of divine love into her heart. High above the chapel, we perceive a painted group of angels separating the clouds to admit the heavenly light. The rays of light which are thus allowed to shine on Teresa and the seraph are made of stucco. Now the symbolism adhering to this part of the composition is, in spite of the intentional perceptual confusions created by illusionistic painting and sculpture, perfectly traditional and readily understood: The heavenly light is the visible sign of the union in marriage of Teresa and Christ. Bernini's iconography is based on traditional images and on Teresa's own description of her mystical union. But how does Bernini make the event our own vision? To begin, there is the incredible lifelike quality of Teresa's face: In it Bernini captures the moment of union, and we can almost hear her moan. Then there is Bernini's usual way of having his figures obliterate the separation between their own space and ours: We are not sure what spatial plane Teresa occupies; since she and the seraph move freely in depth, they occupy our space; furthermore, her foot and some of the drapery protrude from the imagined frame of the sculpture and reach into the space beyond the niche, the space which is rightfully ours. Even more important is the setting of this central group, for Bernini has designed a vision and yet has surrounded it with reality. Above the doors of the chapel, behind prie-dieus, we see the members of the Cornaro family kneeling as well as discussing the miracle. They are carved figures, yet they are in a real setting, a real chapel. At first we are not sure whether they are real or not; we are almost tempted to join them in their choice location. For a moment, we might almost take this part of the composition to be an early example of pop art: The members of the Cornaro family remind us, after all, of those lifelike dummies in real buses one has seen in one exhibit or another. Yet Bernini is not playing a game, and there is a real motive which takes all this bravura beyond theatricality: Teresa's vision must be recreated in us for it to become real. The stucco perspective behind the Cornaro family makes it appear that they are in church. As a result, their space is an extension of ours; they are concerned with the miracle on the altar, but so are we; in short, their vision is our vision. But why do all these devices strike us with such unerring immediacy? For one thing, Bernini has had the courage to use the sexual implications of the whole tradition of mystical union and, more specifically, the sexual implications of Teresa's own words. She writes that the sting of the arrow of divine love is like the "sweetest caressing of soul by God." [7] Bernini has managed to work his stone into the most sensuous representation of orgasm I know. The beholder, especially if he happens to be male, is quite naturally aroused; in spite of himself, he becomes indecorously involved with what is going on under the drapery; bluntly, he may picture himself as the cause of orgasm.

We are ready now to return to the question of light. What gives Teresa reality, what turns her face to flesh, is the *real* light which illuminates her face. For Teresa's divine illumi-

[7] Quoted by Wittkower.

nation does not come from the painted sky; neither does it come from the sculpted rays; its source is, in fact, a hidden window. This light shifts constantly, and we are made aware of its fleeting nature. Teresa's face can be seen properly only when the light strikes her in the correct way. Thus her momentary vision becomes our momentary vision; it turns into our experience of the supernatural. We must recall, however, that the real light derives its power to transform, to make us believe in the reality of the miraculous, from the religious assumptions which created the artificial rays of light descending from the painted heavens.

For the sake of affect, to give us the power of vision, Bernini has connected all the visual arts into one unified master design. The unity is, of course, created by the affect. Bernini has combined real and feigned architecture, real light with a painted sky, and so forth; and he has connected the beholder with the entire composition by drawing him into its space. In the process, he has broken all, or most, of the rules of the various arts he has used; indeed, he has transcended all the accepted genres. It is thus impossible to experience the composition in terms of our expectations about sculpture, painting, or any of the other visual arts. We are left to our own devices, and we must somehow experience the Cornaro chapel directly, without the predispositions provided by our knowledge of a genre. Yet, in spite of all this, Bernini does not really destroy the frame of his work of art. To begin, our vision of Teresa can be experienced properly only if we stand in the nave, at the exact center of the composition. Further-more, as I have mentioned, our capacity to experience Bernini's work fully, in terms of its total meaning, depends on our knowledge of its religious frame. Bernini still depends on a symbolism which is objective and, to a degree, tradi-tional. He does not obliterate the space between us and the work of art completely; he may draw us into his composition, but the image of light is never totally subjective — neither for him, nor for us.

In spite of Bernini's conservation of an artistic frame, of a system of beliefs uniting the many effects into a single meaning, the Cornaro chapel does create the possibility for irony. I mean irony of the sort I discussed in relation to Gibbon. One hardly needs to be reminded that Bernini's whole method, his attempt to make his work the cause of a real vision, is based on the same epistemological doubt which, a century later, was to make possible Gibbon's irony about visions. What if we come to Bernini's work with the same skepticism which prevents us from accepting miracles? What if we cannot equate orgasm with mystical union? One possible approach, given these eventualities, would be the pedantry of historical scholarship. The scholar would industriously search out all possible iconographical meanings and place the work in its historical and intellectual context. So far the approach is, on the whole, harmless and, who knows, perhaps even useful. But the next step is for the scholar to insist that the work can be experienced only in terms of his historical reconstruction; that we must all make an historical leap and adopt the emotions of someone who actually believed in miracles. It should be obvious that this would destroy whatever possibilities Bernini's art has to convince us of its emotional reality: Bernini works through the affect, or not at all; to come to him with an elaborate rule book for his rhetoric is to deny him the opportunity for destroying that rhetoric. If, then, we come to the work as unscholarly skeptics, what form is our ironic reaction to the miraculous likely to take? Unless we are utter clods, we surely will not laugh at Teresa's outlandish pose. But our experience of the work is likely to be entirely secular, and thus sensuous to the point of distraction. The sensuality should draw us wholly into the composition's orbit, obliterating the space which separates it from us. Yet I doubt that Bernini would have been happy with our reaction; for the cause which has elicited the powerful effect of our sensuous reaction is hardly identical to the cause of the miraculous vision; for the skeptic, only the *real* light will enter the field of his vision; he is likely to look only at Teresa's face, not at the heavens above her. Clearly the work can be experienced in both secular and religious ways. When looked at with the eyes of the irreligious, the work's unity will disappear, for we are likely to gaze only at Teresa's face: The unity of effect will be destroyed by our incapacity to have a total vision of the chapel. But the emotion which results from this partial vision will be, no doubt, more violently powerful, more sensuously intense than that experienced by the believer in miracles. Sex, after all, is more than potent. And here lies the great danger for the church — but also its great opportunity. If the skeptic's experience of Teresa has become life itself, if the obliteration of space has caused that experience to be incomplete, there is always the possibility of its completion in the skeptic's life outside the church, away from his experience of art. The affect produced by Teresa's sensuality might lead to an eventual vision of the miraculous in our ordinary experience. Here, then, is something like the ironic procedure implicit in both Gibbon's history and more so in *The Connection*. The ambiguity of vision, the artist's and spectator's mutual doubt, might lead to an emotional orgy of critical destructiveness. But the emotion, coupled with the openness created by its ambiguity, might lead to the possibility of reconstruction on new terms: in Gibbon, on the basis of humane rationality; in *The Connection*, through the necessities of personal union.

I shall now turn to the most important secular — and

being secular, to us the most relevant — implication of the Baroque's use of light. Let me begin with a question: What might be the result of removing Caravaggio's natural light in *The Ecstasy of St. Francis* from its religious context? What would happen to the natural symbolism if it were not anchored in religious belief? We have already seen one possibility in Wordsworth's use of water. Wordsworth imbues the actual objects he describes (not images he creates) with a private moral significance which he hopes we shall also perceive. But Wordsworth's personal, and secular, symbolism — indeed, his very hope of communicating the symbolism to us — depends on his assumption that the moral order he perceives in nature, though fathomable only through private communion, does have an independent existence. This development can be taken a step further. Consider the assumption of someone like Mallarmé that our ideas of light, or any phenomenon we choose, create images or symbols (the poet metaphysician's jargon begins to proliferate at this point) whose logical relationship is only to each other. This formal verbal order — in someone like Valéry it is almost mathematical — is the only external connection the images make, for whatever meaning we give them must be utterly private. Let me ask another question, one related to my last one: What would happen if we were to take Caravaggio's natural light, now secularized, and turn it to unnatural and irrational use in a realistic setting? Something of this sort does occur in Rembrandt's most famous, and most problematic, painting, *The Night Watch*. The painter and novelist Eugène Fromentin observed long ago [8] that Rembrandt, though working within the Dutch tradition of realistic representa-

---

[8] Eugène Fromentin, *The Old Masters of Belgium and Holland,* trans. M. C. Robbins (New York, 1963). My view of Rembrandt owes much to this sensitive and charming book.

tion and using its highly successful rhetoric, became interested primarily in light; light considered for its very own sake.

Rembrandt's interest in light does not seem to have its source in the formal problems of color or composition; rather, it seems to be the product of some internal, personal pressure. In *The Night Watch,* one has the feeling that the subject got in the way of his private concerns. At first glance, the painting impresses one as the usual Dutch realistic but posed representation of the members of a guild or of the board of governors of some hospital. But a careful look soon puts all expectations formed by the tradition out of mind. What is this group about to do? How did some of the figures get into the group? The faces are much too carelessly executed to satisfy the demands of a group portrait. Furthermore, the composition, the disposition of elements in the grouping, seems quite irrational. But most inexplicably, the beholder is drawn to a small and unidentifiable figure to the left and rear of the painting's center. One's eyes are drawn to it irresistibly because its light dominates the whole canvas. Who is this creature? Is she human or some supernatural appearance? How did she get into the grouping? These questions prove to be irrelevant, for the figure's only meaning is located in its light; indeed, it seems to have gotten in the way of Rembrandt's (no doubt) abstract expressive concerns. Rembrandt attempts to suffuse the objective scene with his subjective vision, and in the process he superimposes himself on his subject and on its innate meaning. Consequently, not only the compositional but also the symbolic value of his light becomes uncertain and can be understood only in terms of Rembrandt's private vision. Our experience of the painting and of the objects it represents inevitably becomes internalized. We are also likely to be more concerned with Rembrandt than with the subject he paints. If we look at *The Night Watch* in terms of the tradition it supposedly represents, it becomes clear that Rembrandt can connect himself to its conventions and to its realistic subjects only through the mediation of his personal vision. In using the tradition he breaks with it, for he cannot really bring his private concerns into rapport with its demands. Thus the painting becomes an experiment in self-expression, and the results seen on the canvas become unsure. Fromentin has formulated the problem with his usual conciseness:

> To me the most positive thing contained in this picture is the interesting testimony it bears of a mighty effort. It is incoherent simply because it attempts many contrary results. It is obscure only because the rendering was uncertain and the conception vague.

One might think that *The Night Watch* is, after all, an action painting.

But is *The Night Watch*, as Fromentin would have it, quite incoherent? Rembrandt does break the boundaries and outlines of his figures. Yet this is, after all, a way of drawing us into the painting. The light itself pulls us past the picture's plane and into its background. The elements which tend to make the composition irrational also draw us in. Consequently, the very act of perception should force us to create a new set of relationships. The coherence thus established will, of necessity, be personal; the beholder's feelings will be either entirely esthetic and formalistic or will involve some profound appeal to an emotion which he cannot quite identify. Fromentin's reaction to *The Night Watch* — and he wrote his comments in the second half of the nineteenth century — beautifully illustrates the difficulty of Rembrandt's task: His paintings had to perform the job of criticism; and the criticism had to be a part of his artistic effect.

[130]

Fromentin, being a painter, had the sensitivity to see that whatever reality there was on the canvas, it was not the ordinary (perhaps extraordinary) Dutch realism. Yet Fromentin looks at Rembrandt's painting with Franz Hals' accomplishments in mind. He does not quite know what to make of his own perceptions — he cannot make a judgment about them —, for they do not add up to a complete esthetic and moral experience. Fromentin (and perhaps we) knows only that he is drawn into the depths of the canvas, that he feels nagged; yet he cannot quite connect with whatever reality the painting might represent, with any specific reaction it might be attempting to elicit. *The Night Watch* must, of course, be taken on its own terms; the painting itself, and its light, is the reality — much as is the world created by *The Connection*. But if we are to attain the capacity of seeing and understanding in Rembrandt's own terms, his work will have to shape us and provide us with new artistic predispositions; rather than foregoing a rhetoric altogether and replacing it with a real world, it will have to recreate our notion of what the real world is; its ultimate task will be to criticize and partially wipe out our pasts. Rembrandt tries to reshape us — and herein lies his modernity — by making us feel dubious about just what our perceptions represent, just how much they relate to the external world rather than our own drives and desires — dubious, in short, about the relationship between cause and effect. He has succeeded all too well in creating a critical effect; alas, he has failed in the task of reshaping future generations in terms of his own vision. Has not every new artistic movement appropriated Rembrandt in some manner? Everyone makes of Rembrandt the secret precursor of his own concerns: The history of art and art criticism has seen Rembrandt the Impressionist, the Abstract Expressionist, Rembrandt the action painter — who knows what the next perception of *The Night Watch*'s reality is likely to be.

In a different way, the matter of creating new perceptual predispositions had also created unexpected difficulties for Caravaggio. By portraying his saints in a realistic manner, he had hoped to effect the spiritual conversion of ordinary people. Unfortunately, the unlearned he had hoped to attract rejected the dirty feet of St. Matthew; they would not accept reality inside the artistic frame. The real significance of this event does not lie in the realm of esthetic perception. For the people who rejected Caravaggio's method did so because the spiritual event he tried to actualize had no reality for them. To be accepted, it had to exist in the realm of abstract rhetoric: in the church, not in the heart and mind of the beholder. The Counter Reformation had clearly not done its work, and Caravaggio, due to his dependence on the intimacy of affect, was not capable of coming to its aid by creating images for the use of mass propaganda. Ironically, Caravaggio's religious paintings became potent enough to transform the beholder's artistic predispositions only when they began to be looked at in secular terms. Once we separate them from their religious meaning, the critical propagandists can, of course, go to work. And, indeed, they have not disappointed our expectations. Some even see Caravaggio as an earlier version of Rembrandt and therefore a great-grandfather of abstract expressionism. All this nonsense aside, it is important for our purposes to remember that Caravaggio, unlike Rembrandt, always tries to lead us from the canvas to the external world, rather than having us linger inside the canvas itself or inside ourselves.

The capacity of perceptual and esthetic predispositions to blind us to reality became depressingly clear after an exercise I recently assigned to my students. I handed them, without identification, the famous scene from Book I of Wordsworth's *Prelude* where the poet, when a boy, steals away in a boat. I asked the students to write a simple description of the physical events in the poem. Here are Wordsworth's beautiful lines:

One summer evening (led by her) I found
A little boat tied to a willow tree
Within a rocky cave, its usual home.
Straight I unloosed her chain, and stepping in
Pushed from the shore. It was an act of stealth
And troubled pleasure, nor without the voice
Of mountain echoes did my boat move on;
Leaving behind her still, on either side,
Small circles glittering idly in the moon,
Until they melted all into one track
Of sparkling light. But now, like one who rows,
Proud of his skill, to reach a chosen point
With an unswerving line, I fixed my view
Upon the summit of a craggy ridge,
The horizon's utmost boundary; for above
Was nothing but the stars and the gray sky.
She was an elfin pinnace; lustily
I dipped my oars into the silent lake,
And, as I rose upon the stroke, my boat
Went heaving through the water like a swan;
When, from behind that craggy steep till then
The horizon's bound, a huge peak, black and huge,
As if with voluntary power instinct,
Upreared its head. I struck and struck again,
And growing still in stature the grim shape
Towered up between me and the stars, and still,
For so it seemed, with purpose of its own
And measured motion like a living thing,
Strode after me. With trembling oars I turned,
And through the silent water stole my way
Back to the covert of the willow tree;
There in her mooring place I left my bark,
And through the meadows homeward went, in grave
And serious mood; but after I had seen
That spectacle, for many days, my brain
Worked with a dim and undetermined sense

CHAPTER THREE

Of unknown modes of being; o'er my thoughts
There hung a darkness, call it solitude
Or blank desertion. No familiar shapes
Remained, no pleasant images of trees,
Of sea or sky, no colors of green fields;
But huge and mighty forms, that do not live
Like living men, moved slowly through the mind
By day, and were a trouble to my dreams.

I remind the reader that Wordsworth had made it his task to
lead people from the nature rhetoric of eighteenth-century
poetry to the actual perception of nature itself. He saw the
rhetorical predisposition as a block to the eye and mind; and
both the latter had to perceive properly if one was to understand nature's moral meaning. For the act of perception had
to reveal our connection to the world outside our sensibilities, thereby making its symbolism real. To understand the
meaning of the lines — that one has to go to the center of
nature to cope with it, that it will pursue anyone attempting
to escape — the reader must have an actual image of the
whole scene in mind. He must *see* that a rower faces the area
he leaves behind, and that a peak which is initially hidden
behind a ridge gets bigger and bigger as one draws away from
it. Almost all my students refused to see reality. To them, a
generation raised on Brooks and Warren, a poem was a
structure of images which were connected only to each other,
and perhaps to some fantasy in their own minds — prefer-
ably sexual. Their incapacity to see rendered them incapable
of connecting with the poem, with the moral import of the
boy's union with nature, and, ultimately, of connecting with
humanity itself. When I see how firmly impressed this false
rhetoric has become (after all, most critics have made the
same mistake as my students), how it falsifies what we see,
and how much our intellectual bureaucrats have been responsible for this, and other, falsifications — it is then that I

understand the necessity of Herzen's and *The Connection*'s advocacy of destruction, the necessity for a humane anarchism. For only the obliteration of those formalisms which have lost all relation to their content — whether the particular formalism is private or public — only their obliteration will create the possibility of honest perception, of human contact, and therefrom a natural sense of form and private and public morality. Only by wiping away the empty rhetoric will the work of art be capable of doing its honest work of reconstructing our perceptions of each other and the world around us.

4

NEW ROLES FOR INTELLECTUALS

It was Alexander Herzen, you recall, who passionately defended the intellectual's chief activity — criticism. Whatever its specific nature, the critical activity itself has, of course, become an historical necessity: It is a function of the history of our philosophy and social institutions which we can hardly escape. But what is the task of criticism? In *From the Other Shore*, Herzen tells us somewhat melodramatically:

The Terror executed men but our task is easier; we are called upon to execute institutions, destroy beliefs, break prejudices, shatter hopes of any return to the past, holding nothing sacred, making no concessions, showing no mercy. Our smile, our greetings are only for what is rising, for the dawn, and, if we are unable to bring it nearer, we can at least point out its approach to those who do not see it.

"We"! Herzen, somewhat hopefully, refers to a group which has no legitimate — perhaps no real — existence as a social entity; his "we" is an epistemological act of faith; it creates a wished-for connection. Herzen's remarks refer to the task of revolutionary intellectuals. In Herzen's view (and I should think, in ours), calling an intellectual revolutionary rightfully constitutes a tautology; for if an intellectual is to carry out his task of criticism properly, he must necessarily be a revolutionary socialist. Were Herzen living today, he would no doubt prefer to be called a social anarchist, for the critical impulse led him to reject all forms of doctrinaire and state socialism. Settling then for our contemporary nomenclature, only an anarchist has the capacity to properly perform the duties of the critic, to destroy properly, for only he has the desire to reconstruct the shambles of history on a humane basis; only he will avoid the traps of bureaucracy; and only he will avoid becoming the artisan of false ideological masks for the status quo — whether these be the doctrines of free trade for industrial capitalism, the historical necessity of the dictatorship of the proletariat for Leninism, or the End of Ideology for the cold war. It is hardly accidental that more than a few former American apologists for Stalin are today's most vociferous defendants of Lyndon Johnson and the American intervention in Vietnam: They have never performed the proper task of intellectuals, for they have always been apologists rather than critics, functionaries rather than anarchists, apologists rather than devotees of truth.

The task Herzen sets for intellectuals may seem extreme, but perhaps it is only so in its rhetoric. For Herzen loathed unnecessary violence; and indeed he saw that the only useful activity for the critic in 1848, Europe being busy destroying itself, was to "point out its [the dawn's] approach to those who do not see it." The task may be painful and result in little apparent success. At one point, Herzen compares himself to a man of intellect during the decline of the Roman empire: It was obvious that the rush of events had emptied most institutions and their ethical foundations of any objective content; that the political elites were in the process of mutually destroying themselves, each other, and, for good measure, an incomprehending mass of human beings. The man of intellect could see with sufficient clarity just what was dying; yet how was he to join what was on the horizon? How was he to participate in the rise of Christianity? His very intellect, his critical capacities, forbade him to do so. Thus neither the old nor the new was available to him, for they were both lies. Herzen's judgments were quite similar to those Gibbon made about the proletarian and irrational origins of Christianity. The significance of their insight is that it recognizes an unavoidable split, at certain historical moments, between the intellectual and the community. Truth may have different meanings for different classes, and none of these may be available to the intellectual. For Gibbon the situation of the Roman man of learning was, of course, parallel to that of the eighteenth-century man of reason: He was necessarily and hopelessly cut off from the possibility of community. And is this not the situation of the intellectual who is confronted with the people of *The Connection?* These cast-offs critically destroy, by their very existence, the society into which we step upon leaving the theater: Who can believe in that society after the experience of the play? Yet their irrationality and their total separation remove their perception of possibilities from our own line of vision. But Gibbon's attitude is not the only one; although Herzen may be unsure of the future, although he may not be able to commit himself to whatever develops, he can yet try to understand, to be open, to possibly point the way.

Herzen's awareness of the intellectual's lonely position was crystallized by the failure of politics during the revolutions of 1848: It taught him that to collaborate with the state, or even to use the state, was not only to sacrifice one's critical faculties and one's freedom, it was also to remove oneself from the possibility of communal reunion. Some years later he expressed these feelings in a letter to Tchitcherin:

Do you grasp the difference? You, as a teacher, want to teach, to direct, to herd your flock. We, like a flock that is becoming conscious, do not want to be herded, but want to have our own village courts, our own representatives, our own delegates, to whom we can entrust the management of our affairs. That is why the authority of the government is an insult to us at every step, while you applaud it as your predecessors the priests applauded the temporal power. You may even differ from it as the clergy has sometimes differed from it or like people quarrelling on board ship: however great the distance you may be, you are still in the same boat, and for us, laymen, you are still on the side of the government.

Civic religion — the apotheosis of the state — is a purely Roman idea and in the modern world, principally French. It is consistent with a strong state, but is incompatible with a free people; through it you may get splendid soldiers, but you cannot have independent citizens.[1]

The "we" of *From the Other Shore* has expanded. There is no separate community of intellectuals, no shepherds, but only one community, a flock, arrayed against the state. Herzen's letter is, alas, little more than heroic rhetoric. It was written from an exile which was nearly complete, for unlike Engels, Herzen had little opportunity for political activity, and most of his contacts were not with the flock, but with other exiled intellectuals.

That politics had begun to fail in its traditional function of unifying men under just laws and institutions was central, we have seen, in the political thought of Rousseau. *The Social Contract*, after all, was the product of Rousseau's acute awareness that the law of nature had ceased to be the law of man. In writing *The Social Contract*, and in making his suggestions for the proper government of Poland and Corsica, Rousseau hoped that the proper use of intellect could lead to the establishment of a natural community by political means. Eventually he rejected the political effort of the Enlightenment, for he came to see the critical intellect as one of the

[1] Quoted by Herzen in his *My Past and Thoughts: The Memoirs of Alexander Herzen*, trans. C. Garnett (New York, 1924).

chief reasons for the disruption of our sense of community, for the loneliness of the intellectual. Rousseau rejected intellect itself, for he saw it as the most important cause of human unhappiness. Out of these self-denials, or self-indulgences, come his various attempts to establish connections in an asocial and personal way: He marries a simple, illiterate wife, isolates himself, and attempts to commune with nature. But he fails, inevitably, for there is no tearing oneself from historical realities; they invariably insist on becoming personal. Rousseau keeps writing, and *The Confessions* is, after all, his great effort to convert us; its self-justifications are an attempt to convince us of the justice, of the public utility, of his hitherto private moral code.

For Herzen, the very failure of politics, the evident snares of the state, all those elements which led Rousseau into isolation, pointed to the proper public role for the intellectual. He must, first of all, help to destroy the state: This is not a matter of moral commitment, for his very intellectual faculties, his capacity to see the truth, should inform him of this simple human necessity:

No one believes any longer in these packed juries which decide men's fate blindfolded and allow no appeal; nor in the social order that protects only property, that deports people as a measure of public safety, that keeps a standing army, be it only a hundred men, which is always ready to pull the trigger at the first command, without asking why. [*From the Other Shore*]

Who is to question the dissolution of this? But for the intellectual there is the necessary task of reconstruction. This is not to be done by the formulation of elaborate social schemes commissioned by benevolent monarchs; nor will it be the result of constitutions imposed by the fiat of right reason; it surely will not be accomplished by the snide contempt for the ordinary man of someone like Voltaire: To take these

[143]

paths would be to move even further from the possibility of community. But here is Herzen conversing with Galakhov:

"You are misled by categories not fitted to catch the flow of life. Think carefully: is this end that you seek — a programme, an order? Who conceived it, who declared it? Is it something inevitable or not? If it is, are we mere puppets? . . . Are we morally free beings, or wheels in a machine? I prefer to think of life, and therefore of history, as an end attained than as a means to something else."

"You mean, in short, that the end of nature and history is just — you and me? . . ."

"Partly; plus the present state of everything existing. Everything is included in this: the legacy of past efforts and the seeds of all that is to come; the inspiration of the artist, the energy of the citizen, and the rapture of the youth. . . ." [*Ibid.*]

Herzen's words derive from the skepticism, the doubts concerning a rationally organized body of knowledge, which I discussed earlier. This doubt, created by intellect, ironically limits the possibilities of rational conviction and brings about the necessity of affect. And here rests the problem for intellectuals: how to bring about the communion wished for by Herzen; how to do so with one's intellect; yet to somehow have this happen freely and spontaneously through some hoped-for change of heart. But have I not described the tasks of social anarchism?

The anarchist's task is to seek the unification of self, nature, society, and the work of intellect. He must manage to understand the history which has fragmented our reality; and having understood, he must point to the possibilities of connections in the present. But the task is not as grandiose as it sounds. Since no rational scheme is likely to carry much conviction, since the present is open, the drafting of master plans necessarily puts a limitation on our freedom; worse, it is a violation of reality. Our epistemological studies have taught us that there is no philosophy of history. We now live with the awareness of permanent change, change which is undirected; and since there is no conceivable end to the process, the intellectual's job (the task of rational criticism followed by reconstruction) promises to be permanent. If he does not become the conscience of whatever develops, then who will? These are tasks to which an intellectual should be drawn by the very awareness of the effects of rationality. The division of labor is, after all, the work of intellect; it is part of the general process of rationalization which Weber has described so well; a process which has created, as an aspect of the division of labor, the role of intellectual. A man of learning may, of course, choose simply to perform his assigned task in the division of labor; he may choose to ideologically justify all aspects of the division, to be a bureaucrat, or to separate himself totally. But he will, in these eventualities, deny intellect its natural work of criticism; he will violate his own nature. In short, he will stop performing his natural public role, and therefore forfeit the name of intellectual. But playing a public role may, after all, involve work of a very private nature. Perhaps poetry, for example, is more than the cultivated game T. S. Eliot called it; who knows but it might be a necessity, as Matthew Arnold once claimed, for our very survival.

No other technique for the conduct of life attaches the individual so firmly to reality as laying emphasis on work; for his work at least gives him a secure place in a portion of reality, in the human community.[2]

Freud's solution to the problem of human separation is, not unexpectedly, typically bourgeois. But who would argue with it if one's work were, indeed, related to the human community? Freud, quite naturally, also understood that work sepa-

[2] Sigmund Freud, *Civilization and Its Discontents*, trans. and ed. J. Strachey (New York, 1962).

rates men from each other and in doing so creates their greatest resentments. Whatever exalted ideas men of learning may have about themselves, they do work. Now it is a commonplace that most modern intellectuals have little sense of their work giving them any real sense of attachment to the community, or to reality itself; indeed, they rather tend to feel that their work will almost necessarily cut them off. Thus Jack Gelber, in writing *The Connection*, obviously felt he had to go beyond the task of being a playwright, that he somehow had to bring reality into his play if he were to establish a meaningful relationship between himself and his characters, himself and his audience. This loss of confidence in the possibilities of intellect, the sense of separation from one's audience, is to a large degree the consequence of the bourgeois revolution and the decline of the patronage system which followed.[3] In the eighteenth century, artists and intellectuals tend to drift away from the aristocratic connections which had once kept them alive. Dr. Johnson's ringing declaration of independence from patronage in his famous letter to Lord Chesterfield marks, on the whole, the end of an era. But there is a price to be paid for this release from bondage. As they become independent, intellectuals tend to create new forms of association; if they are not to connect with the aristocracy, at least they will do so with each other. At best, this can lead to associations based on belief in an idea or in a cause; at worst, it can result in the isolation of a coterie. In any case, independence will tend to lead to the separation of intellectuals from society. The court drama of the Renaissance may be the work of an overrefined coterie, but it is a coterie which has its roots in the artistic and intellectual life

[3] On this, I have learned much from Karl Mannheim's "The Problem of the Intelligentsia. An Inquiry Into Its Past and Present Role," *Essays on the Sociology of Culture*, ed. E. Manheim and P. Kecskemeti (London, 1956).

of the aristocracy. The price to be paid for attachment to a social class may be a lack of intellectual cogency and artistic vigor; it will not be a sundering of all social connections. The man of intellect could, in any case, choose to be the propagandist for the bourgeois revolution or the fading aristocracy. But surely the skeptical theory of knowledge, having helped to create the intellectual's role, will make it somewhat difficult to claim that the bourgeois or aristocratic class position is the law of nature. To make his task the propagation of a class ideology would turn the man of learning into a hired flunkie or an ideologue deprived of his skeptical freedom. For the former, there is the excuse of the desirability of money; for the latter, only the failure to see enough of the truth — a failure of intellect. The matter is illustrated aptly in the contrast between Swift and Defoe, both of whom wrote political propaganda for the Earl of Oxford. Swift, who had social ties with the aristocracy without being of it, did his job out of conviction. For one thing, he was not really a professional writer. Swift's failure, as he somewhat ruefully came to see, lay in his inability to see that he was being used. Defoe, on the other hand, had to write in order to stay alive. His political convictions were opposed to those of the Earl of Oxford's, and when coming to collect his money and get his instructions he entered by the back door. Yet he was willing, quite consciously, to tell any conceivable lie, to even act as an agent provocateur by editing and writing a newspaper opposed to the Earl of Oxford's ministry. It seems like a heavy price to pay for one's independence from patronage; an even heavier one to pay for the reestablishment of social connections.

One of the incidental results — perhaps one of the causes — of the bourgeois revolution has been the growth of sociological self-awareness. We have all become aware that we are members of social groupings, that we belong to a social class. Ironically, men of intellect constitute the last group to become aware of its identity as a class. Not until the eighteenth century do they seem to realize that the division of labor has separated them not only from their social origins but from the class system itself. As a result, the intellectual who takes his proper task to be the pursuit of intellect (rather than the ideological justification of class interest) will be rewarded with the thankless tasks of analysis and criticism. Since the dominant skepticism creates doubts about the shape of the external world and the forms of institutions, the intellectual's speculations are likely to turn either to epistemology: the determination of reality, the simple (perhaps complex) truth, or to utopianism: the construction of social plans based on the insights of intellect. But if the intellectual wishes to go beyond these lonely tasks to the possibility of social effect, he will need to do so through some form of direct contact, through some version of social activism. To return to Freud, the most direct way of accomplishing this would seem to lie in making one's work part of the general social effort. Yet we have noticed the difficulty of doing so, and still maintaining one's commitment to intellect. When that most moving of all professional revolutionaries, Blanqui, who eventually spent thirty-seven years of his life in jail, was asked to name his occupation at one of his many trials, he answered, "a proletarian." [4] By "proletarian," he apparently meant all the lower working classes. But he also included himself: the declassed, and therefore socially isolated, intellectual. The only possibility of renewing one's social ties through work, of transcending one's sense of uselessness, lay in the obliteration of the class system itself.

But why the feeling on the part of revolutionary intellec-

[4] See Arthur Rosenberg, *Democracy and Socialism* (Boston, 1965).

tuals like Blanqui that it is necessary to identify directly with the community? Why the avoidance of all political institutions? Briefly, it seems to be the only way of making contact and yet retaining one's skeptical and critical faculties. If both the concern for truth and some humane notion of how to conduct one's life are considered matters of importance by the intellectual, he is not likely to find the demands of politics very congenial. Consider the manner in which intellectuals were attacked for coming to the defense of Dreyfus. The truth of their charges against the government was seldom denied, for it was considered to be irrelevant. They were vilified, instead, for undermining the love of god and country, for subverting the accepted notions of morality — in short, for putting the truth about one human being ahead of the preservation of the status quo. Yet the reactionary attack on the intellectuals was entirely to the point. Though many of the Dreyfusards simply thought of themselves as the defenders of truth and justice, they were unwitting subverters of the political order, of received ideas. And rightly so! This, after all, is the proper task of intellectuals. Anti-Dreyfusards like the literary critic Brunetière had the honesty, at least, to admit that an absolute commitment to the conservation of political institutions might force one to tell an occasional lie and that this was not an entirely noble activity.

Not so today. We have managed to find men of learning who make lying sound like one of our nobler activities; it might, Herman Kahn would assure us, even be scientific. Need one go into Heidegger's justifications of Hitler or Sartre's apologies for Stalin? They are of little interest, except for the philosophers' claims that they are a higher version of the truth. Such are the ways of existential commitment; such the paradoxes of making connections in a value-free universe. More immediately relevant is the recent example of Arthur

Schlesinger, Jr. In his history of John F. Kennedy's presidency, Professor Schlesinger revealed that he had lied to the press as part of the grand strategy of the Bay of Pigs incident. When asked about this by a reporter for *The New York Times*, Schlesinger — who, one remembers, was supposed to represent the scholarly conscience of the Kennedy administration — not only justified his own lies in terms of public morality but even congratulated *The Times* for also having lied in the interest of the government. The lesson should be clear (it would have been obvious for Blanqui): If the man of learning is to put himself in the service of political leaders, he will do so at the expense of the principles of scholarship. Professor Schlesinger, unlike Heidegger or Sartre, did not seem to feel the need to deal with this difficulty. What are ideological justifications to the pragmatic scholar?

If the man of learning happens to be, unlike Professor Schlesinger, no more than an ordinary journeyman, if he does not have the ear of those in high office, his turn from the ivory tower to political involvement most likely will be accompanied by a transformation from the role of scholar to that of expert — or to use the less flattering designation, bureaucrat. As a result, the whole notion of truth becomes irrelevant to his task. He will, no doubt, defend his service to the welfare state, and to its cynical social engineering, on the basis of "social science." The official theory of this social science is best summed up in some phrase like "The End of Ideology," a well-known essay of Daniel Bell's. The essay, as every undergraduate knows, assures us of the sanity, health, and rationality of opportunism and condemns the intellectual's dedication to causes as a form of irrational pathology. It never seems to occur to Bell that his ode (one cannot call it rational argument) to opportunism might be an ideological mask for his own special status as spokesman for the welfare state and the political prop for its economy, the cold war. Most recently Bell has been assuring us that automation poses no real threat to the economy. I trust those who have lost, or are about to lose, their jobs are well reassured. But of greater interest to the scholarly community, Bell has lately become one of the editors of a new journal, *The Public Interest*. The journal seems to be officially devoted to those men of learning involved in government operations. Now we all need our journals; but one is slightly taken aback by the frankly propagandistic nature of the venture. Why the public rather than the scholarly interest? But what is there to make one blush if it is all part of the common pursuit of social science? The cold war also requires a sense of scholarly dignity. Bell's journey from the staff of *Fortune* to the Department of Sociology at Columbia and, at last, to *The Public Interest*, does not cover as much ground as he would like to think. None of these stations of rest, I would guess, is much concerned with the scholar's personal commitment, with his private attempt to discover the truth. Of what importance are these to progressive management, to social science, or to *The Public Interest?*

The fact is that Bell's ideology fills a need. The supposed heirs of Blanqui — no, rather Louis Blanc, as we shall see — the heirs then of Blanc have, at present, a class interest to defend, for they have become members of an affluent bureaucracy. Defending this long wished for status and the welfare state which maintains it may well involve perpetrating the lie of the country's well-being, or the salving of one's conscience with the ideological soporific of "The End of Ideology." Whatever the ideological mask, it indicates the end of the man of learning's search for community, for the only connection the bureaucrat makes is with an abstraction — the state. From intellectual to scholar-expert! The change marks the loss of the critical faculty and the failure of that skeptical theory of knowledge which created the class of intellectuals

The ready movement of the scholar from the university to the government bureaucracy should hardly come as a surprise. After all, a prominent university seems happy to tender the reward of a prominent chair to Professor Schlesinger for his patriotic — though, to a disciple of Reinhold Niebuhr, perhaps tragic — lies. The university itself is, after all, one of our best schools for bureaucracy; one might even refer to a stretch in the service of one as on-the-job training. Even those scholars, teachers, and administrators with the best of intentions are functionaries whose task is the reconciliation of students to the technical and human demands of the society which will absorb them upon graduation. We have always assumed that the most significant connection between teacher and student lies in the mutual search for truth. Our work will create human contact if it gives us a sense of its own significance, if it helps us to better see the truth. Under these conditions — and we still find them in isolated pockets here and there — the idea of a community of scholars will become a reality. But at the present time, our associations are generally based on the *pretense* that our work has some relevance to the pursuit of truth. And most of us are quite aware of this. It is reflected in the language we use: We speak of "jazzy experiments," of "swinging analyses," but not true ones. We know that the research projects we spend weeks "working up" and for which we receive sizable grants are rarely directed toward general enlightenment; instead their objectives are likely to be the furthering of the war effort or the enhancement of one's personal status. An article in *PMLA* might, after all, result in a job offer from a more prestigious university. Or simply think of the jump in status accorded both students and professors after the launching of Sputnik. The predictable result is that any meaningful contact among students and professors will rarely occur through the mediation of work but through the establishment of personal relationships and by means of extracurricular activities like the peace and civil rights movements.

When Randolph Bourne referred in 1915 to the American undergraduate's lack of philosophy,[5] he conferred a judgment not upon the failures of the individual student but upon the social function of the American university itself. Little except the educator's public rhetoric has changed since Bourne's time. We only need to add that Bourne should not have excluded professors from his judgment: Perhaps they lack philosophy more than most undergraduates. This too is a function of the university's institutional demands, the social purpose it fulfills: the needs of the society are hardly for a greater quota of philosophical intellectuals. But here is Bourne on the subject:

The university produces learning instead of steel or rubber, but the nature of the academic commodity has become less and less potent in insuring for the academic workman a status materially different from that of any other kind of employee.[6]

The university has, in fact, become that typical product of late capitalism, the corporation. What provides a clearer sign of this development than the tendency of our university presidents to be — if not in title, at least in effect — industrial managers? Be they scientists or humanists, electrical or social engineers, their job will still be to manage a large capitalistic enterprise.

What are we to expect from the university if, indeed, its

[5] Randolph Bourne, "The Undergraduate," *The World of Randolph Bourne*, ed. L. Schlissel (New York, 1965).
[6] "The Idea of a University," *ibid.*

institutional machinery is a product of capitalism? What motives are likely to guide its actions? Werner Sombart has remarked that, "The spirit of the economic outlook of capitalism is dominated by three ideas: acquisition, competition and rationality." [7] This will serve admirably as an explanatory theory for the academy's various activities. I shall, for the moment, examine only the effects of rationality on the activities of the scholar; a close look at the effects of acquisition and competition might prove to be embarrassing beyond endurance. The tendency to rationalize all aspects of our lives is, Max Weber has taught us, part of a general historical process which has shaped both the consciousness and the institutions of the Western world. The same process has also given rise to our dominant skeptical theory of knowledge, to our doubts, and thereby created the role of intellectual. But the continuing progress of rationalization — furthered by the very intellectuals it created — has turned the intellectual workman into a bureaucrat; it has made him the chief executive of capitalistic rationality. It might prove useful to see how well the academic's activity fits some of Weber's notions of bureaucracy. Here is his definition of the thing:

Bureaucracy may be defined as that type of hierarchical organization which is designed rationally to coordinate the work of many individuals in the pursuit of large-scale administrative tasks.[8]

Would anyone but the most innocent or self-serving apologist argue that this is a fairly apt description of any large university? The individual pursuit of scholarship is a luxury we may be afforded; but the true being of the university, its permanence, is located in its offices, whether academic or ad-

[7] Werner Sombart, "Capitalism," *Encyclopedia of the Social Sciences* (New York, 1930–1935).

[8] Max Weber, "Bureaucracy," *From Max Weber: Essays in Sociology*, trans. and ed. H. H. Gerth and C. Wright Mills (New York, 1958).

ministrative, and their assigned tasks. The office must fit into some rationalized scheme, and what better way to test its rationality than to shape its work to the capacities of a computer. The individual holding the office not only becomes superfluous, he is positively in the way of fuller rationalization. "Once established and having fulfilled its task," Weber tells us, "an office tends to continue in existence and be held by another incumbent." Has anyone recently heard of the demise of a professorial chair with the retirement of its incumbent? The office exists as a rational idea; the professor, like all flesh, will only die. But allow me to take that back: The "professor" does not die at all, for his official task is completely separate — or, ideally, ought to be — from his private concerns. Weber most aptly remarks that "bureaucracy segregates official activity as something distinct from the sphere of private life." Whatever social contact academics have with their fellow office workers (fellow department members, if you will) it is surely on the basis of that office itself, not on mutual intellectual interest. For in a bureaucracy, the nature of the office's task is not of major importance; the academic's chief concern is rarely scholarship or teaching. As Weber puts it: *"Office holding is a 'vocation.'"* [My italics.] He continues:

This is shown, first, in the requirement of a firmly prescribed course of training, which demands the entire capacity for work for a long period of time, and in the generally prescribed and special examinations which are prerequisites of employment.

Now this fittingly describes the first major step the student must take in joining the academic community, the ritual of the doctorate: It is his initiation to the vocation of holding an office. The second major step is, of course, the attainment of tenure in one's office. And here too Weber provides us with a bureaucratic rationalization:

Entrance into an office . . . is considered an acceptance of a specific obligation of faithful management in return for a secure existence.

How then is the academic to discover the sense of community through his work? How are his personal relationships shaped by his academic pursuits? Weber has some chilling words on the subject:

It is decisive for the specific nature of modern loyalty to an office that, in the pure type, it does not establish a relationship to a *person*. . . . Modern loyalty is devoted to impersonal and functional purposes. Behind the functional purposes, of course, 'ideas of culture-values' usually stand. These are *ersatz* for the earthly or supra-mundane personal master . . . they provide an ideological halo.

The halo, in the academic expert's case, is provided by the ideal of independent scholarship, the notion of science. The master? The impersonal demands of capitalism — the Big Connection.

Men of learning have provided the needed machinery for creating an abstract monster, a monster which forces the academic into the unpleasant position of becoming a perpetual critic if he is not to be the technician or teacher of bureaucracy. The man of learning will have to deny himself the satisfactions of integration into society. For integration on these terms will mean to give up the goals of intellect, the goals of philosophy and science, and to devote oneself, with more or less enthusiasm, to the manufacture of those functionaries, industrial cadres, rocket experts, and writers of scholarly articles needed by the Big Connection. We shall all be hooked. How better illustrate this than by pointing at the intimate connections between the university, big business, the foundations, and government. There seems to be a constant shuffling of executives among these institutions: Think of MacNamara, Bundy, Kaysen, Rusk, to name just a few members belonging to the upper echelons. A bureaucratic office requires a scholar-expert, whether that office is located at the Ford Motor Corporation or at the Institute for Advanced Studies. But we need not really look this far up in the hierarchy. After all, the trip to Washington, the afternoon spent consulting on Route 128 have all become part of the generally accepted routine. They give the academician status, a sense of his importance to the community — and, incidentally, money for the comforts of the upper bourgeoisie. A warning is in order. The man of learning who unthinkingly accepts these means of integration will almost necessarily become the apologist for the whole process. I do not state this as an hypothesis, but as a fact. Consider the implications of the general failure of social scientists to participate in the various protests against the government's policy in Vietnam; or consider, further, the considerable number who not only remain silent, but who take it on themselves to act as the government's apologists by lending academic dignity to lies which even *The Wall Street Journal* refuses to swallow. Once more, we need hardly be surprised. The dynamics of bureaucracy, as Weber has shown us, demand loyalty to the office. Besides, one does not become Undersecretary of Urban Affairs, for example, by taking one's master to task. What I find most curious is that the capitalist academic functionary beautifully meets the demands Lenin made of intellectuals: If the intellectual is to become more than a parasite, Lenin pontificated, if he is to become a productive worker in the socialist community, his labor must be at the service of the proletariat. It should be remembered that for Lenin the terms proletariat and socialism really meant the party apparatus and state capitalism. The scholar who willingly submits himself to these demands (and unlike scholars in the West, few Russian ones have much choice about it) admits to the failure of intellect; he sees a role neither for himself nor for the general intellectual pursuit he supposedly represents. And so he joins the community, perhaps cynically, by giving up the traditional functions of scholarship, by doing work which is essentially nonintellectual. It is an odd development for a process which began with the Cartesian doubt about the foundations of our knowledge.

THE TIES WHICH UNITE MEN, Rousseau has told us, may turn into chains. They will do so, one expects, if men feel their natural bonds to have been irrevocably broken. It is fair to assume that for most of us this is unfortunately the case. Whatever the exact history or prehistory of the sundering of men's social ties, the process begins with our sense of separation from nature. As the problem of knowledge becomes an unavoidable component of our consciousness, we begin to see the possibility of the law of man not being the law of nature; moreover, the possibility is likely to harden into an unquestioned assumption. It was this assumption, after all, which helped to create the Cartesian doubt and all the consequent attempts to still it. But this is merely the beginning of our difficulties: For if we feel our own natures to be separate from Nature itself, we shall soon feel dissociated from other men. This feeling will create an awareness of — more accurately, an obsessive concern for — all those social categories, natural and artificial, which divide the community of man. For us the most relevant concepts of social classification, and therefore division, are the notions of social and economic class. However they are grounded in the nature of reality, these classifications are a creation of intellect. Their divisive effect on men's social ties has led to the separation of men of learning from the community. For once the community feels doubts about the natural origins of its social ties, it will look to those who have some kind of special knowledge; it will seek the counsel of men who have been blessed (or cursed) by the gods, by nature, or by intellect with an understanding of those laws and modes of action which will give us the capacity to rejoin nature and the community of men. Because their knowledge is beyond the common understanding, these individuals are removed from ordinary social intercourse. In its attempts to make connections, the intellect inevitably creates new distinctions.

The separation of the man of special knowledge is to be seen in the role the shaman plays in a primitive society. The very features which are the source of his divine secrets — his having visions, his being a spastic, and so forth — set him off from the rest of the community. More relevant to the concerns of a political society like ours is the role traditionally played by the sage.[9] His special knowledge and his authority (whatever the latter's source) have generally been used to give legitimacy to the status quo, thereby binding men, more or less voluntarily, to established institutions. The sage's popular authority largely rests on his separateness, on his having powers of insight which are beyond those of ordinary men. Kings have always been served, and their actions legitimized, by their official wise men; today our leaders' sages are the academic experts, the men of knowledge who surround the depredations of the state with the halo of independent scholarship. Of course, the sage's special status may also serve to justify the introduction of new religious, social, and political ideas. Think of how carefully Calvin, and the leaders of

[9] My observations on the role of the sage are based on Florian Znaniecki, *The Social Role of the Man of Knowledge* (New York, 1940).

other Protestant sects, based their reforms on both the exhaustive scholarly analysis of the Bible, and on the special textual insights allowed the saint by Grace. Let me pursue this in relation to the sects' social teachings. At first, groups like the Levellers and Diggers based their ideas for communal revival and reform on a proper (in their eyes) interpretation of the Bible. For the sacred text, the word of God, had to replace the vanished authority of religious and political institutions. But the same epistemological skepticism which led to this development leads to yet another turn of the screw: This concern with the theory of knowledge eventually leads to the primacy of the scientific method in not only the realm of nature but also the realm of man. Thus the justification of social ideas by special knowledge will need to be secularized — as, in fact, it often enough has. The socialist sage may derive his knowledge from religious sources (as was generally the case in Great Britain before the twentieth century), but he is more likely to give his doctrines the ring of authority by assigning their origins to the scientific method. These secular sages know the scientific truths which will bind men into a natural community; but their knowledge turns them into a separate group — the class of modern intellectuals.

In his much publicized exchange of letters with Einstein, Freud expressed the hope that an association of independent thinkers dedicated to the search for truth might soften the harsh demands of the death instinct, lead men toward the goal of a community based on reason, and thus prevent future wars. But Freud recognized this wish to be hopelessly utopian. In any case, what would the moral objectives of these thinkers be? What if their science should tell them — as John Dewey's experimental method told him about World War I — that wars are among the more useful methods of binding men's communal ties? The association of men dedicated to rationality might, of course, simply accept the moral objectives of the society: They are there, a part of reality, and the man of learning's task, we are often told, is either to systematize or to teach them. But what if the members of Freud's association should be interested in the truth itself rather than the method of rationality? If they should be concerned with the value of a society's moral norms? If they should feel, further, the desire to unite men on a humane basis? If these are their concerns (and I should think them elementary), they will have to be nothing less than critics as well as analysts of the status quo.

The consciousness of our separation from nature and from other men as well as the awareness of the class system itself were anticipated by the development of that most puzzling of literary forms — pastoral.[10] Pastoral apparently grew out of a sophisticated aristocracy's reaction to the rise of urban civilization and to the latter's inevitable social divisions. It should be useful to look at Freud's analysis of our reaction to the development of civilization:

> If civilization is a necessary course of development from the family to humanity as a whole, then — as a result of the inborn conflict arising from ambivalence, of the eternal struggle between the trends of love and death — there is inextricably bound up with it an increase of the sense of guilt, which will perhaps reach heights that the individual finds hard to tolerate. . . . The sense of guilt [is] . . . the most important problem in the development of civilization and . . . the price we pay for our advance in civilization is a loss of happiness through the heightening of the sense of guilt. [*Civilization and Its Discontents*]

The instincts of love and death no doubt provide us with a somewhat shaky foundation for an explanatory theory. But

[10] Most of my ideas on this subject began to develop during the many puzzled, and delightful, hours I have spent with William Empson's *Some Versions of Pastoral*.

Freud's basic social insights are true enough: As civilization expands and becomes more and more rationalized, there is an increase in our sense of guilt; in the midst of larger and larger social units there is an increased sense of the individual's loneliness, his failure to connect. And the most obvious sign of separation in an advanced civilization is, of course, the class system — the division between high and low. Pastoral attempts to assuage the aristocrat's sense of guilt over both his separation from nature and from the lower classes. It tells us that man is like nature; we therefore accept things as they are and reconcile ourselves to the status quo. Pastoral ennobles what appears to be ignoble; it enhances the ordinary by lending it the dignity of an aristocratic art. The high (aristocrats) by pretending to be the low (shepherds) justify their own ignoble actions, while reconciling the low to their miserable lot by ennobling the nature of their work, by converting it, in fact, to artistic play. Early Christianity, in attempting to reconcile the poor to their worldly lot, appropriated the notion of pastoral. This can be seen, most clearly, in the idea of Christ the shepherd: an idea which not only lends dignity to the poor by granting them heaven, but which also attempts to fob off poverty as the most desirable of all states. Most important, Christianity derives our unhappiness, our sense of communal division, the class system itself, from the loss of that ideal pastoral setting, the Garden of Eden. This explanatory account, with its hope for a possible return to Eden, has lent the notion of Christ the shepherd its seemingly perennial potency.

For a modern, the explanatory power, and thus the consolation, of pastoral is more likely to be provided by the social sciences, more especially that medley of mysterious activities we refer to as the "policy sciences." Comte's attempt to reestablish medieval Christian institutions on the basis of social science gives an apt insight into the transformation. Our academic aristocrats, the policy scientists — they may be located at a university, at the RAND Corporation, or in the government — assume that things are what they are because of the necessities of the laws of nature. Reality may seem a bit ugly, but if we look at it in the correct way, if we construct the proper models for it, we shall not only discover a hitherto unknown esthetic factor, we shall not merely beautify reality ("Man," I hear the policy scientist exclaim, "what a pretty model!"), we shall manage nothing less than a reconciliation of social phenomena to the laws of nature. And this, most happily, eliminates all guilt, all sense of separation from the natural order. The law of man is once more the law of nature: The policy scientist *knows*, because he, after all, made up the laws, he constructed the models. If we are capable of believing in these laws — and surely we believe much more in anything which calls itself science than any Renaissance aristocrat believed in pastoral — we shall think ourselves capable of dealing with social realities, of absorbing them, even — blessed thought! — of making valid predictions about them. All this is most consoling if the realities to be absorbed and made bearable happen to be enormities like the possibility of nuclear war. Who would have thought that mere intellect could move the same mountains as Christ? Yet we have reconciled ourselves to the possibility of extinction not through anything so irrational as pastoral: We do not suffer from the obvious neuroticism of the fanatic Christian; nor do we live in the unreal world of the Renaissance aristocrat who dealt with the fears of mutability by playing pastoral games; no, we have attained the ultimate rationality — the sanity and realism of Dr. Strangelove.

The varieties of literary pastoral anticipate, as I mentioned, both the man of learning's sense of separation and his secular attempts to affirm our oneness with nature and with other men. Look, for example, at this sonnet of Sir Philip Sidney's. It is one of the poems from his *Arcadia:* a prose narrative which combines mythical history with a pastoral setting, thus giving the aristocratic Sidney a means of converting reality into a game, into an allegory of man's state which the reader may, or may not, take seriously.

O sweet woods, the delight of solitariness!
Oh, how much I do like your solitariness!
Where man's mind hath a freed consideration,
Of goodness to receive lovely direction.
Where senses do behold th' order of heav'nly host,
And wise thoughts do behold what the creator is;
Contemplation here holdeth his only seat,
Bounded with no limits, born with a wing of hope,
Climbs even unto the stars, nature is under it.
Nought disturbs thy quiet, all to thy service yields,
Each sight draws on a thought (thought, mother of science)
Sweet birds kindly do grant harmony unto thee,
Fair trees' shade is enough fortification,
No danger to thyself if 't be not in thyself.

The speaker's ablility to feel at one with nature depends on his special knowledge, on his "science." His capacity to see the system of the woods also enables him to see the system of the universe and, in turn, man's system of morals. These perceptions create in the poet a sense of harmony and cause him to accept readily things as they are — including his own state. But is the matter really that simple? Is the poem's apparent calm a true indication of the problems it raises? Looking at these lines with a little care, we notice that they are a sophisticated attempt to tie classical meters to the English language and to the form of the sonnet. The poem's tone, which is largely established by the formality of the meter, is one of elegant and sophisticated pretense. The whole thing is, after all, a game; a game which can be convincing because of the poem's seriousness and its logical perfection. But the ability of the game to convince the poet, one must remember, does not really depend on the universality of a natural law but on his private act of contemplation, on his going into the woods. This act may readily yield a belief in unity if the poet, who is a scholarly courtier, can accept the image of Queen Elizabeth the shepherdess and the notion of her divine and natural right to rule. Think of the conclusion to John Davies' *Orchestra:* The perfect order of the universe is represented in a conceit picturing a group of courtiers performing a dance around Elizabeth — a dance whose pattern is a reflection of all earthly and heavenly movement. But Sidney's poem will not let us rest with that kind of notion. We may be told that birds lend harmony to nature, but we are also reminded of "thought, mother of science." Whatever the momentary sense of union provided by the experience of the woods, any system of universal order must also render an account to that product of intellect — "science." This makes for obvious difficulties in accepting any of the traditional ways of connecting, including the pastoral mode. And does not the very experimental nature of the poem — the use of classical meters, the unusual rhyme scheme for a sonnet — evince a skepticism toward those traditions which the poet seemingly affirms?

The skeptical doubt about our connections to nature, about the reality of a natural order, is taken a step further in Marvell's "The Garden." We know that the pastoral world of Sidney's poem is make-believe. Yet the possibility of its philosophical allegory allows us to pretend, at least for the moment, that this world is real; we put the doubt out of mind, for a failure to do so would make the pastoral laughable. It is just this incapacity to put the doubt out of mind which makes realistic pastoral poetry, like that of Ambrose

Philips, so laughable to readers of the eighteenth century. The only viable possibilities for pastoral in the eighteenth century were to make the form a subject for unabashed artifice — for example, the work of Pope in the genre; to parody it; to make — as Swift and Gay did — the city rather than the country its subject; or finally — and think of Rousseau — to turn the mode into an instrument for communion of a deeply personal and private sort. These are the difficulties in our relationship to nature (epistemological difficulties made even more acute by industrialism's drive toward urbanization) with which Wordsworth will have to deal. And the literary intellectual will not be alone with the problem. As we shall see, the further men are removed from the possibility of communion with nature, the more problematic the possibility of communing with other men. Thus the problem of creating a community in an urban and industrial setting, of making the feelings of pastoral a reality, will become the master problem of all intellectuals who wish to reach outside themselves, who wish to make their scholarship relevant to life.

But back to Marvell. His doubts about the possibilities of pastoral are expressed in his poem's subtle irony. The poem can draw us into its apparently serious yet self-mocking world because we share the poet's doubt. Compare the ironic possibilities of our sensuous reaction to "The Garden" with the ambiguities of the skeptic's experience of Bernini's Cornaro Chapel and of Gibbon's Chapter XV. Marvell's use of the skeptical doubt is, of course, much closer to Gibbon's: Both must manage a fine balance between high seriousness and humor. In "The Garden," the poet openly pretends that he can leave the world behind. In Sidney's poem, you remember, the world is never actually mentioned; we are simply taken into Arcadia. The real world is always in the background of "The Garden": If nothing else, we are always reminded that it is not nature itself but a formal garden. And so the sense of communion elicited by the poem's physical setting is made possible only by the mind's act of imagination: by its art, not its special knowledge; by its fantasy, rather than the scientific notions (the connective principles) it might formulate.

Mean while the Mind, from pleasure less,
Withdraws into its happiness:
The Mind, that Ocean where each kind
Does streight its own resemblance find;
Yet it creates, transcending these,
Far other Worlds, and other Seas;
Annihilating all that's made
To a green Thought in a green Shade.

Here at the Fountains sliding foot,
Or at some Fruit-trees mossy root,
Casting the Bodies Vest aside,
My Soul into the boughs does glide:
There like a Bird it sits, and sings,
Then whets, and combs its silver Wings;
And, till prepar'd for longer flight,
Waves in its Plumes the various Light.

Of course the poet does not literally believe what he has tried to make us accept. He knows that the connections he perceives, his mind's union with nature, are based on the momentary affect brought on by his sensuous experience.

What wond'rous Life in this I lead!
Ripe Apples drop about my head;
The Luscious Clusters of the Vine
Upon my Mouth do crush their Wine;
The Nectaren, and curious Peach,
Into my hands themselves do reach;
Stumbling on Melons, as I pass,
Insnar'd with Flow'rs, I fall on Grass.

The lines are gorgeous beyond belief: They rape our wills. But they are also ironic and full of amused self-mockery. The poet, for the moment, becomes a child and seems to play in full innocence; he simply accepts that he is only one among the many luscious flowers and fruits. Yet he knows that all this is part of a mythical world:

Such was that happy Garden-state,
While Man there walk'd without a Mate.

Paradise is lost; furthermore, it probably never existed; and the consequent doubt about knowledge creates the intellectual and ironic game — a game of the highest seriousness — the poet plays with us. The procedure illustrates the disjunction between our desires for communion and our scientific concepts of nature. Neither the categories of mind nor the imperatives of our imaginations have any necessary connection to nature. Marvell, the literary intellectual, teaches us a lesson which Hume, in the eighteenth century, was still trying to drive home for philosophy.

The reaction "The Garden" intends to elicit is based on Marvell's acceptance of the status quo. He is content with the imaginary world of pastoral (though he knows it to be false), for he feels no need to change the world itself. Marvell can still accept the pretense of the pastoral tradition, even without its religious underpinning, and live in two worlds. His skepticism does not totally separate him from some kind of communion with nature. But how will the experience of "The Garden" be possible for those who cannot make their peace with the traditional elements which Marvell readily accepts? Not many men of learning and very few skeptics are likely to accept and live with the self-conscious pretense of pastoral. How many will be content with the fanciful connection to nature, with a fancy which is based on the possibility of a momentary Eden of the imagination? The poet's and the reader's difficulties with this traditional notion become similar to those experienced by both artist and beholder when light loses its specific Christian meanings. The options created by our skepticism are varied, and all are bound to be problematic. We can — and most neoclassicists of the seventeenth and eighteenth centuries in fact did — disregard the notion of man's union with nature altogether and concentrate on relationships among men, an activity which might involve politics. On the other hand, we can retreat totally into our private, subjective concerns. Finally, we can concentrate on the communal possibilities of culture and intellect. One thing alone is certain: Traditional pastoral and its political implications become impossible with the general spread of the skeptical doubt. The freedom and openness which this allows will transform the sage — with his certainties about his special knowledge — into an intellectual — with his critical doubts, with the multiplicity of choices created by his theory of knowledge.

His analyses being deprived of certainty, the intellectual will lose the moral authority of the sage. And since the community is not likely to be convinced by the infallibility of his logic, he will be forced to discover new ways of speaking to it. The role of intellectual may eventually carry its own moral authority, but this will happen when the community has absorbed the man of knowledge and turned him into a respected expert. At this point, he will no longer need to convince, for he will be the mouthpiece, not the teacher, of his society. Whatever the intellectual's public role, whatever his method of connecting, his course will largely depend on the theory of knowledge which he and his contemporaries take to be true.

The guiding concepts of pastoral were, on the whole, irrelevant to the intellectual life of the eighteenth century. The difficulties of the mode were, after all, anticipated by the notorious philosophic and esthetic infelicities of Milton's forays into pastoral. Though Milton scholars may attempt to cloud our intelligence with their historical justifications for the literary manner of "Lycidas" and the pastoral parts of *Paradise Lost*, Milton cannot be looked at as a sixteenth-century humanist; he was — and any intelligent reader knows this — Marvell's, not Sidney's, contemporary. Milton writes with an awareness that the law of nature must stand before the court of science, and it is precisely his difficulty in reconciling this historical necessity with the dogmas of Christianity which makes *Paradise Lost* such a moving experience for the skeptic; but this same difficulty also accounts, unavoidably, for the poem's more ludicrous moments, for its occasional unintended descent from pastoral to mock-pastoral. That the law of nature would have to render its accounts to the law of science had already been hinted at in the sonnet by Sidney I discussed earlier; it is this very challenge which Marvell responded to with such wry beauty in "The Garden." Marvell's balanced irony is, of course, irrelevant to Milton's strong Christian commitment; and so the latter must take his pastoral straight, and the metaphor must be taken for reality. But the skeptical doubt is not to be brushed aside: The very existence of pastoral — its assertion of this vision of the literary imagination as a law of nature — bears witness to the doubt's presence. And so eighteenth-century poets may go through the motions of writing pastoral, generally doing so in the manner of Milton; they may also pretend that Newton's laws not only relate the movements of small objects to those of planets but also the law of man to the law of nature. This last belief should, if one gives it any thought, make pastoral entirely superfluous. But then can anyone who accepts the foundations of Newton's science really believe that the rules governing man's behavior are to be found in Newton's equations? And even further, who is to accept the implications of Milton's Christian belief? Can anyone with even a tinge of skepticism believe that the law of science, the law of man, and the pastoral image are all to be subsumed under the law of god? Dr. Johnson, in his comments on "Lycidas," stated rather bluntly what many must have thought:

In this poem there is no nature, for there is no truth. . . . Its form is that of a pastoral, easy, vulgar, and therefore disgusting: whatever images it can supply are long ago exhausted; and its inherent improbability always forces dissatisfaction on the mind. . . . This poem has yet a grosser fault. With these trifling fictions are mingled the most awful and sacred truths, such as ought never to be polluted with such irreverent combinations. The shepherd likewise is now a feeder of sheep, and afterwards an ecclesiastical pastor, a superintendent of a Christian flock. Such equivocations are always unskilful; but here they are indecent, and at least approach to impiety. . . .[11]

Dr. Johnson's well-known doubts about his own faith made his violent outburst almost necessary. For if the doubt is real, pastoral's assertion of belief will always open the possibility of the whole mode being little more than elegant play; of it being a literary myth like any other.

These difficulties are evident — to the point of intellectual and esthetic embarrassment — in James Thomson's "A Poem Sacred to the Memory of Sir Isaac Newton." Thomson, many of whose contemporaries considered him to be Pope's equal, composed the poem a few months after Newton's death in 1727. Newton had in the latter years of his life become a culture hero, thereby giving us an indication of the importance science attained as a principle of legitimation. Newton's place in the national consciousness stood at least equal to that of the latest military hero, his status being akin to that of Colonel John Glenn rather than that of Einstein. I

[11] "The Life of Milton," *Rasselas, Poems, and Selected Prose*, ed. B. H. Bronson (New York, 1958).

doubt whether this situation would have been possible before the eighteenth century, before the passing of traditional pastoral as a live possibility for men of learning. Thomson's poem praises each of Newton's scientific discoveries in high Miltonic style. But the real importance of these discoveries seems to lie in their apparent confirmation of the causal principle's universality. It is small wonder that learned men beset by epistemological doubts should make Newton the hero of causality rather than one of the unwitting villains who helped to take the sails out of the principle. Look at a few of Thomson's lines on the subject:

Have ye not listened while he bound the suns
And planets to their spheres, the unequal task
Of humankind till then? Oft had they rolled
O'er erring man the year, and oft disgraced
The pride of schools, before their course was known
Full in its causes and effects to him . . .
O wisdom truly perfect! thus to call
From a few causes such a scheme of things,
Effects so various, beautiful, and great,
An universe complete!

But the importance of Thomson's poem does not lie in his praise of Newton's reduction of all effects to a single cause. If we look at the poem with some care — of which it is, unfortunately, not very deserving — it becomes clear that it is an example of pastoral and that it attempts to exploit that mode's inherent presuppositions about man's relationship to nature. Think of the implications of writing a poem of *public* praise (a literary monument which is to join the deceased to an admiring public) for a man of science in terms of pastoral! The poem seeks to unite science and its philosophy — that is, the law of nature — with the law of man and the law of god. Thomson, and many of his contemporaries, believed that this followed from Newton's laws, from their apparent guarantee of a totally objective order in a universe where the motions of all objects are connected. Take the following:

And what new wonders can ye show your guest,
Who, while on this dim spot where mortals toil
Clouded in dust, from motion's simple laws
Could trace the secret hand of Providence,
Wide-working through this universal frame? . . .
All intellectual eye, our solar round
First gazing through, he, by the blended power
Of gravitation and projection, saw
The whole in silent harmony revolve.

Thomson would have us believe that a good look through the telescope followed by the proper formulation of an equation add up to a revelation of, a renewal of faith in, the harmonious universality of Providence; all elements of man and nature are united, and we are subjected to Thomson's unintentional parody of Milton's rhetoric, a rhetoric which supposedly joins the sublimities of nature to the grandeur of Newton's *Principia*. But has this rhetorical coupling really been earned? The answer for the following lines should be obvious:

In a soft deluge overflows the sky.
Her every motion clear-discerning, he
Adjusted to the mutual main and taught
Why now the mighty mass of water swells
Resistless, heaving on the broken rocks,
And the full river turning — till again
The tide revertive, unattracted, leaves
A yellow waste of idle sands behind.

Why are those sands idle? By what right has Thomson made them human? We are told that a universal law of motion controls the movement of the tides, a fact which seems to call for Thomson's sublimities. But in what way is this law connected to man? Why does the tidal recession it explains leave "A yellow waste of idle sands behind"? These are not simply matters of Thomson's incompetence as a poet. They point to a difficulty of belief so fundamental that it must make serious pastoral rhetoric sound ludicrous. Any reader concerned with the philosophical issues so blandly raised by the poem must finally ask just why the moral law, the law of man, must be in harmony with the movements of the tides and heavens. Thomson is aware of the difficulties, for even though much of his poem assumes that the moral law is implicit in the scientific law, his overt statements about the matter tend to be oblique. Witness the following:

Did ever poet image aught so fair,
Dreaming in whispering groves by the hoarse brook,
Or prophet, to whose rapture Heaven descends?
Even now the setting sun and shifting clouds,
Seen, Greenwich, from thy lovely heights, declare
How just, how beauteous the refractive law.

Thomson attempts to join the beauties of nature with those of science. But we ask once more, By what right? Why does the landscape "declare" the existence of a law? Thomson, I suspect, is as busy attempting to pull the wool over his own eyes as over those of his readers. Notice his use of the word "just." Clearly the word, from its context, is not being used in its moral sense — as, for example, in the expression "He is a just man"; rather, it is meant to indicate something like exactness or precision. Yet the implication that scientific elegance somehow relates to morality is clearly there. This does create difficulties; and Thomson, it would seem, is afraid of making the claim overt.

Instead of proceeding to establish the relationship of the scientific pursuit to morality, the poem lamely winds up by attempting to impress the reader with Newton's impeccable personal morality:

Oh, speak the wondrous man! how mild, how calm,
How greatly humble, how divinely good,
How firm established on eternal truth;
Fervent in doing well, with every nerve
Still pressing on, forgetful of the past,
And panting for perfection. . . .

Just how Newton's goodness is supposed to relate to his
"panting" for the truths of science is something we are never
told. Since Newton is a culture hero, since his heroism makes
science a principle of legitimation, Thomson must leave us
with at least an intimation of the moral life's relation to the
quest for new scientific truths. What harm in hinting that a
revolutionary smashing of the old science implies a reaffirma-
tion of the old moral beliefs? In this way Newton would seem
to resolve the skeptical doubts which beset both epistemology and the foundation of morals. And so his memory becomes an example for the youth of his country, a rallying
point for the lovers of truth and conventional morality:

Exalt the spirit of a downward world!
O'er thy dejected country chief preside,
And be her Genius called! her studies raise,
Correct her manners, and inspire her youth;
For, though depraved and sunk, she brought thee forth,
And glories in thy name! she points thee out
To all her sons, and bids them eye thy star;
While in expectance of the second life,
When time shall be no more, thy sacred dust
Sleeps with her kings and dignifies the scene.

The poem ends as any conventional pastoral elegy should.
But Thomson's rhetoric unfortunately descends to the level
of propaganda; what is more, given the subject matter, the
propagandistic tone is quite unavoidable. For these lines contain an ominous anticipation of the attitude which proclaims
that science and scholarship are a national asset, a weapon in
the battle against an immoral enemy. The poem is full of

hints that Newton and British morality are involved in some kind of grand strategy directed against the evils of French Cartesian science. Rational argument will not really make this point; therefore Thomson's attempt to convert pastoral to the rhetoric of propaganda. But how many scientific intellectuals, how many men of learning beset by skeptical doubts, are likely to swallow Thomson's bland assertions of these traditional connections? Will pastoral in this form really wash down? We cannot believe in the poem's connection of the scientific with the moral order through the mediation of nature, for it forgoes the attempt to make this connection real — whether in terms of rational argument or sensuous experience. The poem asserts its truths, backs them up with some more assertions about god, country and the beauties of nature, and hopes that enough conditioned responses will be roused so as to elicit the acquiescence of the reader. In short, the poem will not convince; it will only confirm. We must believe its propaganda to begin with; if we do so, the poem's Miltonic rhetoric will strengthen our belief. But with this rhetoric emptied of its religious belief (recall that this is a poem about science), are its pastoral flights likely to sound like sublimities to the skeptical man of learning? I doubt their capacity to emotionally convince, for example, an Encyclopedist like Diderot.

To perform its poetic work, pastoral will have to radically change its approach to the performance of its traditional tasks. It might, of course, simply abdicate a serious confrontation of its difficulties and become an elegant game to be played by the idle courtier. But this withdrawal from the philosophic and communal issues of pastoral will become an expensive sport, for surely there is some significant relationship between the somewhat ludicrous pastoral frolics of Marie Antoinette's shepherds and shepherdesses, and the coming of the French Revolution. A renegade from the Enlightenment like Rousseau will try, somewhat desperately, to actually lead a pastoral existence; but since he is very far from being a noble savage, his attempt to relate morality to nature only serves to increase his doubts. After all, the very need to make his extreme commitment was fathered by uncertainty. So he inevitably finds himself at war with his own philosophic principles, for they have no emotional basis he can discover. Once we understand Rousseau's difficulty it becomes clear why he exerted such a strong influence on Kant's attempt to relate man's moral law to the law of nature. Kant's grand attempt to formalize the natural foundations of pastoral's assumptions is representative of a master task taken on by the Enlightenment and its often unwilling heirs: to not only reunite men with nature and with other men but to do so in terms of our very ways of knowing — our epistemology and science. The task will encounter obstacles placed by the skeptical doubt; these will require detours from which we have yet to return to the main road.

Diderot's Encyclopedia, you recall, represented the first great corporate attempt to assert the reality of moral universals on the basis of the scientific pursuit itself. Its objective was to confirm, by means of an activity shared by all men of knowledge, those basic moral, social, and epistemological connections loosened by the prodding of skeptical doubts. The task seems to be staggering, demanding of its executors nothing less than the arrogance to reverse history. The *Encyclopedia* was, in fact, anything but regressive. For its attempt to reestablish connections did not involve the traditionalism of pastoral; it insisted on pursuing its objective according to its own rules, the rules of science. In attempting to convince its readers of the unity of science and the moral law, the *Encyclopedia* dropped the pastoral scaffolding of Thomson's poem. But there is a logical trap in this commitment, for to assume that the realm of fact implies the realm of value is to ignore the implications of Hume's analysis of causality.

Just why did Diderot consider editing the *Encyclopedia* to be a task of the first importance? Why was it considered desirable for the intellectual community to collaborate on the gathering of thousands of facts? In his *Preliminary Discourse*, d'Alembert invoked the usual Baconian reasons. "The Encyclopedia," he tells us, is "the work of a society of men of letters." This society of intellectuals is united by its common scientific task:

> The work whose first volume we are presenting today has two aims. As an *Encyclopedia*, it is to set forth as well as possible the order and connection of the parts of human knowledge. As a *Reasoned Dictionary of the Sciences, Arts, and Trades*, it is to contain the general principles that form the basis of each science and each art, liberal or mechanical, and the most essential facts that make up the body and substance of each.

This program would seem to exclude the concerns of morality; they appear to be irrelevant to the task of a scientific intellectual. If this is the case, one wonders why the *Encyclopedia* managed to upset so many people. The fact is that d'Alembert represented only one aspect of the work — the purely scientific — refusing to write anything but the articles on mathematics after the *Encyclopedia* had run into difficulties with the authorities. The union of morals and science hinted at in Thomson's poem is obviously irrelevant to d'Alembert's notion of the intellectual's concerns. This neutral attitude, I suppose, best represents our expectations for a task like the *Encyclopedia*'s; yet Diderot did not think of it in this way. Another look at his entry, "The Encyclopedia," should be more than convincing. Diderot begins his definition thus:

In truth, the aim of an encyclopedia is to collect all the knowledge that now lies scattered over the face of the earth, to make known its general structure to the men among whom we live, and to transmit it to those who will come after us. . . .

So far Diderot seems to be saying much the same thing as d'Alembert; but he continues:

. . . in order that the labor of past ages may be useful to the ages to come, that our grandsons, as they become better educated, may at the same time become more virtuous and more happy, and that we may not die without having deserved well of the human race.

Diderot's emphasis on the morality of knowledge — and the two quotations do not represent isolated instances — is central for an intellectual of the Enlightenment; in fact, it is all but necessary for his peace of mind. We need but recall Rousseau's hysterical reaction to the question posed by the Dijon Academy — "Has the progress of the sciences and arts done more to corrupt morals or improve them?" [12] — to understand how vexing, and therefore most often suppressed, a problem the public effect of the scientific pursuit proved to be. It is through the dissemination of his discoveries, after all, that the man of knowledge makes his connection with the rest of society. But here is Rousseau's reaction to the Academy's question:

The moment I read this I beheld another universe and became another man. . . . What I remember quite distinctly about this occasion is that when I reached Vincennes I was in a state of agitation bordering on delirium. . . . All the rest of my life and of my misfortunes followed inevitably as a result of that moment's madness. . . . All my little passions were stifled by an enthusiasm for truth, liberty, and virtue.

[12] Jean-Jacques Rousseau, *The Confessions*, trans. J. M. Cohen (Baltimore, 1953).

This incident marked, perhaps only symbolically, the beginning of Rousseau's opposition to the encyclopedists, of his rejection of their epistemology. The insight about morality came, significantly, in a moment of intense passion experienced on a country road; yet this insight yielded by the accidents of a moment was real to the point of embarrassment. Rousseau's commitment to a pastoral life was a scandal for the encyclopedists, for it raised an issue which they found impossible to resolve; it made Diderot's endless harping on the morality of knowledge an unavoidable necessity.

A question arises. If Diderot's master concern was for the moral effects of knowledge, why the violent attacks — in spite of protection in high places — on the *Encyclopedia?* I believe that the (generally mindless) critics of Diderot's enterprise had an insight into its nature which the encyclopedists often hid from themselves. The Enlightenment's claim is that its chief commitment is to an epistemology — to the scientific method; whatever else a *philosophe* might consider to be salutary would follow from this. But the opponents of the *Encyclopedia* saw this as a mask for a moral commitment standing in opposition to the status quo. And their insight was correct, although many of the *philosophes* proved to be unaware of it. The encyclopedists' assumption that man's knowledge gives him the capacity to shape the world implies that the world can, in fact, be changed. Consider Diderot's surprisingly frank words:

Today, when philosophy is advancing with gigantic strides, when it is bringing under its sway all the matters that are its proper concern, when its tone is the dominant one, and when we are beginning to shake off the yoke of authority and tradition in order to hold fast to the laws of reason, there is scarcely a single elementary or dogmatic book which satisfies us entirely.

These are the reasons for the gathering of knowledge. But just how is this knowledge to undermine authority? The answer lies in the use of a scientific method:

This is the way to lead people, by a series of tacit deductions, to the most daring conclusions. If these cross references, which now confirm and now refute, are carried out artistically according to a plan carefully conceived in advance, they will give the *Encyclopedia* what every good dictionary ought to have — the power to change men's common way of thinking.

Diderot's emphasis on the possible effect of cross references seems, on the surface, to be no more than an application of Hume's empiricist theory of knowledge: the mind is presented with impressions and then proceeds to make natural and simple associations. Changing "men's common way of thinking" would seem to involve a change in their way of knowing rather than in their commonly held beliefs. Thus there is, it would appear, no overt attack on institutionalized authority, only on the traditional theory of knowledge. The authorities saw through this, as can be seen in their attack on the epistemological work of Helvetius:

Society, Religion, and the State present themselves today at the tribunal of justice in order to submit their complaints. Their rights have been violated, their laws disregarded. Impiety walks with head held high. . . . Humanity shudders, the citizenry is alarmed. . . .

It is with grief that we are forced to say it: can one conceal from oneself that there is a project formed, a Society organized, to propagate materialism, to destroy Religion, to inspire a spirit of independence, and to nourish the corruption of morals? . . .

In the picture that we have just drawn of the principal maxims of this work [*De l'Esprit*] you are seeing in fact, Messieurs, simply the principles and detestable consequences of many other books published earlier, especially the Encyclopedical Dictionary. The book *De l'Esprit* is, as it were, the abridgment of this too-famous work, which according to its true purpose should have been the book of all knowledge and has become instead the book of all error. . . .[13]

---

[13] Quoted in Arthur M. Wilson, *Diderot: The Testing Years, 1713–1759* (New York, 1957).

Their dismal ranting aside, the opponents of the *Encyclopedia* had the intelligence to understand that the *philosophes* were converting an approach to knowledge into a moral weapon. The collaborative effort needed for this task was possible only because a group of men felt they were united by their common commitment to learning and truth. And this, with little philosophical justification, they tended to see as a moral commitment which grew out of the principles of science. Diderot put it aptly:

> An encyclopedia ought to make good the failure to execute such a project hitherto, and should encompass not only the fields already covered by the academies, but each and every branch of human knowledge. This is a work that cannot be completed except by a society of men of letters and skilled workmen, each working separately on his own part, but all bound together solely by their zeal for the best interests of the human race and a feeling of mutual good will.

But why should a dedication to scholarship lead to good will and the best interests of humanity? Consider, for example, Rousseau's reflections on the activity of the *philosophes:*

> The taste for philosophy relaxes all the bonds of esteem and benevolence that attach men to society. . . . Soon the philosopher concentrates in his person all the interest that *virtuous* men share with their fellow men: his disdain for others turns to the profit of his own pride; his self-love increases in the same ratio as his indifference for the rest of the universe. Family, fatherland, become for him words empty of meaning; he is neither a parent, nor a citizen, nor a man; he is a philosopher.[14]

Rousseau's aggressive statement may have been motivated by personal spite, it may have the sound of a fatuous primitivism, but it is based on philosophical and psychological difficulties which are real enough for the *philosophes.* The arrogance of assuming that the devotion to a scholarly subject gives one the capacity and right to prescribe a society's

[14] Quoted by Wilson.

conduct can be seen, most unattractively, in much of Voltaire's work. The natural function of a skeptical epistemology would seem to be criticism, not the promulgation of moral codes.

Diderot does not really justify his moral claims for the encyclopedists as a group. He simply asserts, once more, that these men are *"bound together by zeal for the best interests of the human race and by a feeling of mutual good will,* because these motives are the most worthy that can animate the souls of upright people and they are also the most lasting." This is as bald, and unscientific, an assertion of value as any moralist might desire. Diderot would like the encyclopedists to unite science with morals by acting as a special interest group whose primary concern is the propagation of knowledge. They are to be independent intellectuals without political or academic ties, whose social connections are made by the public effect of their scholarly pursuits. Yet if there is to be a public effect, reactions of a political nature will be unavoidable; in fact, Diderot used both his connections with prominent public figures and an occasional bit of political trimming to keep himself out of major trouble. But he always avoided the obvious (and fatal) step of putting his scholarship at the service of the regime: a policy which seemed reasonable if the scientific pursuit was to have its proper influence on society. Diderot, whatever the nature of his occasional compromises, insisted that the *Encyclopedia,* unlike the academies, remain the voice of men of learning who were entirely independent of the government.

Diderot's foresight, perhaps simply his good fortune, is to be seen in the almost comical fate of the ideologues — a loose grouping of intellectuals who were surely the heirs of the *Encyclopedia.* The ideologues' association was based on a common belief in an epistemology: Condillac's sensationalism, or "ideology." The ideologues believed that all ideas, including moral ones, could be analyzed into sensations. From these modest, even if untenable, beginnings they reasoned that if men were taught the proper principles of knowledge and thereby learned how to analyze their ideas into perceptions, they would, by an inevitable process of association, reach the conclusion that republicanism is the only possible form of government. Only empiricism's prestige can explain a group of intelligent people coming to such conclusions on the basis of Hume's theory of knowledge. Clearly Condillac's theory of sensations served to legitimize a moral commitment which is in no way deducible from the assumptions of empiricism and sensationalism. The rationality of their arguments aside, the ideologues did have their effect during, and as an aftermath of, the French Revolution; intellectuals as a group, armed with their notion of an independent science, had attained a measure of influence; and having done so, they illustrated that traditional institutions had lost the power to relate systems of knowledge to public action. Only the skeptical intellect (the property of the ideologues) could give legitimacy to the actions of any government which had put aside the traditional trappings of authority. Skepticism can serve the status quo only out of cynicism, not out of commitment to the results of its critiques. Thus to understand the situation of the ideologues is to gain an insight into the legitimizing function which intellectuals serve for governments today.[15]

The Law of the Third Brumaire decreed that analysis—the translation of ideas into sensations—was to become the chief instrument of pedagogy in the *écoles normales*. Courses of

[15] Some of the historical detail concerning the Ideologues is derived from Charles Hunter Van Duzer, *Contribution of the Ideologues to French Revolutionary Thought* (Baltimore, 1935).

lectures to be given by members of the National Institute of Arts and Sciences were to convey the latest knowledge in terms of "ideological" analysis. Quite naturally, this proved to be meaningless in the various sciences, as the lecturers simply held forth on their special subjects. But in the civics courses taught at the *écoles normales,* analysis simply served as a mask, an epistemological legitimation, for republican propaganda. Napoleon, not unexpectedly, saw that once the ideologues had permitted themselves to be used, that once they had allowed independent scholarship to become the tool of political action, there was no logical barrier against their pedagogical principles—that is, their skeptical epistemology—being exploited by anyone in power. Thus he courted the ideologues with a great show of interest in scholarship. He was elected to the Institute in 1797, and on the eighteenth Brumaire most of his colleagues fully expected him to create a republic led by philosophers. They discovered soon enough that Napoleon wished to use ideology for the propagation of his own principles. The ideologues resisted; yet they had brought Napoleon's cynical exploitation on themselves. His actions were no more than an aftermath of the ideologues' coupling of epistemology and political stance. Napoleon eventually abolished the class of moral and political science at the Institute and thereby revealed the connection between the moral law and the law of nature to be shaky at best. The dedication to science, the ideologues learned, did not necessarily imply a commitment to a moral course of action; nor did it involve men in the affairs of the community on the basis of a moral commitment: Analysis, after all, is also a necessary adjunct of power politics.

Those intellectuals who are the heirs of the Enlightenment, ourselves included, will be forced to struggle—endlessly, generation after generation—with Hume's separation of matters of fact and relationships of ideas. The fate of the ideologues should have made this clear for the nineteenth century; clear, that is, for anyone unwilling to repeat old philosophical errors. Intellectuals simply cannot wriggle away from the following question: Does the commitment to a philosophical method imply a moral stance, a program of social and political action? Diderot faced up to these difficulties (or almost did so) in the infuriating ambiguities of *Rameau's Nephew*. The work is Diderot's report of a conversation between himself and Rameau, the famous composer's nephew. Rameau conducts his life in accordance with his own version of the utilitarian moral code, his only concern being with the fulfillment of his own sensual needs. We should remember that many of Diderot's colleagues maintained that empiricism dictated the adoption of utility as the sole foundation for morals. Diderot's feelings on the subject were mixed, to put it mildly; consider his reaction to a verbal bout with Rameau:

As for me I hardly knew whether I should come or go, laugh or get angry. I stayed, wanting to turn the conversation to some subject that would drive out of my soul the horror that filled it. I was beginning to find almost unbearable the presence of a man who could discuss a dreadful deed, an abominable crime, in the way a connoisseur in poetry or painting discusses the fine points of a work of art — or as a moralist or an historian points out the merit of an heroic action. I felt gloom overwhelming me.

But why the density of Diderot's gloom? Rameau would seem to be no more than a superstrategist of sensuality. Of course, the point at issue is that Rameau's strategy is refined by the insights of skeptical philosophy; his concern for knowledge is not even faintly related to a "zeal for the best interests of the human race"; science, in this case, serves to make more readily available the expertise needed for more luxurious freeloading. The Enlightenment's theory of knowledge clearly leads to bigger and better meals. Rameau's virtuosity in matters of technique eventually wins Diderot's grudging admiration; yet the principles of philosophy can obviously not be left to the demands of the stomach. Hence Diderot as follows:

> Your performance is unsurpassable [said I]. But there is one human being who is exempted from the pantomime. That is the philosopher who has nothing and asks for nothing.

Brave; yet insufferably stuffy! Imagine Diderot making this speech to the utilitarians of *The Connection*, who might easily count Rameau as a fellow hipster. When Diderot opts for the disinterested philosophy, is he being scientific? Or is he making a choice based on an assumed value? The conversation continues with a discussion of Diogenes' austere manner of life:

MYSELF: He went back to his tub and did without.

HE: Do you advise me to do the same?

MYSELF: I'll stake my life it is better than to crawl, eat dirt and prostitute yourself.

HE: But I want a good bed, good food, warm clothes in winter, cool in summer, plenty of rest, money, and other things that I would rather owe to kindness than earn by toil.

MYSELF: That is because you are a lazy, greedy lout, a coward and a rotting soul.

HE: I believe I told you so myself.

Diderot's admonitions are just enough, but his principles have not really given him the right to make them. Obviously, he had some insight into the flimsiness of his own position, for he makes himself sound like a pompous gasbag, an insufferable killjoy. It is Rameau's unashamed and frank sensuality which attracts us, and which we feel cannot be readily dismissed by moralistic twaddle. Rameau, rather than Diderot, seems to be the devotee of truth; furthermore, the former seems most faithful to the latter's skeptical principles. Yet the consequences of Rameau's faithful adherence to these principles should leave us with something of the horror felt by Diderot. For Rameau finally reveals that the grief he feels over the death of his beautiful young wife derives from nothing so unphilosophic as sympathy; rather, he had been hoping to satisfy his sensual needs by pimping her off to the highest bidder.

The transition from sage to scientific expert, a transition engendered by the skeptical doubt, has put the modern man of learning in an almost untenable position. His knowledge — more, his very attitude to that knowledge — separates him from the ordinary congress of the community, from its received moralities; yet the community needs his scientific bent of mind. The danger lies in the fact that a method of knowing and investigating can, after all, be used for anything. For example, the moral neutrality allowed Rameau by his posing as the scientific expert *par excellence* not only frees him from the dogmas of conventional morality but from those of conventional art as well. The freedom and realism Rameau attains as a consequence are positively bracing; they enable him to challenge the status quo and to unmask the moral pretenses of his society. The price paid by Rameau is in his separation from the community as well as his incapacity to do anything which goes beyond criticism. Yet what might be the expense of using one's scientific expertise for satisfying the demands of the community? The same process of rationalization which gave birth to the procedures and objectives of science also fathered a stepchild: bureaucratization. In our time, a bureaucracy cannot exist without its scientific experts; and so it absorbs them into its communal hierarchy, into its class structure. The sociological consciousness of the encyclopedists is, after all, not so far removed from the sense of communal status attained by modern scholar-experts. The latter are at a far remove from Rameau's almost pathetic amorality. Does not the modern expert consider himself to be at the service of his society's moral goals? Few bureaucrats can afford the psychic expense of admitting to themselves the amorality of their tasks; nor will cynicism about the performance of one's routine help one to settle into the comforts of communal belonging. But in the exchange of Rameau's pathos for the confidence of status — that is, with the intellectual's submission to the imperatives of rationalization and bureaucracy — the capacity for free and clearly reasoned criticism is likely to get lost. The options for the man of learning do not seem to allow for a commitment to both his society and the principles of his science, except on terms set by the society itself. And just what happens to the notion of objective research in the latter case? The intellectual might have to respond with an irrational, and often unattractive, moralistic commitment like Diderot's. Diderot's editing of the *Encyclopedia* seems, finally, to rest on one moral imperative: that the progress of science, of knowledge in general, is a good. And most of us tend to accept this as dogma; in fact, we are likely to excuse almost anything on its basis.

The common reactions to the dropping of the first atomic bomb should illustrate the point well enough. Consider President Truman's reflection on the grand event: "The greatest achievement of organized science in history." [16] At the time, Dwight Macdonald — who felt separated not only from the national purpose but from most of his fellow intellectuals — was one of the few with a clear insight into the sources of Truman's statement. *"The bomb,"* he wrote,

is the natural product of the kind of society we have created. It is as easy, normal and unforced an expression of the American Way of Life as electric iceboxes, banana splits, and hydromaticdrive automobiles.

[16] Quoted in Dwight Macdonald, *Memoirs of a Revolutionist* (Cleveland and New York, 1958).

The point being that we consider any product of science —
even of organized and bureaucratized science — to be of
value; the bomb represents a scientific advance like any
other, and the intellectual's task is to do his share in having
our side manufacture it first. Just how have so many men of
learning been able to justify their role in making mass
slaughter possible? How have they reconciled their work with
the encyclopedists' notion of an independent science? The
rationalization, as Macdonald pointed out, derives from the
very principles which make an independent science possible:

> Yet they all accepted the "assignment," and produced The
> Bomb. Why? Because they thought of themselves as specialists,
> technicians, and not as complete men. Specialists in the sense
> that the process of scientific discovery is considered to be morally
> neutral, so that the scientist may deplore the uses to which his
> discoveries are put by the generals and politicians but may not
> refuse to make them for that reason; and specialists also in that
> they reacted to the war as partisans of one side, whose function
> was the narrow one of defeating the Axis governments even if it
> meant sacrificing their broader responsibilities as human beings.

Macdonald's virtue lies in his insight that the idea of scientific neutrality — and it is relevant in its application to social
scientists and humanists as well — may serve as a mask for a
moral and political commitment. The production of, and
apology for, the bomb hardly add up to the kind of moral
commitment Diderot had in mind; yet it is implicit in his
assumption that the dedication to scholarship, in and for itself, constitutes a social and personal virtue. Diderot's clarity
of mind, coupled with his honesty, kept the *Encyclopedia*
from being exploited by the government; yet his philosophical position did not really support this stand.

It strikes me that it is Diderot's sanguineness about the
uses of knowledge which keeps him from being our contemporary. It is Rameau — and, who knows, he may be Dide-

rot's double — who sounds like a modern intellectual, who seems to have an awareness of the difficulties of his position. Rameau lives with those doubts concerning the uses of knowledge which are the natural outgrowth of skepticism. Diderot, on the other hand (and here the similarity to Thomson's picture of Newton should be obvious), still embodies some of the attitudes of the sage: By means of his special knowledge he justifies certain "truths"; and it is this act of rationalization which establishes his relationship to the community. There seems to be no doubt that scientific progress is a good, and that the duty of the intellectual is to put himself at its service. The step of finally offering one's services to the government or to the bureaucracy is smaller than we think: Diderot, in apparent innocence, eventually allowed himself to be used by Catherine the Great; in our time, men of learning have found a second home in the defense establishment. The dangers should be obvious. It is all too easy to assume that *our* cause is just (or worse, that any moral judgment is irrelevant) and to offer one's expertise for the purpose of justifying and glorifying — freedom?

The dissolution of the old social connections, the questioning of hierarchies, created a number of pressing difficulties, both social and intellectual, with which eighteenth-century men of learning were forced to come to terms. Diderot's *Encyclopedia*, indeed the whole attempt to apply or relate the scientific endeavor to society, represents a general effort to resolve the ironies evident in Marvell's approach to pastoral. What "The Garden" wryly accepts, the *Encyclopedia* tries to eliminate; for the latter claims to be connecting the moral law to the pursuit of science, the intellectual's function to the progress of society. Diderot's passionate interest in technology is not accidental: The products of technology are the most immediate social expressions of science; as such, their general effect will serve as the social test for scientific progress. Diderot saw clearly enough that the rise of the industrial middle class was tied to developments in technology. But he and most other intellectuals concerned with progress failed to notice that another social application of science, the "science" of society itself, served as a mask for the economic depredations of this middle class. The concepts of social science served as a justification for the literal destruction of pastoral in England; they made acceptable — indeed, converted into a law of nature — the compulsory movement of masses of people from the country to the city. Perhaps only a conservative like Oliver Goldsmith, with his sentimentalities about old institutions, was capable of expressing the proper degree of moral indignation about the human expense of technological progress. Not surprisingly, his feelings were expressed in a poem, "The Deserted Village." The imperatives of progress are not readily argued against in formal discourse; often they permit little more than the make-believe of pastoral. It should be more than evident today that the pretenses of free-trade economics to the status of science and moral neutrality really served to lend some measure of respectability to class interests. But a strong sense of detachment from current intellectual fashions was needed to perceive this in the eighteenth century. Indeed, the most deadly criticisms of Thomson's attempt to relate science to morals, of his pastoral frauds, were made by literary men who felt little, if any, commitment to the dogmas of the Enlightenment.

THE MOST NOTORIOUS OF THESE CRITICISMS was (and has been for more than two centuries) Swift's pamphlet, *A Modest Proposal for Preventing the Children of Poor People in Ireland From Being a Burden to Their Parents or Country, and For Making Them Beneficial to the Public.* This mock economic treatise still seems to touch an exposed nerve; the root of the pain might be buried in the very ground from which the perpetual misinterpretations of this work seem to sprout. Swift's primary concern was not with the issues of poverty or population but with the attitude of the pamphlet's fictional author. Irish starvation had been ignored on the basis of free trade — a notion which had almost obtained the status of a scientific law. The author of the pamphlet is obviously proud of his role as a social scientist:

As to my own part, having turned my thoughts for many years upon this important subject, and maturely weighed the several schemes of other projectors, I have always found them grossly mistaken in their computation. It is true a child just dropped from its dam may be supported by her milk for a solar year with little other nourishment, at most not above the value of two shillings, which the mother may certainly get, or the value in scraps, by her lawful occupation of begging, and it is exactly at one year old that I propose to provide for them, in such a manner as, instead of being a charge upon their parents, or the parish, or wanting food and raiment for the rest of their lives, they shall, on the contrary, contribute to the feeding and partly to the clothing of many thousands.

The author uses the language of science; this, in turn, lends his proposal its tone of neutrality; he steps back from the subject on hand, he is independent, and he analyzes the given problem with exemplary disinterest. We, of course, are expected to feel that this attitude is beneficial, that it is needed for the good of humanity. The pose prepares us for the proposal itself: that the children of the Irish poor be slaughtered in order to grace the dinner tables of the well to do. A whole catalogue of economic reasons, backed by statistics, assures us of the rationality of the scheme. The author concludes the pamphlet thus:

I profess in the sincerity of my heart that I have not the least personal interest in endeavoring to promote this necessary work, having no other motive than the *public good of my country, by advancing our trade, providing for infants, relieving the poor, and giving some pleasure to the rich.* I have no children by which I can propose to get a single penny; the youngest being nine years old, and my wife past child-bearing.

The author has allowed the cool rationality of a "realistic" social science to carry him as far as it will; he has the courage to pursue the logic of his scholarship, to "think about the unthinkable." What he consequently proposes ought to strike us with horror, at the very least. Yet we believe in the validity of the scientific method; and doing so, how are we to find fault with the author's procedure? Is there anything wrong with the objective study of a social problem? The point Swift attempts to make, it should be clear, is that the disregard of moral and emotional factors implied by the social scientific stance, far from being realistic, is the supreme unreality. Furthermore, by reducing something so elementary as human suffering to an occasion for the study of economic statistics, the author has severed his own connections with his fellow men; for not to be enraged in the face of needless mass starvation, not to see through (worse, to even provide) the ideological masks justifying official inaction — this constitutes the supreme perversion of the skeptical intellect, thus making the intellectual's role irrelevant to the *human* needs of the community.

The problem is, of course, ours; it is as central to the intellectual and artistic concerns of the present as it was of the eighteenth century. There is little need to discuss in detail either the methodological pretenses of our social sciences or the kinds of activity they shield: We all have our favorite horror stories. But one cannot readily dismiss the example of Herman Kahn. After initially approaching his prose with a measure of seriousness, one hopes that he is, after all, being Swiftian. Dr. Kahn, much like the author of A *Modest Proposal,* assures us that nothing less than a passion for the general benefit of mankind motivates his work; it is solely for our benefit that the unthinkable must be made rational. To accomplish this, Kahn cannot really use rational and scientific procedures: We all know by now that the sport of nuclear strategy involves a kind of reversion to the madness of childish fantasies. No, he must exercise his fancy and come up with a species of imaginative literature which gives the appearance of being rational. This he manages rather neatly by using the imagery and structure — not the substance — of science. Kahn's *Thinking About the Unthinkable* [17] begins with the pretense that something akin to a scientific model provides a solid foundation for his speculations. But what awaits us is much more imaginative: the "scenario." (That this term should recall Genet's *The Balcony* is more than apt.) The higher rationality of the diplomatic strategies which are the fruit of these "strange aids to thought" (I use Kahn's phrase) should be evident from the following:

This does not mean there would be no checks upon Soviet action. Aside from the ever-present fear that calculations, however rationally made, might prove wrong, there would remain another deterrent. We might take a leaf from the Soviet book and destroy some Soviet cities, coupling this with a demand that the Soviets desist from further violence. The Soviets could retaliate by destroying some of our cities, pointing out that since they had the greater resolve they were unlikely to back down first, and we had therefore better acquiesce in the surrender of Europe. At this point both nations would be engaging in a super-destructive game of chicken.
     As stupid and bizarre as this game of chicken may seem, under the assumption of mutual Countervalue over-kill [I admonish the reader to pay close attention to this basic scientific assumption.

[17] Herman Kahn, *Thinking About the Unthinkable* (New York, 1962).

L. K.], it would be less stupid and bizarre than initiating an all-out Countervalue exchange. Obviously, the "controlled" city exchange might escalate into an all-out spasm war [war, sex, and the orgasm: the imagery of centuries of love poetry has been absorbed by this elegant scientific concept. L. K.] as a result of anger or miscalculation or some other event. Such drastic action is obviously inappropriate for minor provocations. It is, in fact, hard to imagine a "controlled" city exchange or similar limited Countervalue attack being used more than once in two generations. If used once, the shock might be sufficient to cause drastic and irreversible changes in the international order which would make repetitions unlikely. At the least it would provide a powerful impetus toward a satisfactory arms control plan. . . . A Controlled Reprisal or nuclear show of force need not be designed to kill many people. It could even be a spectacular fireworks display (such as exploding a megaton bomb at 200,000 feet over Moscow or Washington).

The scientific status of these remarks on atomic diplomacy should be self-evident. But lest the reader think that Dr. Kahn is solely concerned with the abstractions of game theory, I shall allow myself the luxury of further quotation. *Thinking About the Unthinkable*, stand assured, takes the fate of all humanity for its subject; we have, after all, made a measure of social progress since the days of Swift. Here are some of the author's speculations about the aftermath of atomic war:

However, objective studies also indicate that this environment would not be so hostile as to preclude, at least in the long run, decent and useful lives for the survivors and their descendants.

People in a postwar world following a large war would for a time have to get by on a much lower standard of living than that to which they were accustomed. We must remember, however, that our standard today is far higher than preservation of life requires. Studies . . . indicate that after the first year or so, assuming there is a successful reorganization, the standard of living . . . would be higher than the standards prevalent in the U.S. between 1900 and 1930.

The concept of a "policy science," of which Kahn's work is representative enough, has its source in the attempt of Enlightenment intellectuals to legitimate their social and political activities in terms of the scientific pursuit. To a degree, the rise of these intellectuals as a special interest group coincided with a depressing development for modern statecraft. By the time of the eighteenth century, the dominant task of national governments had clearly become the mobilization of resources for the waging of current or imminent wars. Men of learning have been victimized by, but have also profited from, this circumstance; for the making of policy in the modern warfare state demands expertise; and who is more fit to supply it than the intellectual looking for a social role? The role of policy expert is, of course, liable to prove somewhat restrictive to the skeptical intellect. Yet it is this latter attitude to knowledge, the attitude which created the class of intellectuals, which seems to demand that policy be made scientific. But there is a paradox in the very notion of a "policy science" which makes the whole activity a mockery of scientific procedure. "Policy" implies a commitment; it involves the making of choices on the basis of what is considered to be the good. "Science," on the other hand, implies the neutral search for knowledge, the commitment to an epistemology and a method of research. The result of this contradiction can be seen in Kahn's work: The policy expert remains a scientist by turning the waging of conflicts into a formalized game. There is, unfortunately, a difficulty which the game theoretician must face at some point: The testing of his theories might involve a human expense which is likely to be more than trivial.

These difficulties are dramatized with a frightening clarity of purpose in the Enlightenment's fictional masterpiece, Laclos' *Les Liaisons Dangereuses*.[18] The work could easily serve as a model for the policy sciences. It begins, signifi-

[18] Choderlos de Laclos, *Les Liaisons Dangereuses*, trans. P. W. K. Stone (Baltimore, 1961).

cantly, with a quotation from Rousseau's *La Nouvelle Hél-oïse*. Rousseau had demonstrated that men required a sense of society, an awareness of social norms, to have the capacity for moral action. But in the novel the aristocratic hero and heroine, Valmont and the Marquise de Merteuil, are cut off from the possibility of acting in a social context. For them the classic ideal of the aristocracy, glory, can be attained only in the exploits of the boudoir; the old metaphor of love as war has been given a new twist by the political realities of the Enlightenment. And so seduction becomes an elaborate game of diplomacy and of war. Power is marshaled for the enactment of one's sexual fantasies. Consider, for example, these words of Valmont:

> So far, my love, you will, I think, have been pleased with the orthodoxy of my method: you will have seen that I have in no respect diverged from the true principles of an art that is, as we have often observed, very similar to that of warfare. Judge me, then, as you would Turenne or Frederick;

or those of the Marquise:

> As for me, I shall admit that one of the things that most flatters me is a lively and well-executed attack, when everything happens in quick but orderly succession; which never puts us in the painfully embarrassing position of having to cover up some blunder of which, on the contrary, we ought to be taking advantage; which keeps up an appearance of taking by storm even what we are quite prepared to surrender, and adroitly flatters our two favourite passions: the pride of defence and the pleasure of defeat.

To carry on their campaigns, these warriors develop a set of scientific strategies which claim to be no more than objective studies of society — a society whose chief occupation is war. Here is the Marquise explaining her experimental procedures to Valmont:

> But I, what have I in common with these empty-headed women? When have you known me break the rules I have laid

down for myself or betray my principles? I say "*my* principles" intentionally. They are not, like those of other women, found by chance, accepted unthinkingly, and followed out of habit. They are the fruit of profound reflection. I have created them: I might say that I have created myself.

At my entrance into society I was still a girl, condemned by my status to silence and inaction, and I made the most of my opportunities to observe and reflect. . . . I paid little attention, in fact, to what everyone was anxious to tell me, but was careful to ponder what they attempted to hide.

The importance of this declaration of principles lies not only in the Marquise's epistemology, her insistence on taking social appearance as a mask for deeper processes, but in her declaration — remarkable for its honesty — that she has created her own principles, her standards of social action. The form of her strategies does not derive from the empirically based calculus of pleasures she has worked out. Science has not really created policy; it has merely set the stage for it by neutralizing received morality. To the social scientist measurable facts, not statements of principles, provide the relevant data. The Marquise and Valmont are performing roles in scenarios which they, not nature, have created. Laclos makes this clear in his use of the imagery of the stage and in the characters' frequent quotations from a large number of plays. Similarly, those who act out Herman Kahn's scenarios are hardly doing so in accordance to any set of scientific laws; the scientific jargon simply lends an air of needed legitimacy to their dramatic roles. In terms of any set of traditional humane or moral standards, these roles appear to be monstrous; they offend our sensibilities. The balance of terror established by the Marquise and Valmont needs only the intervention of honest human passion to be upset. Yet the erosion of the foundations of ethics by the skeptical doubt has deprived us of the right to apply reasoned moral standards to these activities. How can one call neutral "scientific"

[199]

activity immoral? The distinction of the Marquise and Valmont, as against someone like Kahn, lies in their refusal to pretend that their activities — that is, their use of power to enforce their principles — are carried out for the greater good of mankind — that their knowledge, their scientific expertise, has anything to do with moral progress.

Where does that leave the program of the encyclopedists? What has happened to the idea of a science which would enable men of learning to be the servants of both knowledge and morality? This master problem of the Enlightenment — and it is our problem, as was indicated by Dwight Macdonald's comments on the atomic bomb — is summed up, with more than a touch of bitterness, in Laclos' ironic "Publisher's Notice," which serves his novel as a preface:

In fact, several of the characters he puts on his stage are persons of such vicious habits that it is impossible to suppose they can have lived in our age: this age of philosophy, in which the light of reason, illumining every heart, has turned us all, as everyone knows, into honourable men and modest and retiring women.

THE ENLIGHTENMENT, THEN, HAS LEFT a legacy of discomfort for most intellectuals. Its freeing effect and its confusions concerning the uses of knowledge have engendered problems which are nearly insoluble. Just what role is the intellectual to play? What, if anything, is his social function to be? The fate of pastoral — its political and social implications for those men of learning who created it — serves as an index to some of the historical possibilities and necessities created by the Enlightenment. For pastoral, given its roots in social pressures, reveals how the private fantasies of literary activity, its play of images and ideas, can become the substance of political concerns. Democratization (that is, a version of pastoral's desire for the equality of high and low) surely becomes the most important political issue facing Europe and America after the Enlightenment. The literary intellectual in search of social connections can hardly avoid being plunged into the struggles which develop; his images are, after all, partially responsible for creating the conditions, the state of consciousness, necessary for those struggles; and so the man of learning's pastoral pretense of high being low will seem like a frivolous irrelevance, thereby losing its capacity to assuage his guilt. Pastoral will have to become a social reality if the intellectual is to create the possibility for connections. But it is precisely in the face of this demand that we become aware of the Enlightenment's legacy of political failure; for it had not provided the means of transforming literary visions into social reality. This separation of ideals and political action has dogged intellectuals to the present day; it provides the background for the many disastrous (because glibly propagandistic) attempts at a political literature in our time and sets the stage for the drastic methods of *The Connection*. The problem is aptly summarized in Marx's comments on the political failures of 1848:

Finally, Lamartine in the provisional government; this was actually no real interest, no definite class; this was the February revolution itself, the common uprising with its illusions, its poetry, its visionary content, and its phrases [19]

The institutional and literary images of democracy, in short, had failed to become the reality of *social* democracy. Perhaps this tells us something about the failures of literature itself; about the incapacities of classical and aristocratic modes to meet the emotional demands of democratic needs; perhaps it

[19] *The Class Struggles in France*, in Karl Marx and Friedrich Engels, *Basic Writings on Politics and Philosophy*, ed. L. S. Feuer (Garden City, N.Y., 1959). All quotations of Marx and Engels are from this volume.

reveals the intellectual's failure to perform the proper job of criticism, his failure to connect with anyone but his peers. The gradual democratization of the ability to read makes the intellectual's role (unavoidably) a social and political one; his first task then becomes the discovery of what shape his involvement is to take. In fact, he must discover — or create — just what his social reality is. This involves nothing less than the formulation of a theory relating philosophical and literary ideas to action: a burden which could become the albatross around the intellectual's neck. But the act of self-discovery demanded by his search for community will give the intellectual the opportunity to stand in the vanguard of social action. For the democratization of education and the sense of freedom from the chains of the past, both inherited from the Enlightenment, make social and political action an open process; and being open, it will be dependent not only on ideas but on ways of executing them.

The Enlightenment had failed — and this was the complaint of radicals like Herzen and Marx — in executing Diderot's program, in having the dissemination of knowledge transform the world. The exercise of intellect had not attained social relevance; nor had pursuits of intellect been metamorphosed into a political force. Part of this failure lay in the inability of both political theory and institutions to keep up with social developments. The irrelevance of pastoral literature for the eighteenth century tells us a good deal about this lag. Political reformers of the eighteenth century evinced little interest in the aspirations of the low, and even less in shoving the high off their perch; indeed, both politics and literature seemed to be almost entirely unconcerned with basic social and political transformations. Whatever the interest shown in the idea of pastoral transformation, it tended to avoid the commitment to social relevance: For example,

Rousseau's pastoral act, though highly serious, was intended to separate him from society; on the other hand, the aristocracy's playing of pastoral games was thoroughly frivolous and therefore irrelevant to any principles of social or political action — indeed, it was a way of avoiding relevance altogether. The eighteenth century tried to have its political reform without any corollary social transformation, for it tended to think of class structure as wholly static, as part of the permanent pattern of general nature. Edmund Burke's political thought — and it summarized both the conservative and liberal strains of the eighteenth century — was close to the heart of Dr. Johnson, the last great proponent of the doctrine of general nature, since the former's solicitude for institutions led to that same wariness of fundamental change which the latter felt of literary novelty. And a similar wariness shapes (surprisingly) the political thought of Voltaire, who was, after all, thoroughly despised by Dr. Johnson for his liberalism. Yet Voltaire's classicism and his consequent belief in general nature should have led us to anticipate the similarity between his and Johnson's politics: this in spite of their significant philosophical differences. Voltaire, and most of the *philosophes*, considered social reform to be the task of benevolent despots; the task of the man of knowledge is to make his discoveries available to these monarchs, to guide them — in short, to make them benevolent. The knowledge of the *philosophes* will lead to reforms in the administration of power, eliminating stupidity and putting reasonable checks on greed. These administrative reforms, it is hoped, will eliminate needless suffering by the exercise of a measure of humaneness and intelligence; yet they will also help to maintain the status quo. It is hardly surprising, therefore, that monarchs like Catherine and Frederick courted Diderot and Voltaire, for these *philosophes* lent their regimes a tone of intellectual respectability without raising the specter of fundamental change. But as any ruler should know, the effects of social forces, of knowledge — even of epistemology — so often tend to make fools of our intentions, to outstrip or disappoint our expectations. Thus we may agree to Marx's claim that the Enlightenment had been an intellectual mask for bourgeois interests; we may further agree that its truths had been bourgeois truths, its science a tool of class interests; yet it had made all future attempts at radical political and social change possible. Unfortunately, and equally unpredictably, the Enlightenment also created the possibility for what Engels aptly termed, "the future conversion of political rule over men into an administration of things and a direction of processes of production." [*Socialism: Utopian and Scientific*] Instead of providing the vanguard for the social realization of pastoral, intellectuals could — and so often did — establish their social connections by becoming cogs in the very machine which their intellects had helped to create.

What we have come to call Romanticism, with all its confused intensities about mysterious connections, was really the last (perhaps also the first) serious attempt of our literary culture to make up for the failures of the Enlightenment. Early Romanticism tried its hand at this momentous task by giving pastoral a new content. To remedy the ills of a civilization in terms of a literary vision — the idea is born of daring, or of despair. But one should remember that early Romanticism — think especially of the work of the Schlegels and of Coleridge — braced itself for its huge task by an act of self-limitation. Did it not become primarily a theory of mind and of knowledge? The theory is neither vaguely mystical, nor even incomprehensible, as is often the case in the speculations of the later Romantics: The examples of Wordsworth and Coleridge should make this clear; indeed, it is firmly rooted in the eighteenth century's substantial accomplishments in the philosophy of mind and the theory of perception. The assumptions at the core of Wordsworth's "Tintern Abbey," for example, form a critique of Hume's philosophy of mind. The mind, the poem tells us, is more than the sum of its impressions; furthermore, it has the capacity to perceive a variety of relationships in nature; and finally, by means of this activity, mind, though it may be largely passive, establishes a significant relationship to nature. In Wordsworth's poem, these assumptions about mental activity have been embedded in pastoral: The proper connections between man and nature can be made only where nature is pure, only where the urban superstructure has not obliterated natural relationships.

> Once again I see
> These hedge-rows, hardly hedge-rows, little lines
> Of sportive wood run wild: these pastoral farms,
> Green to the very door; and wreaths of smoke
> Sent up, in silence from among the trees!
> With some uncertain notice, as might seem
> Of vagrant dwellers in the houseless woods,
> Or of some Hermit's cave, where by his fire
> The Hermit sits alone.

These lines and the poem's entire first paragraph, which they bring to a conclusion, bear a superficial resemblance to eighteenth-century landscape poetry. Most of this poetry (it is often embarrassingly bad) is based on the primitivist notion that pure nature has an objective order which is independent of men and the products of their mental activity. Joseph Warton's "The Enthusiast: or, The Lover of Nature" attempts to illustrate, in its elephantine academic way, that our submission to the forces of nature will result in nothing less than our awareness of its laws, and consequently our happiness. This state is, of course, contrasted to the evils of civilization and of human activity:

> Happy the first of Men, ere yet confin'd
> To smoaky Cities; who in sheltering Groves,

Warm Caves, and deep-sunk Vallies liv'd and lov'd,
By Cares unwounded; what the Sun and Showers,
And genial Earth untillag'd could produce,
They gather'd grateful, or the Acorn brown,
Or blushing Berry . . .

That "Tintern Abbey" derives from this tradition should
be clear. But this, in itself, is of little importance. What matters is Wordsworth's attempt to come to terms with the tradition by taking it out of the realm of a silly academic game
and grounding it in the realities of the mind. In Wordsworth's lines, nature's order becomes real because it is revealed in the perception of the speaker; the very way in
which he beholds the scene gives us evidence not only of the
mind's order but also of the unity of man and nature: The
man-made hedgerows run wild, the grass comes up to the
door, and the smoke from the fire disappears into the
atmosphere — all these being evidence that human action
and nature are necessarily entwined. And it is the mind,
when stimulated by nature, which sees the order in the relationship. Of course, to make the pastoral complete, the
speaker's perception of the scene will have to convince him
that nature is capable of providing us with a foundation for
morals. And indeed, Wordsworth assures both us and himself:

                              Therefore am I still
A lover of the meadows and the woods,
And mountains; and of all that we behold
From this green earth; of all the mighty world
Of eye, and ear, — both what they half create,
And what perceive; well pleased to recognise
In nature and the language of the sense,
The anchor of my purest thoughts, the nurse,
The guide, the guardian of my heart, and soul
Of all my moral being.

But the anchoring of the poet's moral being in an act of perception, of personal contemplation, creates a number of diffi-

culties. Unless we have faith in the uniformity of our perceptions, our moralities will be private — that is, not moralities at all. Wordsworth has taken the whole pastoral act out of the realm of society and most certainly out of the realm of politics. The poem has illustrated that the intellectual (the poet) may tie his own mental activity to nature, perhaps to those who are his intimates (Wordsworth addresses his sister in the poem), or even, if the poem is successful, to his readers. But he cannot relate the knowledge, the morality, he attained through the contemplation of nature to society at large. The danger of Wordsworth's position lies in his capacity, as a poet, to convince us of its validity. He convinces because what he has perceived and felt surely corresponds to something we have experienced ourselves. It is one aspect of the truth.

But can we hold on to or can we rest with this truth? The logic of the events which caused Marvell to carry out the precarious balancing act of his irony has, after all, developed further. Can we really accept the effects of a long moment's perception as a valid theory of knowledge? Even someone so close in time to Wordsworth as Matthew Arnold was incapable of doing so, although he judged Wordsworth the greatest poet of the age. For Arnold the contemplation of nature only yielded one inescapable insight: that morals were not to be derived from it. This is the major theme of Arnold's poetry, a theme he so often explored in a pastoral setting. The implications of this knowledge for the intellectual — and we, like Arnold children of the Enlightenment, know it to be true — are reflected on by Arnold in that most honest, and harsh, poem of the Victorian era, *Empedocles on Etna*. The poem deals with the events which immediately precede Empedocles' well-known suicide. Arnold had chosen to write about Empedocles at some length because he considered this figure from antiquity to be a representative modern, his plight exemplifying "the dialogue of mind with itself." [20] Empedocles, a physician, has dedicated his life to the pursuit of truth. Instead of tying him to the community, his work — of being a disinterested man of knowledge — leads to his exile; for the truth he has discovered is that the gods do not exist. The loneliness of being separated from one's society, the despair of being cut off from significant human connections, might be abated by a Wordsworthian sense of communion with nature. But in the poem this act of perception is possible only for the ignorant shepherd boy Callicles, since he is able to perceive the presence of the gods in nature. His simple songs unify nature and morality, giving Empedocles a mere moment of relief. Empedocles is incapable of making the pastoral pretense; the simplicities of the low are unavailable to the man of knowledge. When he is left to the privacies of contemplation, Empedocles cannot turn to nature but only to his own mind. The monologues which result are a catalogue of all the catchwords concerning despair which we have learned to associate with such elder statesmen of modernism as T. S. Eliot and Samuel Beckett. The reader can make his own (fairly obvious) contemporary associations with the following lines:

> I only,
> Whose spring of hope is dried, whose spirit has fail'd —
> I, who have not, like these, in solitude
> Maintain'd courage and force, and in myself
> Nursed an immortal vigour — I alone
> Am dead to life and joy; therefore I read
> In all things my own deadness . . .
>
> But in mind — but thought —
> If these have been the master part of us —

[20] "Preface to *Poems,* Edition of 1853," *The Portable Matthew Arnold,* ed. L. Trilling (New York, 1949). All quotations of Arnold are from this volume.

Where will *they* find their parent element?
What will receive *them*, who will call *them* home?

But we shall still be in them, and they in us,
And we shall be the strangers of the world,
And they will be our lords, as they are now;
And keep us prisoners of our consciousness,
And never let us clasp and feel the All
But through their forms, and modes, and stifling veils.
And we shall be unsatisfied as now,
And we shall feel the agony of thirst,
The ineffable longing for the life of life
Baffled for ever . . .

And each succeeding age in which we are born
Will have more peril for us than the last;
Will goad our senses with a sharper spur,
Will fret our minds to an intenser play,
Will make ourselves harder to be discern'd.
And we shall struggle awhile, gasp and rebel;
And we shall fly for refuge to past times,
Their soul of unworn youth, their breath of greatness;
And the reality will pluck us back,
Knead us in its hot hand, and change our nature.
And we shall feel our powers of effort flag,
And rally them for one last fight, and fail;
And we shall sink in the impossible strife,
And be astray for ever.

The disease, like modernism, has become permanent. These
lines, though spoken by Empedocles, clearly represent Arnold's sentiments about his own situation. He considers himself and his contemporaries to be the prisoners of the very
freedom (of the truths) which the Enlightenment had given
us; for its truths, engendered by the skeptical doubt, have
placed the man of learning in a position "in which there is
everything to be endured, nothing to be done." ["Preface to
Poems, Edition of 1853"]

This vision of a self-perpetuating isolation, of a progressive
and self-destructive inwardness, represents Arnold's most pri-

CHAPTER FOUR

vate fears. His well-known correspondence with Clough gives a touching account of his feelings:

congestion of the brain is what we suffer from — I always feel it and say it — and cry for air like my own Empedocles. . . . God keep us both from aridity: *Arid* — that is what the times are.

These are sentiments which Arnold feels to be disastrous for both poetry and society. The intellectual who is obsessed by such feelings — and of course he can hardly avoid them — must prevent their becoming the dominant motif of his work; he must go beyond self-expression to the discovery of some fruitful relationship between his work and society. Not to do so is to invite the suicide of Empedocles. Arnold withdrew *Empedocles on Etna* from publication and rejected his own lyric and pastoral impulses: These acts may have been self-denying, they may have cut off creativity, but their purpose was surely to create the possibilities for an art which is both personally honest and relevant to the health of society. Arnold proceeded to devote himself to a criticism which might create the social possibilities for the epic — the poem of action which embodies the sense of a public and national vision; it is a form which the Enlightenment, in spite of its programmatic efforts, had been incapable of making its own.

Wordsworth's attempt to base the foundations of morals on the pastoral vision produced, by its very subjectivity, the means for a revolutionary art. Yet the pastoral vision itself was, at the time, clearly reactionary; it involved, moreover, a denial of social reality. Wordsworth associated the possibility of a new morality with the country and with the peasant. Now at the beginning of the nineteenth century, masses of people were leaving, often against their wills, the country for the city. As a result, nearly all political agitation tended to begin in the rapidly growing urban centers. The ideologies of the urban masses (for example, socialism) were generally rooted in the notion of social class rather than that of the soil.[21] The peasant uprisings of the nineteenth century, which were attempts to assert the primacy of the rural setting, were generally reactionary in character: They were directed, for example, against the power of the city in France and against the liberal gentry in Galicia. If the emotional power of the pastoral vision was to relate intellectuals to society at large, a new version of pastoral, one centered on the city, would have to be developed; and more, would have to shape the consciousness both of the urban masses and the intellectuals. Pastoral based on nostalgia for the country, ignoring urbanization and industrialization, could provide intellectuals with no more than the impetus for despair or political reaction.

Socialism, of course, becomes the typical political theory of the urban masses. Its program of democratization, of making the low high, makes socialism a version of city pastoral. It thus offers the intellectual the possibility of community; for by his pastoral act, by identifying himself with the low and with the life of the city itself, he creates the opportunity for a meaningful connection with the urban masses. Recall Herzen's letter to Tchitcherin which I quoted earlier: Herzen, as a socialist, has identified with the masses; he therefore rejects Tchitcherin's notion of the intellectual as the benevolent shepherd and director of his flock. The urban masses want no guide; they want to speak for themselves. As a result, pastoral can no longer be the aristocrat's or the intellectual's, condescending game. Socialism hopes to make citizens of subjects, giving them the opportunity for the exercise of free choice, and thereby creating the necessary condition, accord-

[21] On this subject, I have found Lewis Namier's 1848: *The Revolution of the Intellectuals* (Garden City, N.Y., 1964) most helpful, though perversely wrong.

ing to Rousseau, for their very humanity. There is to be no high or low — only the authority of the general will. In Marx's version of the theory (and here he differs significantly from Herzen), these goals were not seen as the imperatives of a moral vision but as a necessary historical and social fact — though a fact not yet actualized. Through the agency of industrialism, by its transformation of all classes into the urban proletariat, history is in the process of actualizing the pastoral vision. Because he is the heir of the Enlightenment, the intellectual should have a special insight into this process; having this, he is also given the opportunity of uniting his work (the gathering of knowledge, the discovery of truth) with politics and social action. Intellectuals are left other choices: They may array themselves against history; or they may seek to isolate themselves, their private visions bringing on the inevitable despair. In any case, they will be forced into making a choice, for their roles, not deriving from a settled social scheme, will not reveal themselves with the urgency of inevitability. In 1837 the poet Ogarev, recalling a revolutionary oath he and Herzen had taken in their youth, wrote Herzen this letter:

Friend! our path promises few joys, but much bitterness and many sufferings; yet which of us fears the crown of a martyr? And shall we complain of Providence? It has given us what few possess, a store of inexhaustible felicity. . . . Iskander [Herzen] do you remember that hill, that bank steep and high, under which flowed a quiet river, and beyond the river the city spreading out endlessly? O! I always remember it, when I am happy, and warm, sweet tears swell from my eyes. There we confessed our friendship, indissoluble to the grave, there we declared our best feelings, the best ideas of our youth.[22]

The revolutionary sentiments must be addressed to the city. Although they derive from the friends' experience at the uni-

[22] Quoted in Martin Malia, *Alexander Herzen and the Birth of Russian Socialism, 1812–1855* (Cambridge, Mass., 1961).

versity and from their gentry background, they are given emotional reality by their pastoral setting, by their association with the beauties of nature. During his entire career, Herzen was forced to reconcile his revolutionary commitment with his attachment to the peasant commune. But whatever the ambiguities of his feelings, when he and Ogarev faced the city, Herzen had to make a choice concerning his social role; the choice was to be challenged by doubts and the pressures of events at every turn of his life. Only one thing was certain: No social connection was to be established through the quiet contemplation of nature.

The dominant social fact of nineteenth-century Europe was surely the increasing strength of the urban masses. That many intellectuals sought to identify with the proletariat in the mutual search for a political role seems, given the hindsight of history, hardly surprising. Both the men of knowledge and the unlettered masses had but recently come to a sense of sociological awareness, to a consciousness of their class status; and having come to this awareness, their exclusion from political power seemed all the more irrational and inhuman. Here then was the opportunity for the intellectual to rejoin the community by changing the structure of its politics; the union of the masses' strength with the insights of intellect seemed to make a politics both rational and humane attainable in the near future. In the years before 1848 a revolution seemed imminent; its outbreak merely awaited the proper occasion. When it finally sputtered to its dismal conclusion, it had proved to be yet another example of political action failing to effect a fundamental social change. Yet the consequences of the failure were as significant as any success might have been. For the revolution made the class struggle a reality; its blood etched its hatreds indelibly on Europe's consciousness. The disaster of the intellectuals' involvement in political rule removed them from the exercise of power; as a result, their position in the class struggle, if they chose to join it, could be only on the side of the masses. For to ally oneself with the rulers would involve a capitulation of the critical intellect; clearly such an alliance could be based only on the relationship of master to servant, maker of policy to propagandist and bureaucrat. One other choice seemed to be available to the man of knowledge: to give up, once more, the possibility of community, the possibility of political relevance. In reality there were other options, other possibilities; but the events of 1848, with their immediate and seemingly unavoidable political pressures, had made it difficult to search them out and pursue them with a degree of intellectual detachment. The temptations to give up on the demands of one's critical intellect, simply to ignore the legacy of the Enlightenment, became greater and greater. This situation is, on the whole, still very much ours; the roles available to men of learning seem to have been frozen by the events of 1848, yet the pressures of politics have become ever greater.

Of the many revolutions which unnerved Europe during 1848, the French, because of the variety of roles played in it by intellectuals, serves as a most useful example. The June uprising by the Paris proletariat was an open and spontaneous expression of class hatred; the sheep refused to be herded by their shepherds. When the uprising was crushed and thousands innocently murdered in the interests of "public order," it marked a political failure for most of the intellectuals involved in the revolution: a failure not so much of ideas, but of the ability and means to translate them into action. The group represented by Lamartine, for example, being thoroughly frightened by the prospect of democratization, devoted itself to the establishment of a republic rather than to fundamental social change. Most of the politically active intellectuals were afraid to face the consequences of their ideas. And so they allowed themselves to be used; rather than identifying with the proletariat, they became the functionaries of the republic. The saddest story is surely Louis Blanc's. When put at the head of the Commission for Labor (the Luxembourg), he was rendered ineffectual as a revolutionary leader. When Blanc realized eventually that the republic had used him in order to neutralize the demands for social democracy, he had, in spite of his good intentions, lost all effective contact with the proletariat. Blanqui, on the other hand, was kept out of the government because of his total identification with the masses, and his uncompromising social demands. As a result he maintained a clear view of the necessity for social change, the irrelevance of the republic's institutions to democratization, and the unavoidable realities of power. His demand that the proletariat be armed seemed an invitation to chaos; yet if met, it might have helped to prevent the June massacre and brought about effective social change. Worst of all, the regime succeeded in turning the revolutionary leaders who held office on Blanqui: His name was blackened for his refusal to accept the legitimacy of the republic. Thus when the events of June 23rd erupted, the proletariat was left without leaders and without arms; it carried out its revolt alone, through the momentum of despair. The inability — perhaps the social impossibility — of most intellectuals to identify with the proletariat, of realizing some version of urban pastoral, had led to a revolution which could hardly avoid failure. As Herzen foresaw, the terrible and much misunderstood events left a legacy of mutual distrust between the republic, the intellectuals, and the proletariat. The immediate aftermath was the election of Louis Napoleon; the long-range effects have yet to play themselves out. Who knows but that the events may simply keep repeating themselves.[23]

The reactions of most intellectuals to the events of 1848 were bitter (as Herzen had predicted); their comments full of angry recriminations. Even worse, the disappointments over the failure of intellect to manage political events tended to freeze the capacity for action. Rationality seemed irrelevant to politics, events having been manipulated by pure power; indeed, when the masses became active and attempted to transform the mechanics of political action, they were hardly receptive to the appeals of reason. The future of intellect seemed to lie in the service of power; its chief tasks the manufacture of ideologies to justify the status quo, or of propaganda to reconcile the masses to the state. In short, both the intellectual's commitment to knowledge — the legacy of the *Encyclopedia* — and his commitment to the actualization of a literary image — the vision of pastoral — seemed to have been brushed aside, even worse, exploited, by the brute and mechanical pressures of insensible events.

Yet there were those — most notably Marx and Engels — who did not dismiss the possibilities of rational political action. Their claim was that science had not performed its task well enough, that it had seriously erred in not relating the analysis of nature to the flow of historical events. Arthur Rosenberg has done well in summarizing the reactions of Marx and Engels to the failure of 1848:

In the opinion of Marx and Engels the proletariat must first undergo a lengthy period of development before it would be capable of solving independently the tasks with which history confronted it. In the meantime the workers must submit to the leaders, who, equipped with the achievements of bourgeois sci-

[23] Of the many interpretations of the events of 1848, I find Arthur Rosenberg's *Democracy and Socialism*, though occasionally wrong in detail, most convincing. I follow him in most instances.

ence, are able to point out the correct course of action. Marx and Engels always decided alone and in a completely autocratic manner just what the proletariat should or should not do in a definite situation. They never tolerated or even took notice of any opposition from "narrow minded" workers.

Imagine Herzen's likely reaction to these proposals; they are, after all, much like those he attacked in his letter to Tchitcherin. The apparent harshness of Marx and Engels derives, quite clearly, from their belief in a "science" of history which must be used (its results being incontestable) in the analysis of political events. The laws of historical change, determined by the forces of production, dictate the relationship of intellectual to proletariat; consequently, to dissolve the class system before the appropriate change in the forces of production has taken place would be an invitation to failure and political chaos. Meanwhile intellectual and proletariat must play their separate roles. Engels describes the process:

In proportion as anarchy in social production vanishes, the political authority of the state dies out. Man, at last the master of his own form of social organization, becomes at the same time the lord over nature, his own master — free.

To accomplish this act of universal emancipation is the historical mission of the modern proletariat. To thoroughly comprehend the historical conditions and thus the very nature of this act, to impart to the now oppressed proletarian class a full knowledge of the conditions and of the meaning of the momentous act it is called upon to accomplish, this is the task of the theoretical expression of the proletarian movement, scientific socialism. [*Socialism: Utopian and Scientific*]

This "theoretical expression" — in effect, the formulation of the proletariat's rules for political action — is the task of intellectuals; this is their historical role. The social separation which results is only temporary, for the demise of capitalism will not only heal the split between theory and practice but it will also eliminate all divisions of class. Thus a form of pastoral union will have become a social fact, and the intellectu-al's role been made superfluous.

There is something oddly utopian about Engels' expecta-tions, yet it strikes me that both he and Marx had learned the following practical lesson from Rousseau: Humanity will not readily be moved to political action by rational argument alone. Thus the intellectual's task, if he is to have any real effect, is to see beyond, to cut deeper, than the rationalities of practical politics and the superficial urgencies of the mo-ment; he might have to ignore, with a measure of cruelty, the masses' demands for an equal voice in shaping their own fate. For unlike the masses, the intellectual knows the sci-ence of history; his knowledge of social processes allows him to determine what is truly practical, what marginal or irrele-vant. As a scientist it is the intellectual's duty to assert these truths, even at the expense of his momentary estrangement from the masses. Herzen, as we have seen, rejected the arro-gance of this position with some passion. Yet was he alto-gether opposed to it? Recall his argument that there are times when a man of learning must withdraw from political and social involvement, from all action, and wait patiently for the appropriate historical moment. But Herzen's insight led him eventually to the rejection of all political institutions — of the state itself — as conceivable instruments of effec-tive social action. Instead, after reflection on the events of 1848, he developed his theory of the Russian peasant com-mune. Herzen's views on the commune are not to be con-fused with the reactionary nostalgia of the Slavophils, nor do they involve a primitivist abdication of intellect. Indeed, as the following excerpt from his *Memoirs* should illustrate, Herzen considered the commune to involve a reconciliation of both intellect and moral vision with the demands of social practicalities, with the imperatives of the present:

[218]

The foundations of our life are not memories, they are the living elements, existing not in chronicles but in the actual present; but they have merely survived under the hard historical process of building up a single state and under the yoke of the state they have only been preserved not developed. . . . Only the mighty thought of the West to which all its long history has led up is able to fertilise the seeds slumbering in the patriarchal mode of life of the Slavs. The workmen's guild and the village commune, the sharing of profits and the division of fields, the mir meeting and the union of villages into self-governing *volosts*, are all the corner-stones on which the temple of our future, freely communal existence will be built. But these corner-stones are only stones . . . and without the thought of the West our future cathedral will not rise above its foundations.

Herzen's reference to *"our* future" is significant, for it points to his *willful* identification with the commune: an act which is based on a fundamental moral commitment, not on the necessities of historical and social science. As such it helps to define the significant difference — especially for our time — between Herzen and Marx-Engels. The latter consider scientific activity to consist of the determination and analysis of historical necessities; for Herzen, on the other hand, historical necessities do not exist; science — indeed the whole tradition of skeptical thought — rather than dictating what is to be done, gives us the intellectual freedom to determine what the possibilities of the moment are; it gives us, in effect, the opportunity of choice. That social action demands the making of moral choices, Herzen took to be axiomatic. Thus he avoided the illogic, and the implicit moral abdication, of the Encyclopedists' projected science of society, a science which would reveal all choices (and therefore all social processes) to be determined by the iron law of causality. The demands of his involvements, the pressures of events, seem to have taught Herzen the lesson of Hume's reflections on the foundations of ethics — that all moral judgments are based on a fundamental commitment to some notion of social utility. Herzen, of course, left little doubt about the nature of his own social commitment. We can now rest assured that Herzen's earlier appeal for the destruction of the past was not made in the name of a totally undirected freedom, nor was it the bitter fruit of political failure; no, the appeal came out of a social anarchist's vision of the possibilities of the future, of man's need for choice. This vision of an open future, born of the skeptical doubt and the insights of social analysis, gave Herzen the capacity for meaningful criticism, a criticism which was able to sort out significant issues from political trivialities, which had the strength to destroy what needed to be destroyed.

IT SEEMS CLEAR THAT SINCE the events of 1848 — perhaps earlier — any intellectual honest enough to face political realities ought, sooner or later, to reach the conclusion that his responsibilities are best met in the act of criticism. This in itself tells us little. We have yet to ask, What kind of criticism? The answer is far from obvious. What, after all, are the possibilities for critical discourse given the corrosion of faith in rational political procedures? Rather, intellectuals will need to turn to the social and psychological determinants of political activity: to the general quality of their society's life, to the elements which constitute culture. To expand the domain of criticism over so wide an area is to put a nearly unbearable burden upon its practitioner. If he is to be the judge of a culture, by what rules is he to make his judgments? According to what ideals, what programs, is he judging his society's stated objectives? If the man of learning is to be some sort of critical anthropologist, there will be no specific area (no precise task) which will be his special province, to which he can devote his energies; the bulk of the critic's activity is likely to consist of endless discussions over just what is to be done, over his own role, and over the general principles which underlie each of his public acts.

Such are the burdens of criticism. Moreover, they have been steadily reinforced by the special problems of the literary intellectual. By the middle of the nineteenth century, the notion of a static set of literary rules had lost the small degree of authority which had survived the persistent thrusts of the Enlightenment. Both Diderot and Lessing had felt that the rules were still of some relevance to their own audiences. But how did they answer the needs of a newly literate public? What conceivable relevance could critical judgments based on the rules have to an audience not grounded in the classical tradition? Thus the pressures of social change put Hume's philosophical insight — that esthetic as well as moral criticism is not based on the dictates of reason but on those of sentiment — in the social arena. The general acceptance of Hume's analysis, or anything like it, clearly undermines the notion that any formal theory (any set of rules) has the capacity to carry critical conviction by itself. Consequently, the critic needs to shape his public's taste; perhaps even create it; indeed, he must become a cultural critic. Whatever else the demands of this task, it should be obvious that it involves a moral and social commitment of some sort.

The social and philosophical pressures which I have just discussed were instrumental in making cultural criticism the dominant mode of literary discourse during most of the nineteenth century. These same pressures have hardly abated; yet our criticism has abandoned its cultural tasks. There are numerous causes underlying the current interest in formalism; indeed, many of the changes it has introduced in our critical procedures have been salutary, others even highly needed. Yet don't these changes — with their emphasis on mechanical and neutral tasks — also reflect the bureaucratization of our intellectuals? For our critics have largely shunned the task of well-reasoned and committed cultural criticism for the safe amusements of literary epistemology, for endless formal analyses, and, if at all interested in the human context of literature, for the supposed neutrality of an academic social science. This submission to the tyranny of the cultural fact, this refusal to shape, or perhaps create, the fact itself strikes me as an abdication of one's moral being — of one's very capacity to make choices.

The example of *The Connection* has shown us that the modern work of art needs to perform the task of cultural criticism: It must educate its audience to a new set of responses, to an acceptance of the new connections it creates. Thus the artist is forced to play a dual role: of creator and of critic. Baudelaire, in both his criticism and his poetry, exemplifies the necessity for carrying this double burden; indeed, he seems to thrive under it. He assumes that each of his poems performs a critical act, "since criticism," he informs us, "comes from the body of art itself." [24] The first lesson of Baudelaire's remark is that formal criticism has nothing to teach the work of art, since criticism's rules come out of the art work's very constitution. But the implications of the remark reach a good deal further than this, for Baudelaire believes that the work of art is engaged in the continual performance of a critical act: It is the judge of the world's culture, destroying philosophies which it finds to be moribund and replacing them with new connections. The task of the symbolist poet, after all, is to discover the principles

---

[24] Charles Baudelaire, "What is the Use of Criticism?," *Flowers of Evil and Other Works,* ed. and trans. W. Fowlie (New York, 1964). All quotations of Baudelaire are from this volume.

which relate all phenomena, all feelings, all experiences. And so Baudelaire's famous sonnet "Correspondences," in demanding that poetry interpret the *world's* symbols, poses one of the many critical tasks to be performed by the work of art.

But what of criticism proper? When effective, the act of criticism has the persuasive power of a work of art. "Therefore," Baudelaire tells us, "the best article on a painting could be a sonnet or an elegy." Now it must be made clear that Baudelaire's idea has no relation to the fruity impressionism best represented by Pater's criticism; he does not mean that a critical essay should try to sound like a poem. A proper critical performance is like a work of art because it is a creation which has the capacity to move, to transform, to effect the world and, hopefully, the reader. "Criticism," Baudelaire writes,

should be partisan, passionate and political, that is to say, it should be conceived from a particular point of view, but from a point of view which opens up the largest number of horizons. . . . Stendhal has said somewhere: "Painting is morality put into a form!" If you give this word morality a more or less liberal meaning, you can apply it to all the arts. Since they are always beauty expressed by sentiment, the passion and the dreams of each man, namely variety in unity, or the many aspects of the absolute, criticism at every moment involves metaphysics.

Baudelaire's philosophical bravado aside, the tasks of criticism are clearly cultural. The critic needs to shape the life of his society; the artist, correspondingly, needs to shape individual human beings. Their joint venture is to instill in their audience the capacity to transform ordinary life into an artistic vision, the capacity to imbue common experience with symbolic significance. For Baudelaire, the cultural needs are clear: We must confront — perhaps transform — contemporary reality in terms of the revolutionary possibilities of our arts.

"It is true," Baudelaire writes in "On the Heroism of Modern Life," "that the great tradition is over, and the new tradition is not founded." Baudelaire makes the founding of a new tradition his special task; he intends to replace the classical — for it has lost its emotional relevance — by "looking for what may be the epic aspect of modern life." Thus Baudelaire is engaged in an attempt to make up for the artistic failures of the Enlightenment; more properly, he is ready to exploit the opportunities its failures, especially those of classicism, have created. Recall, once more, that the Enlightenment's difficulties with the epic did not reflect a failure of poetic inspiration but rather the impossibility of making the traditional materials of the form relevant to the eighteenth century. The skeptical doubt will not readily permit the conventional connection between Greek myth and the realities of the present; after all, in our time it has taken nothing less than Joyce's radical modernizing to make the connection at all believable. Yet this same skepticism concerning the relevance of the traditional, the same emphasis on the primacy of present experience, should allow the critic to recognize the possibilities of the contemporary, the epic potentialities of the immediate. Baudelaire's search for the materials of epic is, first of all, an attempt to perceive new connections in the apparent chaos of the modern; but beyond this, it also represents an effort to relate these new connections to the traditional objectives of our arts. As such, it is one more attempt to create a meaningful neoclassicism.

How is the critic to proceed with his task? Where, specifically, is he to look? What is his epic ground? "Parisian life," Baudelaire writes,

is rich in poetic and miraculous subjects. The miraculous envelops us and waters us like the atmosphere; but we do not see it.

The *nude,* a thing very precious to artists, and a necessary element for success, is as frequent and necessary as in antiquity — in the bed, in the bath, in the operating room. The means and the motifs of the painting are equally abundant and varied; but there is a new element, which is modern beauty.

The nude, a traditional subject for artists, on the operating table! Baudelaire tries to explore the significance of this living tableau and does so by converting it into a potential painting; the scene, in effect, is absorbed by his artistic vision. In order to perform its task with a measure of success, this vision must in all cases be guided by the traditional aspirations of the epic. If endowed with these capacities, if educated to this mode of perception, the subject matter of epic awaits us wherever we choose to look. Baudelaire considers some examples:

The display of fashion and the thousands of floating existences which circulate in the subterranean places of a huge city — criminals and prostitutes — the *Gazette des Tribunaux* and the *Moniteur* give us proof that we have only to open our eyes in order to learn about our heroism.

We are far from certain whether Baudelaire is being playful or serious; our doubts about the inherent meaning of both our literary tradition and contemporary reality create the possibility for irony. What are we to think of the new subject matter for the epic? We are not sure — and neither is Baudelaire. His task is to envision it as epic, and to convince us, in the process, that this vision is valid. The likely results of this exercise in cultural criticism are, at best, uncertain; indeed, they may amount to no more than a questioning of certainties about our cultural norms. But is this not the goal of Baudelaire's strange inversion of values in *Flowers of Evil?*

Baudelaire's playfulness, his exploitation of our doubts, lies at the very core of his esthetics — that is, his cultural criticism. The fluidity of our social roles gives him the opportunity to transform our modes of existence, to demand that we too become playful and make of our lives works of art. We are to transform ourselves into dandies and doing so we shall create a new cultural elite. Baudelaire would have us believe that this artistic transformation of the self, this playful creation of a role, serves a function beyond mere self-assertion, beyond the frivolity of Bohemia. Consider the following from one of his explorations of an epic subject, "In Praise of Make-Up":

Who cannot see that the use of face powder, so foolishly anathematized by candid philosophers, has the purpose and the result of causing to disappear from the complexion the spots which nature sowed there outrageously, and of creating an abstract unity in the texture and color of the skin, which unity, like that produced by tights, immediately likens the human figure to a statue, that is to say to a divine superior being? As for the artificial black which encircles the eyes and the rouge which colors the uppermost part of the cheeks, although their usage comes from the same principle, from the need to surpass nature, the result is reached in order to satisfy quite a different need. Red and black symbolize life, a supernatural and excessive life; the black lines give depth and strangeness to the expression, and to the eyes they give a more specific appearance of a window opening unto the infinite; rouge, which colors the high cheekbone, increases even more the light of the eyeball and adds to the beautiful face of a woman the mysterious passion of the priestess.

Irony? Who would doubt it? Yet the purpose of Baudelaire's analysis is highly serious and thus needs to be taken at face value. The artistic transformation of the self and the critic's analysis of that transformation are both cultural acts; indeed, since they attempt to transform our vision of reality, they ultimately involve the possibility of transforming society itself. To create the special possibility for the epic, to change the nature of reality, we must choose both to transform ourselves and to provide ourselves with new ways of seeing what is simply there. These objectives are of such a fundamental nature that their attainment would seem to demand a monumental effort — one surely beyond the scope of traditional artistic criticism. Such are the tasks which Baudelaire has taken on: to transform us; to renew our senses; to enable us to see, hear, and interpret both reality and works of art. This makes him, on the one hand, the publicist for Delacroix and Wagner, on the other, the artistic explorer — the epic poet — of contemporary reality. The objective is to create connections by educating a new audience; the actual result is likely to be the intellectual's further separation, for the very nature of his task necessarily places him in the advance guard.

The critical effort demanded by the imperatives of the cultural situation led Matthew Arnold, the reader recalls, to give up the composition of poetry. *Empedocles on Etna* is one of Arnold's major efforts to make antiquity relevant to the present, to establish a sense of cultural continuity. The attempt was (perhaps predictably) overwhelmed by his private obsessions: Whenever the poem departs from the moving and convincing consideration of personal pain, it becomes a stuffy museum piece; in spite of Arnold's best intentions, its setting neither engages nor absorbs the elementary facts of contemporary reality. Arnold's keen awareness of his poetry's failure to relate, with some degree of conviction, the past to the present provided the immediate impetus for the writing of his criticism. For Arnold's personal failure, as *Empedocles on Etna* made clear, also involved a failure in his cultural setting. Thus the task of his criticism is to create a situation which makes possible the composition of a poetry steeped in the tradition. Now any criticism which attempts to establish continuities must ultimately turn to the discussion of culture.

The modern turn to inwardness, to literature as "an allegory of the state of one's own mind," creates, in Arnold's view, a special urgency for cultural criticism. ["Preface to *Poems*, Edition of 1853"] Criticism's most important task is to defeat this destructive obsession with the self by pointing out new connections, reinforcing ones worth saving, and, above all, by asserting the necessity for, as well as the autonomy of, the critical intellect. The last point leads to Arnold's strong insistence on intellectuals avoiding both the temptations of power and the snares of practical politics. His words are as relevant today as they were a century ago:

> I say, the critic must keep out of the region of immediate prac-
> tice in the political, social humanitarian sphere if he wants to
> make a beginning for that more free speculative treatment of
> things, which may perhaps one day make its benefits felt even in
> this sphere, but in a natural and thence irresistible manner.
> ["The Function of Criticism at the Present Time"]

The truths of cultural criticism cut deeper — are perhaps only peripherally concerned with — the mechanisms of political maneuver; to sacrifice one's intellectual independence to these mechanisms is to sacrifice the very foundation of culture itself.

Arnold's critical position is familiar enough, I assume, not to need general summary. I should like to discuss, instead, several issues of immediate relevance to our own moment and central to my discussion of *The Connection*. Let us begin with an embarrassing question: Just what is the use of criticism? Arnold approaches the issue — and this is one of the marks of his usefulness — with a question derived from his own failures as a poet: Why is the age incapable of producing a unified work of some stature? "Because," Arnold answers,

> for the creation of a master-work of literature two powers must
> concur, the power of the man and the power of the moment,
> and the man is not enough without the moment. [*Ibid.*]

The moment is inauspicious enough to defeat even the most talented. What then lies at the source of our cultural difficulties? "The confusion of the present times is great," Arnold complains, "the multitude of voices counselling different things bewildering." ["Preface to *Poems*, Edition of 1853"] Arnold's words seem to paraphrase the opening sentences of this book; indeed, they set the tone and create the objectives for the whole modern enterprise; they surely provide the impetus for my own critical efforts. For the confusion to which Arnold points is a clear challenge to the critical intellect. Here then is his definition of the critic's task:

It is the business of the critical power, as I said in the words already quoted, "in all branches of knowledge, theology, philosophy, history, art, science, to see the object as in itself it really is." Thus it tends, at last, to make an intellectual situation of which the creative power can profitably avail itself. It tends to establish an order of ideas, if not absolutely true, yet true by comparison with that which it displaces; to make the best ideas prevail. Presently these new ideas reach society, the touch of truth is the touch of life, and there is a stir and growth everywhere; out of this stir and growth come the creative epochs of literature. ["The Function of Criticism at the Present Time"]

This summary of objectives is definitive for the modern era; as such, I take its relevance to be permanent. In the face of our progressive confusions not to be obsessed with one's private concerns, not to discard the Enlightenment's legacy of objectivity — these constitute the critic's responsibility. The commitment to the critical intellect by a saving remnant, Arnold warns us, may be the sum of our available social choices. In spite of his private despairs, Arnold did not consider the cultural struggle to be beyond hope. His expectations were based on the insight that the very inwardness which has created our lack of objective standards, which has generated such confusion concerning our goals, has also created our possibilities. And it is the existence of these possibilities, Arnold warned, which makes criticism a necessity for the modern:

There is so much inviting us! — what are we to take? what will nourish us in growth towards perfection? That is the question which, with the immense field of life and of literature lying before him, the critic has to answer; for himself first, and afterwards for others. [*Ibid.*]

There are two persistent problems, both of oppressive magnitude, which confront the cultural critic once "the iron force of adhesion to the old routine, — social, political, religious, — has wonderfully yielded." [*Culture and Anarchy*] The first concerns the relating of our stores of new knowledge — especially the discoveries of science — to the conduct of our lives; the second involves the intellectual's stand concerning democratization, the leveling of all classes. How these problems are to be faced is implicit in the qualities of mind Arnold requires of intellectuals or critics: "a curiosity about their best self, with a bent for seeing things as they are." The possession of these qualities allows the individual to transcend his class and become the servant of culture — that is, of "the best which has been thought and said in the world." ["Literature and Science"] Thus the man of culture needs to become the servant of all areas of knowledge: science, morals, and esthetics. His job is to make, somehow, the proper connections among them. Arnold's heroic conclusion to "Literature and Science" is a measure of the task's magnitude:

While we shall all have to acquaint ourselves with the great results reached by modern science and to give ourselves as much training in its disciplines as we can conveniently carry, yet the majority of men will always require humane letters; and so much the more, as they have the more and the greater results of science to relate to the need in man for conduct, and to the need in him for beauty.

Good enough! Arnold has at least pointed out that connections are conceivable for the man of culture and that intellect transcends the class system. But what of the pressures for democratization? What of those masses of people demanding equality, ready to be educated in some fashion, yet without any immediate prospects — or even desires — for the attainment of humane learning? The intellectual who is also a democrat finds himself on the horns of a dilemma: His very aspiration to culture separates him from the mass of humanity. For Arnold the way out is to be found, once more, in the nature of the man of culture:

The men of culture are the true apostles of equality. The great men of culture are those who have had a passion for diffusing . . . the best knowledge, the best ideas of their time; who have laboured to divest knowledge of all that was . . . professional, exclusive; to humanise it, to make it efficient outside the clique of the cultivated and learned, yet still remaining the *best* knowledge and thought of the time. [*Culture and Anarchy*]

Arnold proposes no convincing arguments which illustrate that any of these hopes are likely to become historical realities. If there exists a valid argument making science relevant to our moral and esthetic sense, I am not aware of it; Arnold most assuredly does not provide us with one. His critical goals are simply based on the assumption that the theory of knowledge bequeathed us by the Enlightenment, indeed everything we presently know and also what we shall know in the future, must be absorbed by, and made an organic part of, the body of humane learning. The various parts of our learning must be made relevant to our way of life, for men desire to be whole; considering it a moral and esthetic affront to be in pieces, to live in many realms, they yearn to make connections. That men need to be objective, humane, and sensitive to beauty; that these qualities must ultimately lie within everyone's province — these are for Arnold moral im-

peratives. To lend them support there is only the strong will
of the man of culture; to convince us of their necessity there
is Arnold's style. Both sweetly reasoned and full of passionate
irony, it has the appearance, though not the formal substance, of rational argument; yet the style means to envelop
us, to seduce us into a sense of mission or, rather, intelligent
concern. Somewhere Arnold praises Burke for his application
of ideas to politics; yet it is the very decline in rational political discourse which lends Arnold's critical effort its importance. After the events of the past decades, has any intellectual really been able to keep his faith in the power of reasoned political argument? This loss of faith allows Arnold's
literary procedures their credibility. Perhaps it is the task of
our intellectuals to use style as an instrument of social transformation, to diffuse their culture, thereby transforming all
humanity into one cohesive elite. Might not this process involve the actualization of the pastoral image? I give as an
example today's new radicalism in America, though Arnold
could hardly have lived with it in comfort: It has given birth
to a movement built around a style; indeed, it is a form of
cultural criticism. And therein lie the reasons for both its
successes and failures.

A nagging question remains: Considering the long-range
objectives of the intellectual's cultural concerns, what is to
guide his response to those specific issues which demand that
he take a specific stand? One is not sure. Decisions must be
made as the issues come along. But our dedication to intellect surely teaches us that we must not take stands on the
basis of expediency, of predictions concerning the distant future, nor — one should hardly need to say it — on the basis
of any compromise with the truth. On these points, as on
many others, Herzen and Arnold would agree; thus agreeing,
they serve us as exemplars. Herzen and Arnold! My pairing

may seem oddly willful, if not perverse. Yet there is an obvious stylistic congeniality between these men, both being men of culture; and in this case, style is also a reflection of intellectual substance. Culture demands a clear commitment to intellect and to its use for a rational, humane, and politically independent criticism; it further demands that we eschew all dogmatism; and finally, that we vigorously oppose the further spread of a philistine liberalism. In answering these demands, Arnold and Herzen are as one. Clearly I have stressed, with perhaps an unfair exclusiveness, those aspects of both Arnold and Herzen relevant to our own situation. But something much more fundamental accounts for their many similarities: Have I not argued that any intellectual, whatever his specific stance, must be a social anarchist at the core?

Arnold's particular success — it may also be his failure — lies in his ability to express an essentially radical position with the voice of sweet reason. His ideas on social questions are quite similar to Nietzsche's; yet consider the difference in tone, for in this case the tone might have more social relevance than the ideas it expresses. Arnold, like Nietzsche, believes that the intellectual's duty is to see more of the truth, to see it whole, thereby availing himself of the power to change both himself and the world. Yet how is the intellectual to convert others? Or to take the problem of modernity a step further, how is he to convert himself? Arnold's exhortations are written in a language which (and this is a measure of our own disorder) has the sound of a foreign tongue. Nietzsche's virulence seems to be closer to our temper; for the young he has the feel of a contemporary and thus the power to convert. Yet Nietzsche has rarely had the effect he intended: It is the abrasive and deceptively disjointed style which has taken hold — the style emptied of all ideas, of all rationality. Thus Arnold and Nietzsche demonstrate the uncertain prospects of conversion, the treacherous ground on which it forces intellectuals to stand. My discussion of the Baroque has already touched on this problem. Its centrality to the difficulties of modernism should be apparent from even our brief consideration of *The Connection*. But the next chapter will consider the ways of modernism in dealing with the capacity of intellect to convince.

5

TRANSFERENCE

THE DREAM, PERHAPS THE NIGHTMARE, of the scientific study of society has made political and social philosophy the slaves of the objects of their study. Our social philosophers are concerned not with what the objectives of our society ought to be but with what that society is. This development should not be looked at in isolation: It is an integral part of the situation of philosophy itself. One aspect of the dominance of empirical skepticism, as I have shown, has been the breakdown of belief in the possibility of rational argument. This would seem to put philosophy in somewhat of a bind, to put it mildly. If we do not believe in the validity of rationality, how is philosophical argument to proceed? But being human, philosophers tend to find a blessing in what the rest of us might think a curse. Friedrich Waismann's reflections are not untypical:

A philosophic argument does more and does less than a logical one: less in that it never establishes anything conclusively; more in that, if successful, it is not content to establish just one isolated point of truth, but effects a change in our whole mental outlook so that, as a result of that, myriads of such little points are brought into view or turned out of sight, as the case may be. Are illustrations necessary? Once Hume had exposed the fallacies of his predecessors when dealing with the notion of causality he had made it impossible for anyone to think along the lines of Spinoza whose world looks to us strange as the moon.[1]

If that be the case, the objective of philosophical argument would seem to be nothing less than our *psychological* transformation: Rational argument becomes no more than one of the instruments of this grand conversion.

The revolution in philosophy to which Waismann refers was hardly of Hume's making. Hume's arguments about causality were the summation of a congeries of attitudes which had gathered over the course of a century; Hume's spare reasoning gave this development the status of scientific truth. Hume's division of knowledge into the mutually exclusive compartments of matters of fact and relations of ideas formalized the doubts empirical skepticism had created about the relevance of abstract reasoning to our experience of the external world. The doubts concerning the possibility of rationality go, of course, beyond the formal problems of philosophy. "Proof, refutation — these are dying words in philosophy," Waismann tells us; but his notion of philosophy as the transformation of a total pattern of thought seems to indicate that proof is dead, or about to die, in all those areas of thought which had formerly assumed that men might be subject to rational conviction. Some of the consequences of the skeptical doubt are to be seen in the obliteration of space I discussed in an earlier chapter. The process seems to have gone a good deal further in our time. Whereas it formerly revealed itself primarily in artistic and political procedures, it now seems to be a part of philosophical and scientific discourse itself. When Freud, for example, published one of his earliest case studies, *Dora*, in 1905, he made these prefatory remarks:

---

[1] Friedrich Waismann, "How I See Philosophy," *Logical Positivism*, ed. A. J. Ayer (Glencoe, Ill., 1959). All quotations of Waismann are from this volume.

Whereas before I was accused of giving no information about my patients, now I shall be accused of giving information about my patients which ought not to be given. I can only hope that in both cases the critics will be the same, and that they will merely have shifted the pretext for their reproaches; if so, I can resign in advance any possibility of ever removing their objections.[2]

Freud simply assumes that there is no possibility of rational argument in matters which touch us deeply; if we disagree, it is clearly because we are repressing something we wish to hide.

Waismann's notion concerning the nature of philosophical argument is, of course, a reflection of current fashions. As such, it is to be taken as symptomatic, rather than to be argued against. Waismann, we should remember, was one of Wittgenstein's most devoted followers. And it was the later Wittgenstein who was not only the most representative product but also one of the chief propagators of that attitude toward rational argument exemplified by Freud's statement. Philosophy has traditionally been thought of as an agent of our search for order. For Wittgenstein it is a part of the struggle against disorder. Take, for example, his reflections on the nature of philosophical theories:

These are, of course, not empirical problems; they are solved, rather, by looking into the workings of our language, and that in such a way as to make us recognize those workings: *in despite of* an urge to misunderstand them. The problems are solved, not by giving new information, but by arranging what we have always known. Philosophy is a battle against the bewitchment of our intelligence by means of language.[3]

The natural function of that most human gift, language, seems to be the propagation of disease, the induction of be-

[2] Sigmund Freud, *Dora*, ed. P. Rieff, no trans. given (New York, 1963).
[3] Ludwig Wittgenstein, *Philosophical Investigations*, trans. G. E. M. Anscombe (Oxford, Eng., 1958). All quotations of Wittgenstein are from this volume.

fuddlement. This is not the time to go into the more ludicrous aspects of this position; this task, in any case, has been performed by others. Of greater importance is the fact that Wittgenstein's notions were so readily accepted, that they have come to represent the most common procedures of academic philosophy. An element of the attractiveness of Wittgenstein's attitude toward language derives from its promise to eliminate the difficulties of rational argument; in fact, to eliminate philosophy altogether. Wittgenstein informs us that, "We must do away with all *explanation*, and description alone must take its place." Admittedly, this statement is supposed to indicate that philosophy does have its own validity, a validity which is separate from that of science. Yet I find it difficult to believe that there is much left of philosophy if its task is "description alone."

Just what, one is forced to ask, is the purpose of these descriptions? Why are we to give them the name of philosophy? "A perspicuous representation produces," Wittgenstein tells us, "just that understanding which consists in 'seeing connections.'" The task of a philosophical description, it seems, is to rearrange matters and thereby indicate connections which were not initially apparent. What then is the result of this procedure? "It leaves everything as it is," Wittgenstein tells us. We do not seem to have gotten very far. Just where are these connections made? What is rearranged? The connections obviously do not seem to be a part of the external world; they seem to be made, instead, by something inside us, or by language. We are confronted here with the same difficulties which we have previously had to face in Hume. And indeed, Wittgenstein's approach to philosophical procedure derives from the attempt to cope with those difficulties concerning connections formalized by Hume. If we accept the implications of Wittgenstein's position and assume that connections are made by our minds, it is difficult to imagine just how this is done unless we accept the notion of innate ideas. But this is hardly something Wittgenstein would agree to. If the connections are made by language, Wittgenstein's concept of language as a game with an arbitrary set of rules would seem to condemn the process to utter triviality, since it has no natural connection to the external world. What then are the rational processes, the arguments, with which philosophy allows us to rearrange matters; which allow us to become aware of previously hidden connections? Just what is philosophical activity? Here is Wittgenstein on the subject:

The real discovery is the one that makes me capable of stopping doing philosophy when I want to. — The one that gives philosophy peace, so that it is no longer tormented by questions which bring *itself* in question.

The making of connections is clearly irrelevant to what Wittgenstein thinks of as philosophical procedure. Our search for connections — that is, philosophy — is a form of obsessive behavior, and therefore must be gotten rid of. Wittgenstein's description of philosophical insight makes it sound like the end of a bout with psychoanalysis; the problem has been solved, the obsession gotten rid of, when the patient can tear himself away from the analyst, when he no longer needs to ask questions. Can we rightfully call this procedure philosophy? What, after all, is its method? "There is not *a* philosophical method," Wittgenstein tells us, "though there are indeed methods, like different therapies."

Philosophy as therapy! Philosophers, in effect, are to become each other's analysts. One recalls Hume's reaction to his occasional obsession with skeptical doubts: It was to leave the study for the healthy companionship of his friends. The Wittgensteinian approach has, instead, institutionalized the companionship of mutual suffering and made it a part of philosophy; in fact, it has become philosophy itself. The descriptions one has read of Wittgenstein's Cambridge lectures make them sound like an exercise in group therapy; or, at least, like an attempt on the master's part to rid himself of his painful obsessions with the help of his fellow sufferers. Today any major American or British campus is likely to have its Wittgensteinians sitting around a seminar table on Saturday mornings, their heads resting in the palms of their hands, seeking each other's aid in the attempt to discover just what ails them. Not that this is the sole concern of all Wittgensteinians! John Wisdom, the current incumbent of Wittgenstein's chair at Cambridge, while discussing the difficulties of skepticism — "the cramp of conflict," as he calls it — reminds us of

. . . the incompleteness in the description of the proper philosopher as one who tries to cure uneasiness. He may set himself to disturb complacency. So may a psycho-analyst. We may recognize this without forgetting how much philosophy and analytic work by patient and analyst is conflict and the cure of it.[4]

As a contribution to the annals of doctor-patient relationships it might be interesting to recall that though Wisdom was a faithful follower of Wittgenstein, the master apparently could not abide the disciple. If uneasiness and conflict are, indeed, the chief concerns of philosophy, we can now readily understand Waismann's notion that the objective of philosophical argument is psychological transformation. And, in fact, Waismann was another disciple of Wittgenstein's whose personal relationships with the master seem to have been extremely difficult and ambiguous. But here is his description of philosophical procedure:

[4] John Wisdom, *Philosophy and Psycho-Analysis* (Oxford, Eng., 1957).

To bring out what seems to be peculiar to these questions as tokens of a profound uneasiness of mind. . . . The philosopher as he ponders over some such problem has the appearance of a man who is deeply disquieted. He seems to be straining to grasp something which is beyond his powers. The words in which such a question presents itself do not quite bring out into the open the real point — which may, perhaps more aptly, be described as the recoil from the incomprehensible.

Philosophy's chief task, it seems, is the release of anxieties which have been deeply repressed. Waismann's picture of the philosopher reminds one, uncomfortably, of a method actor contorting both face and body in his attempt to speak the unspeakable, to make the audience grasp the incomprehensible. The words which finally emerge may not be to the point at all — at least on the face of it; they are likely to bê a mask for something even more deeply repressed; something which, in turn, will have to be brought to the surface and interpreted. All this seems equally reminiscent of psychoanalysis and the drama of the absurd. But these procedures of modern philosophy, psychology, and drama are related by more than accident.

The search for connections, for order — these, rather than the stilling of our doubts or the surfacing of repressed thought, have been the traditional objects of the philosophic quest. Those philosophers who, like the Wittgensteinians, have given up on the possibility of making rational connections seem to assume that the therapeutic process will leave them, somehow, with a sense, an assurance, of the order of things. But the Wittgensteinians' most important weapon in stilling our doubts, in setting us at ease, is to dissolve connections which we have formerly taken to be real. Their arsenal consists primarily of infinite regress and *reductio ad absurdum* arguments and of the paradigm case. Ironically, these dissolutions of connections are supposed to set our minds at ease. What has, in fact, been dissolved, or at least bypassed, is the necessity for rational procedure. We still need to make connections: We need to do so even in building an argument by paradigm case. But it is precisely the vague and uncertain nature of this kind of argument which shows us that the connections made will have to be intuited; that we have no formal procedures for placing an expression in a sentence which will be paradigmatic. If nothing else, the Wittgensteinians have given us a clear example of how rational connections have ceased to be psychologically convincing. Since rational explanation — indeed, any form of explanation — is little more than a mask for a psychological process, we shall have to be convinced of the validity of connections on some deeper level. Compare this to Freud's attitude to rational argument when used by a patient:

When the patient brings forward a sound and incontestable train of argument during psychoanalytic treatment, the physician is liable to feel a moment's embarrassment, and the patient may take advantage of it by asking: "This is all perfectly correct and true, isn't it? What do you want to change in it now that I've told it you?" But it soon becomes evident that the patient uses thoughts of this kind, which the analysis cannot attack, for the purpose of cloaking others which are anxious to escape from criticism and from consciousness. [Dora]

Whatever connections the analyst, or philosopher, perceives among the fragments of this repressed material, whatever their scientific or rational status, he will have to convince the patient, or interlocutor, of their validity; for the arguments have become incapable of carrying their own weight. The connections will, somehow, have to *feel* sure.

We now have some hint of how the disquieted philosopher might manage to speak the unspeakable; how he might be convinced of the orderliness of the seemingly disorderly. The way out of his obsession, out of his intellectual paralysis, will be provided not by a static logical structure but by an open process. For the Wittgensteinians philosophy has, in fact, become an action, an action built around a more or less permanent dialogue. Do not the Wittgensteinians, after all, speak of themselves as *doing* philosophy? But what is the nature of the process? Waismann tells us the following:

First, we don't *force* our interlocutor. We leave him free to choose, accept or reject any way of using his words.

And again:

We cannot constrain anyone who is unwilling to follow the new direction of a question; we can only extend the field of vision of the asker, loosen his prejudices, guide his gaze in a new direction: but all this can be achieved only with his consent.

Compare this, for the moment, to Freud's description of his clinical procedure:

I now let the patient himself choose the subject of the day's work, and in that way I start out from whatever surface his unconscious happens to be presenting to his notice at the moment. [*Dora*]

The result of this free procedure, the philosopher assumes, will be an evaporation of the problems which were initially beyond speech. I assume that Waismann, and others like him, believe that this evaporation will somehow reveal a pattern of connections which we find convincing. For Freud, after all, this is one of the objectives of any analysis; further, it is what lends analysis its scientific status. This quotation of Freud goes on as follows:

But on this plan everything that has to do with the clearing up of a particular symptom emerges piecemeal, woven into various contexts, and distributed over widely separated periods of time.

But at the end of the analysis, after the difficulties have been cleared up, all the pieces fit; they become part of a meaningful pattern. If the same sort of thing occurs as a result of the Wittgensteinian way of "doing philosophy," the process of psychological transformation has, indeed, earned the right to be called philosophy. But I am not at all sure that this is what the Wittgensteinians are really after. In any case, if new connections are to emerge from this kind of philosophical dialogue, the burden of creating them will not rest on any notion of rational procedure. Wittgenstein and his followers, one recalls, have rejected explanation as an objective for philosophy. The burden will rest, instead, entirely on the individual mind's reaction to the dialogue. For as far as I can see, Wittgensteinian philosophy, unlike Freud's psychology, does not attempt to relate any of the suppressed material it has released to a general theory. In fact, one of the Wittgensteinians' articles of faith seems to be that the quest for general theories is a dangerous illusion, a form of disease.

That philosophy, in order to convince, might have to use means other than formal rational argument is hardly a discovery of the twentieth century. But that the method of rationality, scientific procedure itself, might be no more than an aspect of our psychological transformation, a mask for some deeper process — these are surely typically modern attitudes. They seem hardly possible before the Enlightenment. We ask questions, for example, about the psychological sources of induction, once we have learned that there is in fact a problem, that there is a doubt about the foundation of the inductive principle. And at this point, induction becomes a subject of historical study: when we realize that its form might not be permanent, that it might be subject to change. Thus Marx looks on the scientific pretenses of sociology as a psychological device which rationalizes bourgeois economic and political interests. Furthermore, sociology can have its proper psychological effect — that is, it can convince us of being true, of providing connections — only at the appropriate historical moment. I suppose that Nietzsche provides the most notorious example in nineteenth-century philosophy of the drastic means needed to effect philosophical conversion. His exuberant and puzzling procedures, his attempts alternately to capture and repel us, his "gay philosophy," are all based on his decision to take up the challenge — partially fathered by our historical awareness — to rational discourse, to its capacities to induce belief. His notion that the acceptance of new (and historically appropriate) forms of rationality must be based on deeper psychological processes obviously anticipates Freud. But this is only typical of a general development which can be seen most clearly in literature. But at this point we need to ask why Nietzsche feels the need for a "gay philosophy."

Nietzsche, in his attempt to shock philosophy out of its academic irrelevance to actuality, takes life styles to constitute the most important form of philosophy. He considers the dominant philosophy of Europe — the Platonic notion of Pure Spirit and the Christian glorification of slave morality — to be a type of disease. In the Preface to *Beyond Good and Evil*, Nietzsche observes, somewhat hopefully, that this disease "has been surmounted. . . . Europe, rid of this nightmare, can again draw breath freely and at least enjoy a healthier sleep." [5] The abstract notions of philosophical truth and falsity do not matter in themselves; the preservation of health and life does. As a result, the philosopher's task is not to convince us of a rational truth, but to instill health. And to accomplish this, philosophy must be gay. In *The Genealogy of Morals*, Nietzsche discusses the uses made of the ascetic ideal:

[5] Friedrich Nietzsche, *Beyond Good and Evil*, trans. M. Cowan (Chicago, 1955).

The object is to pry the human soul loose from its joints, to sink it deep in terror, frost, fire, and transports until it suddenly rids itself of all its dullness, anxiety, gloom. What are the roads leading to this goal? What are the most infallible roads? . . . Any strong emotion will do — rage, fear, lust, vengeance, hope, triumph, despair, cruelty — provided it has sudden release.[6]

The task of philosophy is to bring us alive by releasing our suppressed emotions — even if the means of release is provided by the lie of the ascetic ideal. Indeed, the latter becomes the source of gaiety.

The immediate task of the philosopher, under these conditions, ceases to be discovery. He will spend his time uncovering those philosophies which lie beneath the surface; he will tear off masks. When his time comes he will also reveal that Spinoza's pretense at mathematical method is no more than a magical incantation and that Benthamism hides its secret desires behind the façade of scientific method. There is more. For the philosopher must have the courage to see to the very source of our actions and ideas; he must finally see, given the historical opportunity, that "moralities too are but a *symbolic language of the passions*" [*Beyond Good and Evil*] and that the source of all values is the individual's will to power. Once he becomes aware of the nature of his task, the philosopher will be forced, if he is to remain effective, into a radical revaluation of the hierarchy of the sciences. As Nietzsche says, he will "be in a position to demand that psychology be acknowledged once more as the mistress of the sciences." [*Ibid.*] It is the passions, after all, which will have to be examined if we are to deal with our logic; it is a mental disease we shall have to be cured of if the will to power is to be released for its task of creating philosophies.

What then, we ask once more, is philosophy to do? Nietzsche's answer is not surprising:

[6] Friedrich Nietzsche, *The Birth of Tragedy and The Genealogy of Morals*, trans. F. Golffing (Garden City, N.Y., 1956).

The more abstract the truth you want to teach, the more thoroughly you must seduce the senses to accept it. [*Ibid.*]

Philosophy, then, does not strive toward a desired end. It is a continous process: In Nietzsche's case, the process is the recovery of health; in Wittgenstein's, the warding off of disorder, of mental cramp. Nietzsche assumes that the philosopher is an actor; an actor who has learned the psychological lessons of the modern theater. He tries to seduce us — whether into truth or falsehood is, for the moment, irrelevant — with almost every word he writes: The whole thing is a performance, rather than a logical argument. But Nietzsche's objective is, after all, philosophy. And so his seduction takes the form of philosophical discourse. In spite of their apparent disorderliness, Nietzsche's arguments generally follow rational procedures, and they are not readily dismissed on the grounds of logic. But the expression of these arguments is such as to create a personal relationship between Nietzsche and the reader. In *Beyond Good and Evil*, Nietzsche attempts to draw us into a personal confrontation, and eventually refers to "we immoralists." Nietzsche's arguments could be reformulated so as to give them the tone of abstract and impersonal argument. But this would miss the point. Nietzsche, if he is to perform his task at all, must give us the sense of a personal struggle rather than an abstract philosophical one. His only opportunity of releasing our suppressed emotions and giving us health lies in leading us to direct these emotions at him in a personal struggle of wills. Our hates and loves, our megalomanias and angers are all directed at the healer-philosopher. Our philosophical ills have become all of our ills; and, in turn, they are the ills of our society, of the historical moment. It should be clear that something very much like Freud's notion of the transference in psychoanalysis has taken place. Something of the sort, the reader has doubtlessly noticed, also seems to be the chief motive behind the Wittgensteinian mode of philosophy. Before I further pursue the subject of transference, a cautionary note. There is a great difference between the ultimate concerns of Nietzsche on the one hand and Freud and the Wittgensteinians on the other. For Nietzsche, unlike the latter, the results of the transference are directed at the world and its possible transformation. Unlike Freud and the Wittgensteinians, his chief concern is not the mending of individual psyches, nor is it accommodating thought to things as they are. The last thing Nietzsche wants is to offer rationalizations for the status quo: something both Freud and the Wittgensteinians have been accused of with some justice.

One of the difficulties the spectator has to contend with in a performance of *The Connection* is that the events in the play seem to be random. How are we to relate the various incidents to each other? And once we discover what the system of relationships is, how are we to be convinced of its truth, of its correspondence to the real world? Our sense of conviction about the new connective principles will have to be real if we are to relate to events on the stage — or their counterparts in life. If the play is to be meaningful, these principles will have to govern our perception (our sense of organization) of what we shall experience after we leave the theater. This necessity for affect, as I indicated, derives to no small degree from the skeptical doubt about the nature of empirical knowledge, from the difficulties experienced by the causal principle. The events in *The Connection* do not follow an ordinary causal sequence, yet some of us are convinced that there is a reason for that sequence; we might even feel that it represents a form of causality.

In discussing the order of a patient's free associations, Freud noted that if the notion of causality were to be saved, it would have to be modified. Modifications of the causal principle are an old story, and every major shift in physical theory demands one. The triumph of Newton, for example, brought with it an acceptance of functional relationships as a version of causality. But to have something so basic as our notion of causality rearranged will clearly involve some form of psychological transformation; the great scientific discovery, the new way of making our connections, will also have to be an instrument of affect if we are to take it for reality. Now this is something many artists, poets, and novelists knew long before Freud turned it into a commonplace of psychology. Few would argue, furthermore, with the contention that the major aspects of Freud's psychology were anticipated by some of the literature of the nineteenth century. Would it be venturing too much to assume that this literature helped prepare the way — was an instrument of affect — for the eventual acceptance of Freud's notions on the causality of mental events?

In one of the many asides on methodology which are scattered throughout *Dora*, Freud makes the following observation:

I must now turn to consider a further complication, to which I should certainly give no space if I were a man of letters engaged upon the creation of a mental state like this for a short story, instead of being a medical man engaged upon its dissection. The element to which I must now allude can only serve to obscure and efface the outlines of the fine poetic conflict which we have been able to ascribe to Dora. This element would rightly fall a sacrifice to the censorship of a writer, for he, after all, simplifies and abstracts when he appears in the character of a psychologist. But in the world of reality, which I am trying to depict here, a complication of motives, an accumulation and conjunction of mental activities — in a word, overdetermination — is the rule.

I find it curious that Freud should consider his masterful job of construction in *Dora* — one is tempted to call it creation — a dissection of a mental state. In any case, he does not seem to be aware that the task he assigns to the psychologist was most surely carried out by a fictionist like Dostoyevsky — an author Freud had read more than casually. Freud's idea of fiction seems to be based on the classical notion of a rational, linear plot generated by the simple and clear motives of the chief characters. But surely those novelists descended from Richardson — for example, Rousseau, Goethe, and Jean Paul — saw the realistic complication of character as one of their objectives. Consider Dostoyevsky's *Notes From Underground*. The story, which is narrated (rather free-associated) by its chief character in seemingly irrational gasps, angry ejaculations, and nasty reflections, connect the events of the present with those of the past in a surprising fashion. The Underground Man's sense of causal relations seems mad, and the sequence of events (the plot) is every bit as absurd as that of *Dora*. If we are to believe in the narrator's mad logic — in all the apparent contradictions and complications of his character — we must be converted to it. We must go beyond the traditional realistic objective of merely believing in the possibility of that logic, for the story makes such demands on our ordinary psychological and epistemological assumptions, that, if it is to seem real, it will have to become the occasion for an affective change in the reader. If, to put the matter in Freud's terms, a view of the Underground Man's multiple facets leads us to an understanding of his repressed desires, those actions which we had previously taken to be irrational will now appear to be motivated by the causal logic of the subconscious. But for us to believe in the reality of these connections, for us to understand, for example, the significance of the narrator's lies, the story will have to convert us to a notion of mental activity which is not terribly far removed from that of Freud.

Freud's misconception concerning the nature of

nineteenth-century fiction is largely due to his own old-fashioned ideas about storytelling. His case studies are neatly structured, and the time sequence of the events has generally been put in proper order. As Freud readily admits, the tale he tells us is not quite the one he heard. It strikes me that Freud's old-fashioned method of storytelling may derive from his pretense of saving the principle of causality in its old form. The following should illustrate the point:

It is a rule of psychoanalytic technique that an internal connection which is still undisclosed will announce its presence by means of a contiguity — a temporal proximity — of associations; just as in writing, if "a" and "b" are put side by side, it means that the syllable "ab" is to be formed out of them. [*Dora*]

Contiguity, you remember, is one of Hume's rules for the association of ideas. Freud would have us believe that this typically eighteenth-century notion, this mechanical concept of causality, underlies his own practice. His narrative method attempts to give one that impression; the actual details of his reasoning belie him. In spite of Freud's denigration of his own role in making connections, in perceiving widely separated associations, his free use of his extraordinary imaginative powers indicates as great a rejection of eighteenth-century associationism as that of Wordsworth and Coleridge, to put it mildly. For example, Freud's derivation of Dora's dyspnea from her fantasy of sucking a penis is surely one of our supreme illustrations of Coleridge's concept of the imagination as the mind's unifying principle. To construct his derivation Freud relates reality and fantasy, dreams and memories; words are connected to their opposites and are given their proper meaning in terms of puns; Dora's memory of sucking her thumb while tugging at her brother's ear is given meaning in terms of her present condition. To further connect the past with the present, the comments Dora

makes (during the analysis) on the events of the past become, much like the mature Wordsworth's reflections on his
actions as a boy, a part of the narrative; further, her symptoms
take on different meanings according to their temporal context, as the river Wye, in "Tintern Abbey," gains new significance when Wordsworth returns to it after an absence of
five years. Finally, in an almost sublime flight of imagination,
Freud concludes that Dora, at age fourteen, must have felt
her friend Mr. K's erection when he suddenly embraced her
in a hallway. The only evidence for this is that it is a necessary link in Freud's causal chain. And indeed, we believe
it — if we have been converted to Freud's causal logic. At
this point it becomes clear why Freud has gone through the
pretense of working by the old rules of causality and associationism. Although most of the procedures Freud used in his
derivation of Dora's dyspnea were anticipated or hinted at by
Wordsworth in *The Prelude,* Freud cannot hope to convince
us of their validity by quoting the Preface to the *Lyrical
Ballads.* He is, after all, a practitioner of the science of psychology. Though we may value him for his departure from a
mechanical notion of causality, Freud must justify himself
according to procedures which he deems properly scientific.
Only under these conditions will his imaginative — and perhaps true — constructions be accepted as scientifically valid.
Freud, much like Wordsworth, frequently injects comments
on his past actions into his narrative: Wordsworth, in doing
so, sees the events in his life unified — the past related to the
present — in terms of the theory of imagination; Freud, on
the other hand, attempts to give his connections — so similar
in their play of free association to those of Wordsworth —
the status of science. The following observations on sexuality,
placed by Freud just before his derivation of Dora's dyspnea,
make this fairly clear:

A stream of water which meets with an obstacle in the river-bed is dammed up and flows back into old channels which had formerly seemed fated to run dry. The motive forces leading to the formation of hysterical symptoms draw their strength not only from repressed normal sexuality but also from unconscious perverse activities.

We are not quite sure whether the analogy is meant literally or metaphorically. And this is hardly an isolated instance: The concept of force, analogies from mechanics and electricity — all of them involving a classical version of the causal principle — keep making their way almost unnoticeably into Freud's narrative. They are representative of Freud's attempt to define (and justify) his method according to the dictates of a philosophy of science which had, ironically, outlived its relevance to much of the contemporary work in the physical sciences. But for psychology, classical physics provided a mask of legitimacy for the insights of the poets and fictionists, a legitimacy which the power of imagination had surely lost. Strangely enough, today the appeal of psychoanalysis seems to derive from its imaginative insights, from its not giving the appearance of a "hard" science. Freud, I imagine, might not have been overjoyed by this development; yet given his knowledge of defense mechanisms, it should hardly have surprised him.

As Freud proceeds with his derivation of Dora's dyspnea, he must constantly refer to subconscious mental activity and to the general theory of psychoanalysis if he is to make the proper connections. But more important than the analyst's search for truth is the necessity for the patient to feel convinced of that truth. Only then will the scientific configuration which supposedly accounts for his mental activity bear the stamp of reality; only then will the patient, in a manner of speaking, feel cured. The clinical situation corresponds to the Wittgensteinians' notion of philosophical activity: There too analysis leads to the peaceful acceptance of truth and consequently the clearing of mental cramp — or perhaps the other way around. On the surface, this procedure should prove no more difficult than the task of convincing someone innocent of molecular theory that the reaction of sodium and chlorine is caused by the number of electrons in their outer rings. I clearly remember how readily I accepted my high school teacher's explanation, how little doubt I or anyone else in the class expressed. The source of our ready acceptance should be obvious. The teacher's explanation, though utterly fantastic, had the sanction of science; and science was real, though occasionally mysterious. This much we knew from our memories of Hiroshima and Nagasaki. The explosions had seemed fictional, yet they had happened; and science, somehow, had done the job. It was not very difficult to convince us of the reality of atomic structure, since there were no strong defenses to be broken down. Compare this to the difficulty I experienced, for example, in convincing undergraduates to accept the reality of a young girl's hidden sexuality in James's *What Maisie Knew*. At first, most of them simply refused to see its existence in the novel. As a result, they were incapable of making any sense out of the story; the events did not connect, since there were no visible motives for them. Freud's work has, of course, helped to break down partially our culture's defenses against child sexuality; but amazingly enough, they seem to have survived the onslaught of even Nabokov's *Lolita*. Freud's *Dora* was written in 1897; James's novel, it should hardly surprise us, was published in the same year. The similarity of the two works is remarkable, though this is not the place to explore them. Both are works about the hidden sexuality of young girls and the family circles which surround and exploit them; in both, the connections can be made only if we accept the reality of subconscious mental activity. In order to break down our resistance, James developed his later style, a style which, by combining the past with the present, the conscious with the subconscious, breaks down the notion of linear narrative, of an orderly causal progression from event to event. In the completion of this task, James had enough precedents to lean on. His variation lay in the use of a child's latent sexual desires to create new connections; in James's last novels, written after *What Maisie Knew*, the connections were provided, instead, by the elaborate symbolic networks which make these works so difficult to penetrate. But James went even further than this in his assault on our defenses; for if we are to accept something so strange as a young girl's sexual desires for a grown man, his method will have to create some affective change in the reader. James's method, as he explained in the preface to his novel, was to relate all the events through the consciousness of Maisie, yet to couch her thoughts in the language of the reader, thereby giving them the benefit of adult reflection. James forces us to take on Maisie's role; it must become part of us, it must change our perception of events, if we are to understand her actions. For the reader, the result will be either affect, that is a psychological transformation, or a total rejection based on his incapacity to understand or to accept Maisie's logic as real.

Psychological defenses tend to crumble totally or not at all. Freud found himself confronted with this problem in getting his patients to accept the insights of psychoanalysis. The conversion to belief (and faith), the creation of affect, must, after all, be the objective of any analysis. That literature would need to do something of this sort in order to convince had, by Freud's time, become more or less of a commonplace in advanced artistic circles. It is expressed in its maturity by the following words from the elegiac coda to the first volume of Proust's masterpiece; words which were, in all likelihood, first written at about the time Freud was analyzing Dora:

And seeing all these new elements of the spectacle, I had no longer the faith which, applied to them, would have given them consistency, unity, life; they passed in a scattered sequence before me, at random, without reality, containing in themselves no beauty that my eyes might have endeavored, as in the old days, to extract from them and to compose in a picture. They were just women, in whose elegance I had no belief, and whose clothes seemed to me unimportant.[7]

The narrator, Marcel, in a fit of nostalgia, has gone for a walk in the Bois de Boulogne and is now gazing at the Allée des Acacias. It is a setting which had once struck Marcel with wonder; it had united the details of his life and given them meaning when, as a young boy, he stood awaiting the regally staged appearance of Mme. Swann. The parallel to Wordsworth revisiting the banks of the river Wye should be obvious. But Wordsworth's voluntary act of memory only reminds Marcel of the ravages of time, of his incapacity to make meaningful connections between memory and the experience of the present moment. Wordsworth, if we imagine him in the place of Marcel, would gaze at the acacias, recall the past, and thereby renew his faith in the order of his experience. Wordsworth's faith is based, the reader recalls, on his belief that nature has an objective order which is available to the perception of the individual beholder. Despite some of the romantic trappings, there is a classical assumption of orderliness which has not fallen victim to the skeptical assaults of the Enlightenment: One rarely gets the feeling that Wordsworth is struggling with the Cartesian doubt. As a result, the relaxed form of the eighteenth-century meditative poem is readily available to Wordsworth: Unlike most

[7] Marcel Proust, *Rembrance of Things Past,* trans. C. K. Scott Moncrief (New York, 1934).

other Romantics, he is spared the necessity of imposing his own form on experience and thus allows "Tintern Abbey" to wander in a manner apparently guided by free association alone. The order, he knows, will somehow be provided by Nature. And the reader readily perceives it in the poem if he but looks at the physical details of the scene described. They are not as freely associated as it initially appeared.

The act of perception, we have seen, the voluntary inducement of memory, will not renew Marcel's faith. Something beyond this, an experience involving affect, will be needed to make his connections real, to give them emotional validity. Proust's need to go beyond Wordsworth involves more than the ordinary demands made on literature and philosophy by the passing of several generations. Proust, owing to his lack of Wordsworthian faith, sets himself a much more difficult and inclusive task. When I substituted Wordsworth for Marcel in the Allée des Acacias I allowed him to look only at the acacias, not at the passing show of social fashion. In "Tintern Abbey" and in most of his earlier poetry, Wordsworth makes a willful separation between man's social life and nature, between the country and the city. Consider Wordsworth's reflections upon the river Wye. This one follows the detailed description of his perceptions in the opening paragraph of "Tintern Abbey":

> These beauteous forms
> Through a long absence, have not been to me
> As is a landscape to a blind man's eye:
> But oft, in lonely rooms, and 'mid the din
> Of towns and cities, I have owed to them
> In hours of weariness, sensations sweet,
> Felt in the blood, and felt along the heart . . .

The experience of nature allows Wordsworth his sense of order, it renews his faith, because it restricts, indeed wipes out, his memory of "The dreary intercourse of daily life."

Wordsworth's ability to believe in the reality of his connections — rather the connections of his past and present perceptions — rests on his assumption that the neoclassic notion of General Nature is identical to what we ordinarily think of as nature: that is, the country, trees, streams, and so forth. Social experiences cannot really be assimilated to the mind's (or Nature's) sense of order. Proust, of course, attempts to do precisely this. All memories, perceptions, each kind of experience — especially the social — must be connected, must relate to Marcel's sense of order, if that order is to be emotionally real. Consequently, Marcel does not restrict his revisiting of the Bois de Boulogne to a contemplation of the woods, but goes in search of all aspects of his past, including the fashion show put on by Mme. Swann. Now if Proust's attempt to combine traditional and city pastoral — that is, the demands of self and society, the realities of love and politics — is to be emotionally convincing for the reader, if the connections are to be made by us, he will also need to go beyond Wordsworth's attempts at drawing the reader into the poem. Proust's attempt will require something other than Wordsworth's use of the meditative poem and nonpoetic diction. For the reader, as much as Marcel, will have to experience a psychological transformation of some depth, a restructuring of his philosophical assumptions commensurate with a bout of Wittgensteinian philosophy. Surely for most of us, as much as for Marcel, the notion of an objective General Nature has been dead for a long time.

Remembrances of Things Past is a record of Marcel's attempts to regain the boy's lost faith. But it is wrong to say "attempt," for the necessary psychological transformation will be occasioned by the release of involuntary memory, remembrances called up by sense experiences which have not been prearranged, which are not separate from our ordinary lives. Indeed, as we read the book, we are not sure whether the attempt to make the past real will be successful. We are given our first hint of both the problem and its possible resolution by the flood of involuntary memories the aroma of a madeleine evokes in Marcel. From this point forward, as we eventually discover, all memories lead to that overwhelming moment of psychological transformation at the end of the work, the moment when Marcel regains his faith. A subtle progression of events leads to the consummation of affect. Marcel is on his way to a reception given by the Princesse de Guermantes. In front of the Guermantes mansion he strikes his foot against two uneven flagstones; somewhat later, he is surprised by the clang made when a butler strikes a spoon against a plate. Both of these experiences have an apparently unaccountable psychological effect on Marcel, an effect which he cannot understand. When he comes upon a copy of George Sand's *François le Champi* in the Guermantes' library, a book from which his mother had read to him at an important moment in his childhood, his chained memory is freed; his defenses have been broken down, and the connections which were previously hidden and submerged have now come to the surface. Not only do the uneven flagstones and the clang of the plate fall into their proper places in Marcel's memory but further, he now has the ability to perceive meaningful relationships in the apparently random flux of events we call history, in the confused relationships we abstractly designate as society. The psychological transformation has given him the power of philosophy, the power to make connections. All this is most immediately expressed in Marcel's newly discovered faith in his vocation — the craft of literature. The act of self-discovery is consummated in Marcel's capacity to give his private connections reality in the external world. For we now understand that the book we

[261]

have been reading is the product of Marcel's newly discovered vocation; indeed, it is the record of his search for that vocation — this has been the meaning, the order, of his life. Like Dora, whose analysis allowed her "to tear herself free from her father and . . . [be] reclaimed once more by the realities of life," Marcel is reclaimed by reality through his creation of a work of art — a work which lends objectivity to the privacies of his memories, of his inner connections. And we, by the act of reading Proust's book, are also plunged into reality and are hopefully transformed thereby. For the book, although composed of memories, must be read in the continuous present; we are never sure of what events will mean, or whether they will mean anything at all; we must, in fact, experience them and make them a part of our own psychic lives. Only then will there be a possibility of making connections: The result depends on our own psychological transformation, on how an event, an image, or a character has gnawed at our own consciousness with the passing of time. We are now capable of locating Proust's modernity, his difference from Wordsworth, with some clarity. Although Wordsworth attempts to draw us into "Tintern Abbey" 's frame, the poem's objective is to present us with a proper example, a good model, for behavior. Wordsworth asks us to accompany him, and he assumes that our experience of nature will be similar to his. It should be clear that this is very close to the classical notion of poetry's function: to delight and teach. True, we are not expected to imitate the hero's — in this case, significantly, the poet's — actions because we share a common belief in a fixed law of nature; rather we do so because the language of the poem, its manner of description and moral address, has convinced us of the poet's sincerity. But the poem does not attempt to destroy our defenses, to effect some grand psychological change. Its chief task is to reaffirm those humane values in which we all supposedly believe, even though they may have lost their support in the law of nature. Ultimately, the poem must lead us outside ourselves, to the contemplation of nature itself. Proust, on the other hand, surprises us with his almost unnoticeable probes into our sense of what is real, into our very habits of making connections. As his book becomes our reality, we are initially led to a contemplation of ourselves, for our ordinary laws of perception are destroyed, and our total effort must be dedicated to discovering new ones — if there are, in fact, new ones to be discovered. We are forced into the performance of this epistemological task, into the transformation of our very manner of thinking, for the alternative is to give up on the possibility of understanding our experience of the book, the possibility of making connections. The journey we take with Marcel may lead nowhere; it may lead to utter confusion; but once the book has captured us, there is no returning from it. It is this (perhaps unwanted) necessity to deal with an experience, this insidious undermining of our defenses, this demand that we cast off our perceptual chains — it is all these which punctuate Proust's modernity and make him the contemporary of Freud. Proust, rather than standing in opposition to Wordsworth's procedures, draws on them, and brings them to their logical conclusion; a conclusion which is largely based on his insight into literary psychology. If the work of art is to become a part of our lives, if our lives themselves are thereby turned into works of art, and if, following Nietzsche, we recognize that our historical awareness has transformed all modern moralities into artistic creations, then literature will need to transform us, it will need to exploit the psychology of affect in order to perform its persuasive task, thereby assuring us of the reality of our connections. It should be clear, once more, that the process

at work in Proust's novel bears more than an accidental relationship to Freud's notion of transference. Both psychologist
and novelist were forced to recognize the uses of affect by the
intellectual imperatives of their historical situation.

What, precisely, does Freud mean by the notion of transference? Perhaps in matters of this sort it is too much to ask
for precision. If so, it is a matter, I suspect, Freud would not
have readily admitted. Toward the conclusion of *Dora*,
Freud makes his first important attempt to clarify the
emotional events which constitute transference. Here are his
remarks:

> What are transferences? They are new editions or facsimiles of
> the tendencies and phantasies which are aroused and made con-
> scious during the progress of the analysis; but they have this
> peculiarity, which is characteristic for their species, that they re-
> place some earlier person by the person of the physician . . . it
> is only after the transference has been resolved that a patient ar-
> rives at a sense of conviction of the validity of the connections
> which have been constructed during the analysis.

Much of this amounts to little more than Wordsworth's
notion of the past being revived through the agency of
present experience. But to see no more than this is to miss
the point badly. The importance of Freud's remarks lies in
the role prescribed for the analyst: He becomes more than a
clinician, more than the convenient instrument of the heal-
ing process. Something of a deeply personal nature must take
place in the relationship of doctor and patient. To a large
degree, the necessity for this relationship derives from our
awareness of those epistemological problems discussed in an
earlier chapter. Difficulties in relating perception to belief led
to the obliteration of the space between a work of art and its
beholder. The problem of Baroque religious art — an art
dedicated to the strengthening of religious conviction — lies
in the subjective demands it makes upon the beholder; it

constantly asks him to refer to his private experience. Transference, though it needs to eliminate the space between subject and analyst, must go beyond this, for the subject, if he is to experience a restructuring of his very way of making connections, must undergo a psychological transformation of a fundamental nature. Freud explains the psychological necessity for this process in a late paper, "Analysis Terminable and Interminable":

The therapeutic effect of analysis depends on the making conscious what is, in the widest sense, repressed within the id. We prepare the way for this operation by our interpretations and constructions, but so long as the ego clings to its former defences and refuses to abandon its resistances we have interpreted merely for ourselves and not for the patient. Now these resistances, although they belong to the ego *are nevertheless unconscious* and, in a certain sense, they are segregated within the ego. [My italics.] [8]

In spite of the obfuscation caused by the psychoanalytic jargon, Freud's observation strikes me as basically sound. If the fundamental manner of interpreting our experience (that is, our theory of knowledge) is to be transformed, our defenses will have to be broken down and some kind of change will need to occur in our subconscious. Here, then, is one thing which Freud seems to mean by transference.

In attaining its objective — the release and reordering of subconscious material — transference must do more than eradicate the line between doctor and patient; if a basic transformation is to take place, the analyst will have to become part of his subject's reality. But we are still left somewhat puzzled. What exactly happens in this relationship between analyst and subject? In what way does it differ from any strong involvement with another human being? Falling in love, for example. This last question is, quite naturally, of

[8] Sigmund Freud, *Therapy and Technique*, ed. P. Rieff, no trans. given (New York, 1963).

supreme importance in our consideration of transference in a work of art; for, as I pointed out in relation to *The Connection*, there is an emotive danger, an esthetic risk, in taking the action on the stage for reality. And similarly, Freud points out, disaster awaits the analysis which takes the emotions of the transference to be identical to those of ordinary human intercourse. In the attempt to clarify matters, I shall quote and briefly comment on a few passages from Freud's several papers on the subject:

When there is anything in the complex-material (the content of the complex) which can at all suitably be transferred on to the person of the physician such a transference will be effected, and from it will arise the next association.[9]

But, we may ask, why do we need the physician to coax the next association out of its hiding place? The price to be paid seems to be a bit steep. Freud continues a bit further on:

It is undeniable that the subjugation of the transference-manifestations provides the greatest difficulties for the psychoanalyst; but it must not be forgotten that they, and they only, render the invaluable service of making the patient's buried and forgotten love-emotions actual and manifest; for in the last resort no one can be slain *in absentia* or *in effigie*.

As in Proust, a specific occasion — a sense experience, a relationship of some depth — is needed to release involuntary memory. For the reader, this occasion is provided by Proust's own work of art; for the patient, by the analyst. The difference, it would seem, is that the analyst's presence allows the patient to resolve his released emotions. But, we need to ask, just how does this occur? We know that a female patient, for example, should not really fall in love with the analyst, nor should the latter consider the satisfaction of her desires one of his duties. Furthermore, it would hardly do for the patient

[9] "The Dynamics of the Transference," *ibid.*

to resolve his aggressions by murdering his physician instead of his father. Here is Freud's not entirely clear advice:

> The physician requires of him [the patient] that he shall fit these emotions into their place in the treatment and in his life-history, subject them to rational consideration, and appraise them at their true psychical value. This struggle between physician and patient, between intellect and the forces of instinct, between recognition and the striving for discharge, is fought out almost entirely over the transference manifestations. This is the ground on which the victory must be won, the final expression of which is lasting recovery from the neurosis. [*Ibid.*]

The analyst's task, then, is to provide the occasion, the touchstone, for the ordering of the previously suppressed material. If he is to accomplish something of this magnitude, the analyst's involvement with the patient will need to become deeply personal; he must do more than bridge the space between two egos; indeed, he must strike to the id itself. This is the task which Proust set for his novel. But if the work of art, taking the place of the physician, releases the contents of the id, just how, not being a rational creature like the analyst, is it to reconcile instinct and intellect? Just how is it to create order? The modern work of art, owing to its very attempt to strike at the depths, cannot provide the order which, Matthew Arnold has taught us, is a part of any classic. Thus the necessity, created by the modern, for providing new connections cannot avoid becoming an extremely subjective affair. In the case of *Remembrance of Things Past*, the gradual revelation of a strong sense of order creates at least the possibility of the novel fulfilling the obligation of the analyst: to heal by bringing the patient to an understanding of the rationality of events. But is anything of this sort likely to happen during an evening spent with *The Connection?* To indicate the magnitude of the difficulty, we need not take anything so extreme as *The Connection*. The notorious diffi-

culties of defining one's experience of Hopkins' "The Windhover" will serve as an example.

The Windhover [10]
I caught this morning morning's minion, king-
dom of daylight's dauphin, dapple-dawn-drawn Falcon, in his
  riding
Of the rolling level underneath him steady air, and striding
High there, how he rung upon the rein of a wimpling wing
In his ecstasy! then off, off forth on swing,
As a skate's heel sweeps smooth on a bow-bend: the hurl and
  gliding
Rebuffed the big wind. My heart in hiding
Stirred for a bird, — the achieve of, the mastery of the thing!

Brute beauty and valour and act, of, air, pride, plume, here
Buckle! And the fire that breaks from thee then, a billion
Times told lovelier, more dangerous, O my chevalier!
No wonder of it: shéer plód makes plough down sillion
Shine, and blue-bleak embers, ah my dear,
Fall, gall themselves, and gash gold-vermilion.

Father Hopkins composed the poem with the knowledge,
born of modern skepticism, that the conversion to Christianity cannot be effected through logic. The rhetoric of conversion must begin — perhaps end — with an assault on the
senses, for its objective is a basic psychological transformation of the nonbeliever. Hopkins' poem, beginning with its
initial verbal swirl, involves us with the tangible, scrupulously
objective picture of the bird. It is simply there: a beautiful
and frightening object. We alternately love and reject both
its struggle against and ultimate submission to the forces of
nature. Our emotional struggle with the bird should issue
eventually in a transference of our feelings to the poem; a
breaking of our defenses which will result in the release of
suppressed emotions. Hopkins assumed that the release of

---

[10] Reprinted from Gerard Manley Hopkins, *Poems*, 3rd edition, eds.
Robert Bridges and W. H. Gardner, with the permission of Oxford
University Press.

such emotions would lead us to emulate the submission of the bird, and, in turn, the self-sacrifice of Christ. To make the conversion complete, these emotional upheavals will be crowned with our conviction of both the rationality of our own emotions and the rationality of Christian belief itself. But is this, in fact, bound to happen? What is to guarantee that our emotional involvement will be with anything but the bird, the poem, and with ourselves? Just what is to give order and meaning to our released emotions? And why should "The Windhover" make us think of Christ at all? Hopkins became aware of these, and similar, difficulties in the theology which shaped his religious poems. As a result, he eventually placed the now familiar dedication, "To Christ our Lord" (I left it out) at the head of the poem. Hopkins lost faith. And rightly so! For Christ is not in the poem; nor is he objectively imaged in a bird. If he does exist in our experience of the poem, he will need to emerge from our own psyches and from the connections this allows us to make. But where is the analyst who is to direct our emotions to their proper end? Hopkins does make the attempt. But the presence of the dedication is almost bound to deprive the nonbeliever of the possibility of transference.

There is a doubt which should have been nagging at any of us for a good while. Why the imperative to turn from the exclusive concern with the poem itself? Why the need to go beyond the transference? There would seem to be no good scientific reason why our emotions should not remain fixed on the analyst — especially if we can afford the expense. Freud's following comment is remarkable for what it reveals.

For the physician there are ethical motives which combine with the technical reasons to hinder him from according the patient his love. The aim that he has to keep in view is that this woman, whose capacity for love is disabled by infantile fixations, should attain complete access over this function which is so inestimably important for her in life, not that she should fritter it away in the treatment, but preserve it for real life, if so be that after her cure life makes that demand on her.[11]

It should be clear that Freud makes a very strong ethical commitment; and he does so immediately after telling us that there are good *technical* reasons for the analyst denying his love to the patient. Freud's need to make his moral assertion stems from those motives which produced both the irony of an eighteenth-century conservative like Swift and the militant moral stance of an encyclopedist like Diderot. The most significant of these motives is the skeptical doubt: That is, the lack of confidence in the law of nature, in the foundations of causality. The ethical doubts engendered by questions of epistemology demand a strong, willful stance about the moral law — even if that stance is given the mask of the stoic law of nature or of the necessities of science. And these doubts are further reinforced when human motives and human society are made the subject of scientific study: There is, after all, no ready way to move from what there is to what there ought to be. So Freud, in the midst of a great deal of talk about the technical necessities for ending an analysis, makes his ethical assertion. It is a moment of supreme honesty in the history of psychology and social science.

I must now return to a question already posed in a different form. If the work of art effects the transference, then who (or what) is to assert Freud's ethical imperatives? The matter is left to each individual. This may be an opportunity for the exercise of free choice; but it may also be an opportunity for the propagandist, or, worst of all, for our own destructive impulses. This is the danger of the Hopkins poem as well as of *The Connection.* The emotions released by

[11] "Further Recommendations in the Technique of Psychoanalysis: Observations on Transference-Love," *Therapy and Technique.*

these works of art are open to anything; they become the subject of a free-for-all. When turned to social and political action, Herzen pointed out, such undirected passions may have dire, and unforeseen, consequences. The destruction of institutions is necessary if our suppressed human possibilities are to be released. But who is to say what will be made of these opportunities? What guarantee that the ethical commitments made will be humane? The burden put on the individual by the transference may, all too easily, result in its malfunction. Consequently, the analysis — even if it does not lead to a spiteful destructiveness — may be interminable; our involvement with "The Windhover" may become its own end, rather than returning us to life. But I ask again, What is the ethical commitment which returns us to life? What, beyond the transference, is the given task of analysis? The following, I believe, was Freud's last word on the subject:

Our object will be not to rub off all the corners of the human character so as to produce "normality" according to schedule, nor yet to demand that the person who has been "thoroughly analysed" shall never again feel the stirrings of passions in himself or become involved in any internal conflict. The business of analysis is to secure the best possible psychological conditions for the functioning of the ego; when this has been done, analysis has accomplished its task. ["Analysis Terminable and Interminable"]

The psychological transformation has not led to a specific ordering of our lives; much as the philosophical procedures of the Wittgensteinians, it has not provided us with a philosophy. Its task has been much more basic and therefore more insecure. The transformation has occurred in our epistemology, and thereby given us the capacity to confront reality in a more or less orderly fashion. What that order actually is remains uncertain and must be dealt with as the occasion arises. But it should be clear that under these conditions no analysis is ever really terminable; nor does any transference initiated by a work of art ever lead to a logical conclusion. The catharsis of classical drama allows our egos to function realistically, setting our minds at rest, because it reaffirms a set of accepted values. But *The Connection,* for example, is not terminable in this sense. Its release of suppressed emotions may force us to confront reality; it may give us the capacity to make new connections. But we have to wait and see; we must use our new capacities to make decisions and act; in short, our lives, as well as the dramatic action, are unresolved. The play has not really ended.

In one of the methodological asides near the beginning of *Dora,* Freud reflects on this matter of resolution:

It is only towards the end of the treatment that we have before us an intelligible, consistent, and unbroken case history. Whereas the practical aim of the treatment is to remove all possible symptoms and to replace them by conscious thoughts, we may regard it as a second and theoretical aim to repair all the damages to the patient's memory. These two aims are coincident. When one is reached, so is the other; and the same path leads to them both.

Significantly, Dora's analysis never reached a conclusion. And this, despite Freud's claims, was not caused by a malfunctioning of transference. Freud, in this early paper, simply expects too much. He came to understand, further in his career, that there is no end to the effects of transference; the matter can never be resolved with finality. If the pattern of intelligibility can be seen only at the end, then that pattern is in continuous flux, for the end keeps changing with every change in our lives. Thus no modern work of art which attempts to induce the effects of transference will ever be complete, will ever be resolved. Recall the polar opposites of all possible approaches to Bernini's Teresa: the undoubting

Christian view will lead the beholder to a feeling of resolution and to a sense of order; on the other hand, the skeptical view is most likely to result in a rousing of hidden sexual feelings, feelings leading to — who knows where? For the modern work of art there can be no conclusion. The necessity for transference leads it to reach for our emotional depths; it tries to strike at bedrock. But there is no resolution at the bottom, as Freud observed in "Analysis Terminable and Interminable":

The paramount importance of these two themes — the wish for a penis in women and, in men, the struggle against passivity — did not escape the notice of Ferenczi. In the paper that he read in 1927 he laid it down as a principle that in every successful analysis these two complexes must have been resolved. From my own experience I would observe that in this I think Ferenczi was asking a very great deal.

The specific nature of our most fundamental biological fears aside, it seems highly likely that we perpetually build defenses that cater to the demands of these fears. Consequently, if a work like Proust's attempts to strike at our emotional foundations, if it has indeed succeeded in becoming a part of our psychic lives, we shall keep building defenses against it. Furthermore, defenses will be built for rejecting any new attempts at ordering our psychic experience. These defenses will have to be broken down in turn, and thus any new work of art will be obliged to attempt a repetition of the transference. Herein lies one reason for the permanence of modernism.

One aspect of the modern art object's unfinished nature can be seen in the (not untypical) manner of composition of several famous literary works. Much modern literature tends to be autobiographical. The writer looks at his task not as a craft, nor simply as an instrument of self-expression. Rather, the job of composition turns into the writer's search for connections, into his attempt to settle his own doubts about the order and significance of his personal experience. As the writer's life goes on there are new experiences, and they, in turn, order the past in a new way. Take, for example, Wordsworth's compulsive rewriting of *The Prelude*. The many changes made between the versions of 1805 and 1850 were not attempts at autobiographical falsification. Wordsworth's changes, almost invariably, corrected false psychological notes; the memories became ordered, and their connections more real, as further experience placed them in a new psychic context. There is a remarkable example of this procedure in the earlier quoted boating scene from *The Prelude*. Here, once more, are the relevant lines:

When, from behind that craggy steep till then
The horizon's bound, a huge peak, black and huge,
As if with voluntary power instinct,
Upreared its head. I struck and struck again . . .

That is from the version of 1850. The terror of seeing the peak loom up suddenly, leads the boy to attempt his frantic getaway: therefore the violent striking of the oars. Any reading of the whole passage will immediately convince us of the reality of this memory; its psychological justness assures us of its truth. In the version of 1805 the last of the lines quoted above reads, in its initial appearance, as follows:

"I push'd, and struck the oars and struck again. . . ."

Curiously enough, the line first appears *before* the boy has been surprised by the peak. It is wrong; it could not have happened that way. When the line makes its second appearance its lack of surprise dulls the possibility of terror. Wordsworth, with the insight gained from new experience, corrects a mistaken memory. In a much similar way, Proust kept adding new incidents to *Remembrance of Things Past*; and with each new incident, everything else in the work had to be reconsidered and perhaps rewritten. Naturally, the outbreak of World War I demanded inclusion, and its very enormity put most of the novel's social reflections in a new, and historically meaningful, light. The church of Saint-Hilaire — which provides one of the anchors for all of Marcel's experience — only finds its proper place in the novel when it is destroyed during the war. And who knows if this new meaning, this new connection, would not have been changed, in turn, if Proust had lived longer. Both *The Prelude* and *Remembrances of Things Past* are literary works without their own conclusions; their only possible end comes with the deaths of the authors. The logic of this process of composition has been formalized by Wittgenstein. Wittgensteinian philosophers are notorious for not publishing their papers, for they consider the activity of philosophy to be a continuous therapeutic process. Wittgenstein's *Philosophical Investigations* were, quite naturally, published posthumously. Wittgenstein discusses his method of composition in the Preface; his words shed much light on our whole discussion:

After several unsuccessful attempts to weld my results together into such a whole, I realized that I should never succeed. The best that I could write would never be more than philosophical remarks; my thoughts were soon crippled if I tried to force them on in any single direction against their natural inclination. — And this was, of course, connected with the very nature of the investigation. For this compels us to travel over a wide field of thought criss-cross in every direction. — The philosophical remarks in this book are, as it were, a number of sketches of landscapes which were made in the course of these long and involved journeyings. . . . Thus this book is really only an album.

It is an album whose pages we turn, whose contents we use for endless seminars, in the hope of discovering its secret, in the expectation, perhaps, of the manifestations of transference. And so it is with the works of Proust and Wordsworth: They do not really come to a resolution with the deaths of their authors. If they have induced the transference, their struggle to understand the pattern of experience will continue in the reader; nor, especially in Proust's case, will it come to a resolution there. Proust sought to defeat this inconclusiveness, as he attempted to defeat the imperatives of time. In order to perceive the definitive pattern of experience, to understand the immanent logic of nature and human action, Proust set himself the megalomaniacal task of including everything in his work: private and public experience, politics and social gossip, the artistic and the vulgar, philosophy and history, and, finally, time and reality themselves. His ambitions went much beyond those of universal and philosophical history. But the task is, of course, impossible — and therefore the pathos of Proust's desperate attempt to complete it in the last years of his life. For what is everything? The totality of facts changes as we live — and so does the past. Marcel reflects on the subject in a famous passage near the end of *Remembrance of Things Past*:

And in those great books there are certain portions which there has been time only to sketch in and which no doubt will never be completed because of the very magnitude of the architect's plan. How many great cathedrals remain unfinished! Such a book one nourishes over a long period of time, builds up its weaker parts, keeps it safe from harm; but later it is the book itself that grows up, selects our tomb, protects it against false rumours and somewhat against oblivion.

Yet Proust's very procedure does expose him to false rumor and forces him to take the risk which might do harm to his work. Marcel discusses these difficulties as he continues his esthetic reflections:

But to return to myself — I had a more modest opinion of my book and it would be incorrect to say even that I was thinking of those who might read it as "my readers." For, as I have already shown, they would not be my readers but readers of themselves.

. . . Consequently, I would not ask them to praise or dispraise me.

These words, and especially the last sentence, should, if we take them with the seriousness they deserve, bring us face to face with the difficulties of transference as a literary mode.

Marcel's warning not to judge him is very much to the point. If the book's task is to lead to a reading of ourselves, to an induction of transference, just how are we to make an esthetic judgment? We are once more confronted with the ambiguous legacy of the skeptical doubt; indeed, the same legacy which made the nature of judgments a sore point for the ethical and political theory of the Enlightenment. These difficulties are ours; they are, after all, the ones with which we began in our consideration of *The Connection.* The effects of transference almost destroy the possibility for a criticism which goes beyond epistemology to specific judgments. Yet our literature needs the effects of transference if it is to be more than a minor diversion, if it is to attain glory. Recall, for the moment, my earlier discussion of Matthew Arnold. Arnold's poetry, though its chief concern is for just those modern themes which we identify with poets like Eliot, does not strike us as belonging to our time. The source of this effect is located in Arnold's concern for objectivity and order: It leads to his occasionally mechanical attempts to use classical forms. These forms were, quite clearly, a defense against the disorder of Arnold's buried emotions, though the latter came to the surface often enough to give us the depressive atmosphere and the potential disorder of the Marguerite lyrics. Arnold was most determined not to create the conditions for transference, though he recognized its historical necessity. His feelings were so strong, they led him to suppress *Empedocles on Etna,* for he did not wish to induce an emotional orgy which rather than leading to ordered action creates subjective disorder. Arnold finally turned to criticism in order to create the conditions for the creation of what he termed the architectonic. But in vain, for this critical task, though heroic (even necessary), was quite beyond the realm of contemporary possibility.

By discussing transference as a characteristic of the modern, I have not meant to imply that a similar kind of affect has never occurred in classic literature. Surely something of the sort takes place near the end of Racine's *Phèdre*. The example could be multiplied endlessly in the various arts. But the breaking of defenses and the consequent emotional release generally occurs within a tightly ordered sequence of events — a formal structure — which leads us to the recognition of an ordered set of values. The work as a whole thus acts as a guide to the released emotions: The suppressed materials are always kept in bounds, and the transference is hedged. Recall, once more, the effect of the religious context on our experience of Bernini's Cornaro Chapel. When we behold this work from its appropriate vantage point — both physically and religiously — it is physically whole, our perception of it is unified, and our experience complete. The very failure to totally break the frame makes the chapel's dramatic unity, even Bernini's grand conception, possible. But also recall the ambiguity of Bernini's work for those who cannot be firm believers in the possibility of mystic union. And how many of us, today, are? There is no return to the faith in terms of its old foundations; the process, of which Bernini's mode of striking at our perceptions is a part, is irreversible. It is, after all, the result of an historical logic, a sequence of events generated by the skeptical doubt.

As the process hurries on, it will have to answer to the ever greater demands of increased emotional release. And how shall we judge those events which will attempt to induce that increasingly more unattainable release? If we are to remain human, if we are not to become the slaves of the necessity for transference, we shall have to make the attempt, and make it constantly, at moral and esthetic judgment — though there be no grounds for judgment. Since transference will not allow us the peace of emotional resolution, the demand for judgment will be permanent. But consider the following irony: The only thing likely to give us the energy for judgment (to keep us human) is the emotional release brought on by transference. The effort involved is bound to be prodigious, for our historical consciousness has made us aware of the arrogance of our judgments and therefore makes ever greater demands on our psychic energy. Nietzsche has put the matter well:

We are the first era that is truly learned so far as "costumes" are concerned — I mean moralities, articles of faith, esthetic tastes, and religions. We are better prepared than any time has ever been for the Great Carnival, the most spirited Mardi-Gras laughter, the most reckless fun, for the transcendental summit of the utmost idiocy, for a truly Aristophanean mockery of the universe. Perhaps we shall discover here the field for our kind of inventiveness, the field in which we too can be original! Perhaps we can be the parodists of world history, the punchinellos of God! If nothing else living today has a future — perhaps it will be our *laughter* that has one. [*Beyond Good and Evil*]

And indeed, our typical efforts may be the products of lunacy. We may forget about the arts — for they demand judgment and critical effort — and seek release through the joys of LSD, our orgone boxes, or a happening. When worn out by this, why not reject the whole damned effort of being human, lock up our emotions, and let our electronic anodynes do their idiot work. But before we close shop, before we give up on the possibilities of transference, recall not only that it might be a road to sanity — a goal valuable enough — but that for the work of art it creates the possibility of a sublime intensity previously unknown to man.

6

FREEDOM AND ORDER

THE DEPENDENCE OF LITERATURE and philosophical argument on the psychic probes of transference has, no doubt, created the possibility for an unheard of intensity of experience. Yet the results have proved a mixed blessing, confounding our hopes with the prospect of uncontrollable disorder — both in our arts and in our lives. The psycho-analytic process itself frees us — that is, it gives us the possibility of choice — by inducing an expansion of self-awareness. But self-awareness may build emotional prisons for the unwary individual as well; for the knowledge of our own disorder may freeze the capacity for action, thereby making the possibility of choice irrelevant. There is a point in Doris Lessing's *The Golden Notebook* where the novelist-heroine, Anna, despairing of her attempts to record her own experience realistically, decides to mechanically report each event of a single day in her life. Consequently, she passes the given day observing herself, as well as others, obsessively. The result is chaos. The experiment not only changes the events of a day but transforms Anna's attitude to herself; it gives her the sense of losing control, of being the prisoner of circumstance. For while observing herself Anna becomes incapable of initiating actions; events simply *happen* to her.

The Connection's immediate effect on the spectator may be the elation (or depression) induced by a newly acquired sense of freedom. But can the play really bear the burden of this freedom? Implicit in its challenge that we express ourselves freely is the destruction of the roles assigned us by society. Thus the play, exploiting the self-awareness it has induced, goads us into searching out new roles, for it has destroyed the ones with which we entered the theater. But, once more, is *The Connection* really capable of dealing with these demands? I doubt it. By this time, the reader may wonder whether, in the course of my argument, I have not used the play to point entirely too many morals. No doubt I have. But the refusal to carry so large a load is not the play's failure; its incapacities are only symptomatic of our social and esthetic difficulties. The very task *The Connection* sets itself — to dislodge our moral, epistemological, and esthetic assumptions — if brought off with success, creates the demand that it reorder the elements it has managed to disarray. Thus the play is asked to give us answers to the modern problems of ethics, epistemology, and criticism. But surely this is asking a bit much. To attempt all this would only diffuse the play's impact and thus reduce it to impotence; for the job of dislodging our values requires a concentrated psychological effect rather than a balanced attempt to create systematic order. And so, by the very performance of its task, *The Connection* deprives itself of wholeness; as a work of art it is necessarily partial, its structure incomplete. Since it takes a series of erratic stabs at the spectator, its sense of order is, at best, uncertain. Such is the price esthetic order must pay to the emotional needs of the historical moment: Since *The Connection* addresses itself almost exclusively to these immediate needs, its effects are not likely to have any permanence. In turn, lacking a sense of permanence, there is not likely to be any sense of order, and thus the play seems capable only of creating the conditions for change. The permanence of modernism — the perpetual renewal of our emotional needs fostered by our historical awareness — seems to imply the impermanence of our arts. There is thus no continuity in the histories of the contemporary arts: The emotional needs of succeeding moments are dealt with in fits and starts as they arise; their developmental logic is not linear, each instance being treated in historical isolation.

The Connection attempts to make us face the possibilities of freedom by plunging us (perhaps involuntarily) into reality. Instead of leading us to a consideration of *human nature* — that is, our innate capacities — the apparently random activities in the theater force us, for the moment, into an awareness of the world outside our own sensibilities. After all, we can hardly avoid being curious about the strange events going on around us. And herein rests one of the formal difficulties of the modern arts. At the end of *Dora,* Freud considered his patient to have attained a measure of freedom, meaning that she had ended "her flight from life into disease," and therefore "been reclaimed once more by the realities of life." Dora has been thrown into the swirl of experience by the work of science. This would seem to be the very goal of *The Connection,* yet Freud considers works of art to be a palliative, a shield against reality. But is this really the case with most modern literature? Does it not attempt to goad us into a direct confrontation with reality? By freeing us from the old sense of a permanent order, from the notion of an "essential" human being, does it not affirm the primacy of experience?

It can hardly be doubted that the novel has been the dominant literary form of our time. Its origins as well as its development during the eighteenth century were, not unexpectedly, related to the Enlightenment's empiricism, to its concern with the primacy of experience. The earliest novels — those of Defoe and Richardson, for example — pretended to be nonfiction: *Moll Flanders* masking itself as an autobiographical account, *Pamela*, going a step further, as an actual exchange of letters. These procedures released a good deal of creative energy by creating new possibilities for the usable range of emotions; but they created the conditions for artistic chaos as well. Most novels attempt to be a, more or less, realistic record of a life. If most lives — being free and unstructured — tend to be chaotic, what is to be the form of the novels representing them? This is the source of the perpetual difficulties and confusions experienced by modern realism; the source, indeed, of most of our critical cant. Making the novelist's task the forcible imposition of order on the disorganized materials of experience would, of course, resolve all artistic difficulties. But this move demands the payment of a heavy price, for by violating the canons of realism it would defeat the novel's very purpose.

The following entry is found in one of the notebooks kept by the heroine of *The Golden Notebook:*

The novel has become the function of the fragmented society, the fragmented consciousness. Human beings are so divided, are becoming more and more divided, *and more subdivided in themselves*, reflecting the world, that they reach out desperately, not knowing they do it, for information about other groups inside their own country, let alone about groups in other countries. . . . Yet I am incapable of writing the only kind of novel which interests me: a book powered with an intellectual and moral passion strong enough to create order, to create a new way of looking at life.[1]

For Anna, the arbitrary creation of order would involve nothing less than intellectual and emotional dishonesty, a falsifi-

[1] Doris Lessing, *The Golden Notebook* (New York, Toronto, London, 1963).

cation of her deepest commitments and feelings. It is impossible for her to reconcile the demands of realism with the intellectual qualities which she admires in the work of Thomas Mann — "the last of the writers in the old sense, who used the novel for philosophical statements about life." But perhaps Mann, more obviously than any novelist who has set himself a lesser task, points up the difficult relationship of realism to the traditional demands of art. *Doctor Faustus* is on one level an old-fashioned realistic novel: Its account of several lives is not only thoroughly believable but deeply moving as well. But then the endless philosophizing! The oppressive symbol-mongering! Does the order thus created really have much to do with the novel's life? Or is it no more than the artist's arbitrary imposition of his own concerns on his characters' experience? Mann's procedure is, at best, difficult to accept.

Today's most clamorous advocates of realism are, I suppose, the practitioners and theorists of the *nouveau roman*. The movement has so nearly buried us under its avalanche of theories that the few childish ideas implicit in the fiction itself now have the appearance of unfathomable profundities. Alain Robbe-Grillet, for example, has managed to bypass the significant problems raised by Doris Lessing's protagonist in the most simple, if ostrichlike fashion; for the goal of his novels is to give no more than a completely objective report of experience. What seems objective to Robbe-Grillet might, of course, strike the philosophically innocent reader of novels as being slightly fantastic. Robbe-Grillet apparently assumes that the mind is a blank on which experience impresses a series of pictures; after relating these impressions to each other by the principles of simple association, this blank somehow proceeds to construct hypotheses about the external world, thus figuring out (perhaps) just what is going on. Accepting this theory of perception can make the novelist's task either boringly simple or impossibly difficult. Robbe-Grillet's typical procedure, exemplified by *The Voyeur*, is to record the succession of pictures — both present perceptions and old ones stored away — flashing through a single mind and to allow the reader to reconstruct the sequence of events taking place in the external world.

It should be obvious that Robbe-Grillet's method is an unintentional parody, perhaps the *reductio ad absurdum*, of the empiricist theory of knowledge. Recall Hume's notion that the mind is no more than a composite of sense impressions, its only creative power being their juxtaposition. This drastically wrong view of how we acquire knowledge may have been justified by the specific historical context of the Enlightenment, but as Noam Chomsky has somewhat tartly observed:

There is surely no reason today for taking seriously a position that attributes a complex human achievement entirely to months (or at most years) of experience, rather than to millions of years of evolution or to principles of neural organization that may be even more deeply grounded in physical law.[2]

Yet the position has dominated modern psychology for years; worse, it has managed to influence much of the advanced thinking in contemporary literature. The results have usually been disastrous; indeed, often enough they have been utterly mindless. Both the *nouveau roman* and its somewhat elderly progenitor, the literature of the absurd, derive from the implications of empiricist psychology. Both *genres*

[2] Noam Chomsky, *Aspects of the Theory of Syntax* (Cambridge, Mass., 1965).

assume that the mind is incapable of making meaningful connections, thus leaving all sense experience in discrete units which, of themselves, have no pattern, no sense of order. Thus any literature which claims to be realistic and therefore faithful to the true principles of psychology must also, of necessity, be disordered. Now Hume had the good sense to see that there was something wrong with the empiricist philosophy of mind; that, in any case, the mind would generally manage to discover connections in almost anything, no matter what the actual degree of randomness. One cannot say the same for most contemporary theorists of the advance guard.

Clearly, the empiricist theory of knowledge has played a far from trivial role in the development of our literary forms. Its influence derives from its rejection of Descartes' claim that the form of our knowledge is innate. During the latter half of the seventeenth century, most British literary theorists began to reject the French neoclassical rules; in their stead, they stressed the direct examination of experience, which was to yield those rules which reflect the permanent features of human nature. The British critics' rejection of the arbitrary French rules, seemed to imply, as well, a rejection of Cartesian metaphysics in favor of good sense and the primacy of experience. Whatever their origin, the neoclassical rules were validated by French critics on the basis of the mind's innate structure: The forms of literature, they claimed, somehow correspond to (or are determined by) the form of the mind. Now the latter strikes me as being, in some way, obviously true. Yet the rules were so blatantly opposed to the dictates of common sense that a philosophy of mind which was at least arguable — and probably true — found itself dismissed out of hand. The associations ordinarily made between literary theory and the philosophy of mind, the passions thus aroused, are most richly illustrated in Swift's *The Battle of the Books* and *A Tale of a Tub*. In both, the neoclassical rules are not only satirically associated with the notion of innate ideas but, in turn, with religious enthusiasm, atheism, scholasticism, materialism, madness, and a host of other evils. It may seem ironic but hardly illogical that Diderot — whose commitment to the Enlightenment Swift would have despised — was also to associate the rules with innate ideas, rejecting them on the basis of the empiricism he shared with Swift. Further, Diderot considered Richardson's fiction, with its emphasis on experience and its disregard of neoclassic literary theory, to be his ally in the battle against the persistent influence of Descartes.

In spite of its illogicalities, the commitment of eighteenth-century men of letters to empiricism allowed literature a salutary sense of freedom, thus making large areas of experience, hardly touched on previously, accessible to all the arts. Yet in our time the literary consequences of empiricism have been corrosive. The notion of art as an experimental report of experience, combined with the unfounded assumption that we attain knowledge in an unstructured way, must eventually lead to chaos. There is an equal portion of pathos and comedy in Robbe-Grillet's need to bypass the implications of his own theories; he does so by taking the easy way out of the dilemmas posed by literary realism. *The Voyeur* is a work of elegance, precision, and order because Robbe-Grillet cheats: He abandons his empiricism and shamelessly manipulates the novel's protagonist, Mathias. To accomplish this, while yet remaining true to his literary theories, Robbe-Grillet makes some odd assumptions about our way of ordering knowledge. Mathias' perception, through which we see everything in the novel, has apparently been structured by a few childhood experiences. For example, he sees many objects in the shape of a figure "8," a perceptual set which relates to his early obsession for tying pieces of string in the usual manner. Curiously enough, even Mathias' journey around the island on which the novel's action takes place is in the shape of an 8. What results is the facile and mechanical ordering of an eighteenth-century *conte* [3]; an ordering based on the severe limitations Robbe-Grillet places not only on Mathias' perceptions but on the kind of mental activity he is capable of performing. We are not exactly certain about the succession of events in *The Voyeur:* Like Mathias, we must construct hypotheses. Yet this is of little importance, for what matters is the elegance of the arrangement, that the details fit as neatly as the clues in a detective story. Indeed, the novel's only subject seems to be epistemology rather than a concern for reality itself. But this strikes me as being disingenuous, if not downright dishonest; worse, it reflects a refusal to confront the complexities of human experience. Robbe-Grillet's demonstrably false and somewhat silly assumptions about our ways of attaining knowledge are, after all, little more than an excuse for his refusal to deal with the actual, and perhaps unwieldy, capacities of the mind. Thus the novel, in spite of Robbe-Grillet's claims that it consists of nothing more than objective reports, is turned into a trivial game of making mechanical connections — connections emptied of all meaning and human relevance.

Toward the conclusion of *The Golden Notebook,* Anna records the following:

[3] Nathalie Sarraute in *The Age of Suspicion* (New York, 1963) has claimed that the new novel's sole concern is with surface. Its lack of interest in character or psychological analysis allows "the literary object . . . to recapture the full outlines, the hard, smooth, finished aspect of fine classical works." It is curious to reflect that the psychologism scorned by the new novelists was instrumental in dissolving the old, and played out, classicism: That "finished aspect" often enough hid an empty interior.

I said to myself: I must write a play about Anna and Saul and the tiger. The part of my mind concerned with this play went on working, thinking about it, like a child moving bricks about a floor — a child, moreover, who has been forbidden to play, because she knew it was an evasion, making patterns of Anna and Saul and the tiger was an excuse not to think.

Similarly, Robbe-Grillet's fictional procedures (his patterning) constitute an abdication of both intellect and feeling. His version of reality is a falsification of experience, since it avoids almost everything which is pertinent to how we act, feel, make choices — in short, to how we live. Why anyone concerned with more than trivialities should evince any interest in the *nouveau roman* — and Robbe-Grillet is easily its most competent practitioner — is beyond me. That these molehills have been made into mountains, that they are taken as serious representations of, and statements about, how, we live, must surely reflect an abandonment of will, an evasion of human concern. Perhaps the matter is an unhappy symptom of the increasing impotence felt by today's literary intellectuals.

The freedom we owe the Enlightenment has also increased the possibility of chaos; its prospects have become real, and, as a result, we often respond with an obsession for order. *The Voyeur* is typical in this respect: Its devotion to objectivity for its own sake would seem to court total disorder, yet in performance its formalism is as strict as that of any neoclassic work painfully adhering to the rules. Cultural criticism, as I pointed out, developed in response to the prospects of disorder. Arnold's conclusion to his "Preface to *Poems*, Edition of 1853" should serve as an apt reminder of the problem's permanence:

If it is impossible for us, under the circumstances amidst which we live, to think clearly, to feel nobly, and to delineate firmly: if we cannot attain to the mastery of the great artists — let us, at least, have so much respect for our Art as to prefer it to ourselves: let us not bewilder our successors: let us transmit to them the practice of Poetry, with its boundaries and wholesome regulative laws, under which excellent works may again, perhaps, at some future time, be produced, not yet fallen into oblivion through our neglect, not yet condemned and cancelled by the influence of their eternal enemy, Caprice.

The Preface was Arnold's farewell to poetry. Recall that Arnold's abdication stemmed from his devotion to the classical idea of poetry as an imitation of reality; that, consequently, order in his poetry could only follow from order in the world, from the avoidance of chaos in life. The critic's task, then, is to create a world rational enough to warrant the poet's imitation. Arnold's admonition, we know, has rarely been heeded.

One modern development which derives from our sense of chaos is the notion that the chief task of poetry (of the arts) is to create its own autonomous order. Indeed, one of the more tiresome clichés of contemporary poetry is that a poem's identity — its state of being — is determined by the formal relationships it establishes amongst its own components. The whole tradition of Mallarmé bears witness to the pervasive influence of the idea. The theory implicit in this sort of poetry is most obviously reflected by our formalist criticism: It considers the elements of structure to constitute the poem's literary reality, thus reducing the task of criticism to the analysis of the formal order of images, sounds, plot, and so forth. How well a poem submits itself to this kind of analysis becomes, inevitably, the measure of its excellence. The immediate, and most visible, literary consequence of this critical mode in America was the flowering of a generation of poets — I refer, of course, to the disciples of John Crowe Ransom — whose works accorded with the formalist canons of the New Criticism, avoiding, as a consequence, any sub-

[293]

ject which raised the possibility of disorder — that is, anything which is vital to the management of our lives.

The ordering of life, rather than its imitation, was central to the goals Baudelaire set for poetry. He had, of course, been anticipated by the similar ambitions of many Romantics: The argument of Keats' "Ode On a Grecian Urn" will serve as an example. But Baudelaire's concern for the contemporary — for the immediacy of his surroundings, for the apparent chaos of city life — set the tone for so much later poetry, that we recognize it as being modern, of our own time. Baudelaire's search for order — expressing itself in strange juxtapositions, the use of synesthesia, and the exploration of odd areas of experience — is unconventional with a purpose, for it intends to shock us into a recognition of our difficult task, of the many connections which are to be made. The approach might, quite readily, degenerate into the solemn contemplation of colored ribbons, an activity already popular during the eighteenth century, or the performance of smell concerts, a diversion of mid-nineteenth-century Paris; worse, the attempt to shock might simply become an end in itself. Baudelaire spares us such trivializing, for he is convinced of the presence of hidden connections, secret meanings, which may be discovered by the poet's dedication to his very special task. His search may lead to the performance of psychic experiments, forays into the occult, even to the use of drugs. Once again, Baudelaire's seriousness of purpose — most especially when at play — helps him to avoid mere self-indulgence; yet the peculiar direction of this search for a hidden order, its implicit nonsense, makes childish abuses almost unavoidable. Has not the faddish pursuit of the occult been the bane (almost the undoing) of the advance guard for over a century?

We are told that experimentation of this sort is freeing. I

do not doubt it: The exploration of odd emotional and perceptual states does create unheard of possibilities; it gives us the feeling of an unbounded spaciousness. Yet the effect may be oddly restricting. The obsession with the occult is, after all, likely to remove most human activities — especially those performed in a social context — from the domain of art: that is, from the pursuit of order. I point to the drug-induced insanity of William Burroughs' *Naked Lunch*, if illustration is needed. But to turn to the more serious concerns of Baudelaire, the difficulties are apparent even there, for his survey of strange areas of feeling leads him to make connections which are intensely personal, bordering on caprice. In Baudelaire's poems, the most arcane insights take on the guise of a public act (one in which we may share), because his surprising flashes of understanding are given direction by the most strict formal procedures: His use of traditional stanzas and meters represents more than a way of holding the pieces together; it is, in fact, an attempt to escape the prison of his own idiosyncrasies. The dangers courted by an exclusive dependence on one's private sense of order are even more apparent in Baudelaire's prose poems. The scenes they portray are held together and given their meaning only through the strength of Baudelaire's vision, the persistence of his own sense of order. In the hands of someone with a lesser sense of artistic decorum, something like "The Poor Boy's Toy" could simply degenerate into a straining after odd effects, its lack of meaning matched by the chaos of its form.

The necessity to impose one's personal sense of order on experience seems to be almost unavoidable. It derives, to a degree, from the response of the early Romantics to the loss of faith in rational literary form: Coleridge is not untypical. He managed to resolve the thorny contradiction between the poet's major tasks — the honest representation of experience and feeling and their formal ordering — by his theory of the imagination. The latter is a *natural* mental faculty, available to all men, which has the capacity to perceive and create order of a degree far beyond simple associationism. The advantage of the theory is that it seems to allow the poet an escape from the necessity of performing a willful and private act: His capacity for complex organization derives, after all, from a universal operation of the mind, an innate idea. But unlike Descartes, Coleridge provides us with no formal, and therefore universal, procedures describing mental activity. And so the faculty of imagination appears to be something vaguely personal, a private gift of special individuals — of poets. Consequently, when the theory is put into practice, it creates dangers which we have already encountered in Wordsworth. The only thing which holds *The Prelude* together is the inescapable presence of Wordsworth's personal vision: It gives the poem uniformity of tone and thus convinces us that the life of the poet is an organic, and meaningful, whole. Further, we are capable of accepting Wordsworth's tone (his private sense of order) because it is, in most instances, relevant to the mainstream of our own experience. Contrast this to the unity, the consistency of tone, in Van Gogh's paintings: The work records a life which has been ordered by an obsessive vision of reality; a vision which borders on absolute privacy. Van Gogh's insane, and practically irresistible, swirls dominate everything; they are his reality, and, as such, they falsify our common experience. The paintings are — and this provides their order — a painfully beautiful record of one individual's pathology.

It should be clear that the attempt to order the external world may turn into an expression of solipsism. The obsessions of the self may, after all, constitute the only power which is capable of organizing our experience. On the other hand, our inability to make rational connections which derive from our own being — from our needs, from our own sense of humanity — may lead to the arbitrary imposition of formal schema on reality, schema which seem to bear no relation to the mind's innate order. We may be led a step further and conclude that all social habit (that is, the condition of almost all human contact) is without meaning, since the forms of society, perhaps society itself, seem to be unrelated to our internal structure. Finally, we are led to the conclusion that all evidence of order in the external world — indeed, all events, everything which occurs — is totally arbitrary.

I take these conclusions to be indefensible; indeed, irrelevant to the way we lead our lives. Yet they represent feelings which are real enough, which form a substantial part of all our nightmares. As such, these attitudes demand consideration; since they are irrational, they need to be derived from (and placed in) their historical context, as, in fact, I have been attempting to do. The substantial body of literature which has given voice to these feelings is usually referred to, in our current jargon, as the "absurd." The manner, one can hardly call it a style, has become everybody's favorite parlor game; ordinarily it has merely involved a submission to caprice, which quality, Arnold told us, is the death of poetry. Yet there is more to the matter than this. For some time, both solipsism and the desire to impose an arbitrary order on experience have represented an intellectual stance of a most compelling nature, its strength deriving from a concrete and significant historical development: the progress of that inwardness implied by the skeptical doubt. Reasonably enough, a literature of some substance has been generated by these attitudes — not only in the recent past but over the last two centuries. This literature has been saved from caprice, thus warranting serious attention, whenever it has been willing to ask questions about the relevance of both its philosophical speculations and formal experiments to actual human concerns.

In the course of an admiring essay on Samuel Beckett, Robbe-Grillet proposes that the chief characteristic of Beckett's work is its objectivity: The objects and the people on the stage are simply there; they are what they are. "In *Godot*," Robbe-Grillet writes, "there is no more thought than there is beautiful language." [4] Oddly enough, these words are intended as praise. Robbe-Grillet, somewhat capriciously, imposes his own esthetic on Beckett's play. If his claim were true, Beckett would be no more than another trivializer of the absurd. As a matter of fact, Beckett's plays are important precisely because they lack objectivity; they embody a personal vision whose intensity lends them their dramatic interest and form. But that *Endgame*, for example, should depend for its sense of order on the obsessive pursuit of a private vision raises the very problems I have just discussed.

Near the beginning of *Endgame* [5] there is this exchange between the play's two main characters:

HAMM: (*anguished*): What's happening, what's happening?
CLOV: Something is taking its course.

The game of chess is being played out. There is a set of rules which determines the characters' each move; yet they are not entirely conscious of what these rules are, obeying them helplessly as they assert themselves in some mysterious fashion.

[4] Alain Robbe-Grillet, *For a New Novel: Essays on Fiction*, trans. R. Howard (New York, 1965).
[5] Samuel Beckett, *Endgame* (New York, 1948).

An understanding of the moves is out of the question, there being no apparent relation between the rules of the mind and those of the world, the sequence of thoughts and that of actions. Hamm and Clov do not need to make Descartes' skeptical pretense, for they are, in fact, embodiments of the Cartesian doubt: It is their emotional reality. What do they know? That they doubt and that they suffer, the mutual presence of these two states, we shall see, being problematic. Outside of themselves — who knows? There is only the doubtful evidence of the senses to depend on. Like good empiricists, they have to build a world from their sense impressions. And so Clov, Hamm being blind, spends a good part of the play looking out of windows and at the audience through a telescope. He makes the discovery that all is "zero"; for if Clov begins with the skeptical doubt, depending wholly on experience for his epistemology, there will be no way of relating his sense impressions to each other, to himself, or to the external world. Thus for Hamm and Clov the doubt persists: It persists because the evidence of the senses provides them with no guarantee against it; left to themselves, the senses are incapable of deriving rules which reliably describe the relation of mind to perception, mind to the external world. Consider the following:

HAMM: If you leave me how shall I know?
CLOV: (briskly) Well you simply whistle me and if I don't come running it means I've left you.

But does it? At play's end the audience knows that Clov, although he has not responded to Hamm's whistle, is still on the stage. How is the blind Hamm to know?

Their skeptical doubts have left Hamm and Clov in a world composed of their unrelated perceptions. Now Robbe-Grillet would forbid the playwright or novelist to charge this situation with anxiety or, indeed, any feeling: Doing so would amount to no more than an indulgence of humanist sentimentality; it would have no relation to objective fact. Yet this is simply not so, certainly not in *Endgame* and, Robbe-Grillet's claims aside, not even in *The Voyeur*, where it is impossible for the reader not to feel the pathos of Mathias' hopeless struggle to make sense of his chaotic impressions. As for Hamm and Clov, they are, of course, incapable of accepting their situation. At one point in the play, "Clov begins to pick up the objects lying on the ground." "What are you doing?" asks Hamm. The answer: "Putting things in order . . . I love order. It's my dream." Clov does no more, or less, than give expression to a basic human impulse — and both he and Hamm are, after all, recognizably human, not bundles of perceptions. Yet where are they to discover the order which constantly eludes them? They discuss the matter:

HAMM: Nature has forgotten me.
CLOV: There's no more nature.
HAMM: No more nature! You exaggerate.
CLOV: In the vicinity.
HAMM: But we breathe, we change! We lose our hair, our teeth! Our bloom! Our ideals!
CLOV: Then she hasn't forgotten us.
HAMM: But you say there is none.

The classical notion of nature — that is, the concept of an ordered and meaningful world — represents no more than a faint possibility, a vague hope, for Hamm and Clov. Nature's only perceptible regularity appears to be their wasting away. But what is the meaning of this inevitable process? Of what relevance is it to anything apart from Hamm and Clov? The innate longing for order is foiled, with dispiriting regularity, in its attempts to connect consciousness with dead matter: "There's no more nature." What does the mind's passion for order have to do with the external world?

Doubt has not been for Hamm and Clov the beginning of understanding, as it was for Descartes. The significance of their verbal difficulties should now begin to emerge with some clarity. Words are incapable of assigning meanings, for both the mind and the external world (where "something is taking its course") appear to function according to separate sets of rules. What is more, it is impossible to derive meaning from experience alone: "Imagine if a rational being came back to earth," Hamm asks, "Wouldn't he be liable to get ideas into his head if he observed us long enough." Surely not, given *Endgame*'s empiricist assumptions; forming concepts requires mental capacities far beyond the simple association of perceptions. Thus Beckett's "absurd" verbal procedures reflect a good deal more than the simple wish to play childish games, for they are generated by philosophical beliefs, whatever their formal validity, whose emotional foundations are real enough.

If nothing else, at least the yearning for order, both in the self and in the external world, seems to be actual. But given the disjunction between mind and the events of the world, who is to know whether any order perceived by Hamm and Clov actually exists? "I once knew a madman," Hamm tells Clov,

who thought the end of the world had come. He was a painter — and engraver. I had a great fondness for him. I used to go and see him, in the asylum. I'd take him by the hand and drag him to the window. Look! There! All that rising corn! And there! Look! the sails of the herring fleet! All that loveliness! He'd snatch away his hand and go back into his corner. Appalled. All he had seen was ashes. . . . It appears the case is . . . was not so . . . unusual.

Similarly, each attempt at creating order made by Clov or Hamm reflects, without fail, the world of their private obsessions. Hamm's initial utterance in the play is, "Me — to play." The words refer both to the moves made in the end-game and to the role being played by Hamm. The necessity to create a role and, consequently, order is illustrated by the running story Hamm tells on himself. The following makes the point:

CLOV: Oh, by the way, your story?
HAMM: (*surprised*) What story?
CLOV: The one you've been telling yourself all your days.
HAMM: Ah you mean my chronicle?

To create a role for himself — to give himself an identity — Hamm must have a past, he must be a character placed inside an historical narrative. But we do not know whether his story is to be believed, for it is outside Hamm's immediate field of perception: The events of the past seem to lie beyond the possibility of belief; they are neither true nor false. And so the following lament:

HAMM: I was never there.
CLOV: Lucky for you.
HAMM: Absent, always. It all happened without me. I don't know what's happened.

There can be no meaningful relation among any sequence of events (that is, order) in Hamm's life, for he can make no causal connections, construct no narrative leading from the past into the present. In their search for order, Hamm and Clov are reduced to an acceptance of the arbitrary rules of the game ("something . . . taking its course") or to an equally arbitrary imposition of their own vision upon the world. And indeed, they do see the world as ashes.

But why this particular vision rather than another? The question is of some importance because *Endgame*'s dramatic power does not derive from the comic disjunctions created by its philosophical assumptions but from the unrelieved starkness of Hamm's and Clov's suffering. Its reality is the one thing they never doubt: Yet, what is its source? Is it really to be derived from their philosophic concerns? Or from their frustrated desire for order? The play itself will not permit these facile connections for it puts us in the presence of a misery so overwhelming that it is beyond rational motivation. For example:

HAMM: Yesterday! What does that mean? Yesterday!
CLOV: (*violently*) That means that bloody awful day, long ago, before this bloody awful day.

Clov's outburst takes place directly before he makes the following observations about meaning:

I use the words you taught me. If they don't mean anything any more, teach me others. Or let me be silent.

Do difficulties concerning meaning or even the impossibility of communication, call for Hamm's and Clov's sheer physical revulsion from life? Do they call for the following reaction?

HAMM: A flea! Are there still fleas?
CLOV: On me there's one . . .
HAMM: (*very perturbed*) But humanity might start from there all over again! Catch him, for the love of God!

If the source of the difficulty is to be located in the problem of meaning, why such overwhelming disgust, rather than the (perhaps painful) twinges of Wittgensteinian mental cramp?

The answer, it seems clear, lies in the nature of Beckett's private obsessions: The connection between a nagging philosophical problem and the extremes of suffering is made both in his mind and by his feelings. If such is the case, why should anyone but Beckett — or someone similarly aggrieved — at all care about the play? Here, then, lies Beckett's dramatic task: If the plight of Hamm and Clov is to have its appropriate effect, the connection of thought to feeling, of semantic difficulties to physical disgust, must become a reality for the audience. Beckett is charged with convincing us that the madman's vision of ashes is, if not our vision of the moment, at least one which we find conceivable. Making us laugh at illogic is fairly easy game; convincing us of its emotional and philosophic seriousness is quite another. To do so, *Endgame* will have to resort to transference in attaining its end. This being the case, who would accuse Beckett of playing capricious games? His unusual — indeed, extraordinary — dramatic and verbal procedures intend to accomplish nothing less than the transformation of the logic with which we order reality.

The play's ending will serve as an example. Beckett has, throughout, been trying to convince us that there are no endings, that human lives, having no apparent pattern, do not develop. There is no conceivable resolution implicit in *Endgame*'s pattern of action or in the makeup of its characters. Yet we do anticipate resolutions; the notion is so deeply ingrained as to be an element not only of our dramatic expectations but of our expectations concerning life itself. In order to change our attitudes, Beckett must play on the very predispositions with which we enter the theater: therefore his use of methods which give the appearance of illogic, of a language which seems both artificial and disjointed. As the play proceeds, it is impossible to tell whether it is approaching its end: clearly, it could go on endlessly. Given these circumstances, who can think of a logical conclusion? Suddenly, this surprising development:

CLOV: Let's stop playing!
HAMM: Never! Put me in my coffin.
CLOV: There are no more coffins.
HAMM: Then let it end! With a bang! Of darkness! And me? Did anyone ever have pity on me?
CLOV: What? Is it me you're referring to?

HAMM: An aside, ape! Did you never hear an aside before? I'm
         warming up for my last soliloquy.

When at last Clov, rather than Hamm, begins the soliloquy,
he breaks into formal dramatic speech. Looked at in isolation, sentences such as, "Here's the place, stop, raise your
head and look at all that beauty," read more like natural
speech than anything else in the play; but listened to in the
play's context, they sound utterly false and are clearly intended as parody. And so Hamm's and Clov's attempts to
draw events to a formal conclusion simply dissolve, for they
cannot be taken seriously: Logic will not readily allow itself
to be imposed on a world of illogic without it being turned
into farce. Forgetting dramatic formalisms, Hamm must
proceed to the true ending — which is no ending at all. He
throws the whistle, which he has been using to call Clov, to
the audience. It is their turn to keep the game going, for the
play has prepared them for the contemplation of its final
tableau: Hamm sitting in his chair, a handkerchief over his
head, while Clov stands near the door, apparently ready to
leave. Yet who knows? It is impossible for Hamm to determine whether Clov is there or not. The audience, in turn,
will never know what his intentions are: Its task is surely
not to bring the play to its end but to consider the relationship between men's unnamed miseries and their passion for
order.

THE THEATER OF THE ABSURD's claim of Georg Büchner as a
grandparent is hardly in the order of a surprise: Practically
everyone has. The history of the theater has included numerous versions of *Woyzeck*, all, no doubt, equally valid.
Scholars probably consider this confusing state of affairs

with alarm, but Woyzeck's several interpretations — as naturalist, political, or psychological drama — might simply be a
necessary function of its experimental nature. The play is
composed of a series of short, spare, and starkly realistic
scenes; being nearly autonomous, they can be shifted almost
at will. Büchner's death before completion of the play leaves
us at the mercy of its editors: We are certain neither of its
ending nor of the precise order of its scenes. Yet this hardly
matters. Which is not to say that my intent is to put Woyzeck in the company of some of our more ludicrous experiments in randomness: for example, the book or musical score
whose pages can be shuffled at will. Woyzeck's randomness
— though it may, like its modern offspring, have originated
from the skeptical doubt — is hardly intended as an invitation to disorder. Quite the contrary: The play, if nothing
else, demands that we give the problem of order our most
serious consideration.

The play's opening finds Woyzeck, an ordinary soldier,
shaving the Captain, and listening to his half-ironic sermon:

Easy, Woyzeck, take it easy. One thing after the other! You're
making me dizzy. You'll finish up early and what'll I do with ten
minutes on my hands? Use your head, Woyzeck. You've got
thirty years to live. Thirty! . . . What are you going to do with
that horrible stretch of time? Figure it out for yourself, Woyzeck! [6]

It is a question of ordering one's life; and being a modern,
Woyzeck will have to "figure it out" for himself ("*Teil Er
sich ein*"). While Woyzeck keeps responding in mechanical
fashion, the Captain accuses him of leading a disorderly life;
the accusation, interestingly enough, leads to the following
sermon:

[6] Theodore Hoffman's translation of Woyzeck, printed in *The Modern Theatre*, Vol. 1, ed. Eric Bentley (Garden City, N.Y., 1955),
though dull, is generally accurate. I have changed serious distortions
and have included an occasional German word for the sake of clarity.

You have no morals. Morals! That's what a man's got who behaves morally! Understand? It's a good word. You went and got yourself a child without the blessing of the Church, as our right reverend chaplain put it. "Without the blessing of the Church." Now I didn't invent the phrase.

The Captain's connection between immorality and disorder is apt, for Woyzeck rushes about like a madman in order to meet the expenses of keeping his mistress. Clearly, if morality is to be the source of human order, the play will need to consider some aspects of the Enlightenment's legacy for ethics. Just what, for instance, is the foundation of moral judgment? The Captain seems to assume that there is some sort of natural moral order, embodied in the church, for he "didn't invent the phrase" (*"es ist nicht von mir"*). But who in the play takes the church seriously? Does a moral order indeed exist at all? Morals, the Captain has told us, are "what a man's got who behaves morally" (*"wenn man moralisch ist"*)! The concept in itself is no more than "a good word." These difficulties weigh heavily upon the play, for its principal characters will have to perform actions which involve the relation of instinct to received morality. If both morality and instinct derive from nature, the order of the characters' actions — the choices they make — should hardly be problematic.

When Marie, Woyzeck's mistress, succumbs to the physical attractions of the Drum-Major, she attempts to justify her betrayal of Woyzeck with this consoling bit of sophistry:

I'm such a rotten creature. I could stab myself. Ah, what a world! Everything is going to the devil, man and woman!

Marie, being a creature of nature, has no moral choices available to her: having looked at the Drum-Major, there is nothing to do but to sleep with him. Thus her self-condemnation is quite irrelevant, and her excuse not as lame as it might at first appear. In another scene, after Marie has invited the Drum-Major to lay his hands on her, there is the following exchange:

DRUM-MAJOR: You've got the devil in your eyes.
MARIE: What's the difference?

And what of Woyzeck? Upon discovering these goings-on, he too is forced to puzzle over questions of morality. What is he to do? Does he have the right to make a moral judgment upon Marie at all? They are, after all, not married. In any case, what does the notion of virtue mean to Woyzeck? Here is his answer to the Captain's preachments:

Yes, Captain. Virtue. I don't have much of that. But you see, what happens to us ordinary people — that's just nature. Now, if I was a gentleman and wore a hat and a watch and a cane, and could talk smooth — well, I'd like to be virtuous too.

Thus when Woyzeck vengefully murders Marie, he has surely not done so out of moral outrage. Does his act even involve the matter of free choice? How can we know, given the uncertainty of the causes involved. For Woyzeck, in order to support his child and mistress, has made himself the subject of a curious medical experiment, one which could hardly fail to affect his body and mind. At one point, the doctor conducting the experiment, having been promised Woyzeck's urine, goes into a fury when he catches him pissing against a wall. Woyzeck's understandable excuse, that nature called, is not taken kindly to by the doctor:

When Nature calls! When Nature calls! Nature! Didn't I prove that the *musculus constrictor vesicae* can be controlled by the will? Woyzeck, Man is free! Through man alone shines the individual's will to freedom! Can't hold his water? Have you been eating your peas, Woyzeck? Nothing but peas. Cruciferae. Remember that! This will cause a revolution in scientific thought, I'll blow it to bits! Urea, o.10., Ammonium hydrochlorate, hyperoxidic. Woyzeck, can't you piss again? Go in there again and try.

Free will barely seems to stand a chance against a steady diet of peas. And so, what causal relationship is there between Woyzeck's thoughts and actions? Has he committed murder because of the peas? One might as well put the blame on his paranoiac visions or his economic deprivation. Perhaps, as with his urine, it was simply the call of nature: Woyzeck the natural man! And here is the crux of the play's moral difficulties — and also of its interest: *Woyzeck* has stressed that the state of nature is without moral content. Consider the following incident at a fair visited by Marie and Woyzeck. A barker is trying to convince the audience of his horse's intelligence; the animal, quite naturally, "mounts up indecently." The barker's reaction:

All right, put society to shame! This beast, as you can see for yourselves, is still in a state of nature — not ideal nature of course. . . . Take a lesson from him. But first consult your doctor. It may prove highly dangerous. This has meant: Man, be natural! You are created from dust, sand, and dung. Do you want to be more than dust, sand, and dung?

There are more possible motives for Woyzeck's act than any single hypothesis is capable of accounting for. In spite of the doctor's scientific pretenses, he is incapable of predicting the course of human action. "Anything can happen," Woyzeck tells us. "God! Anything can happen." The absence of causal relationships between events as well as the disparity of intent and completed action make the exact sequence of *Woyzeck's* scenes irrelevant and, of far greater importance, deprive the play of an immanent moral order. As a result, Büchner must empty the play of even the hint of moral didacticism: Its events cannot be ordered on the basis of a moral vision which the author expects us to share with him.

[309]

It would be a lie: a sentimentality arbitrarily imposed upon the events. The characters in **Woyzeck** do not share a common moral code; some, as we have seen, do not possess one at all; those capable of making judgments — and of connecting events — do so as best they can, basing them, ultimately, on their private notion of good and evil. In the case of the doctor, moral judgment is a logical impossibility: Actions have their causes; he explains them, constructs hypotheses, and makes diagnoses. His response to Woyzeck's description of his frightening visions? "Woyzeck, you have an *aberratio.*" A word: It explains nothing, and therefore does not begin to order the events in Woyzeck's life.

We come to this unavoidable conclusion: Both **Woyzeck's** order and its moral significance must emerge from those qualities of insight, from those commitments, which the play awakens in the spectator. In short, its performance is a moral experiment, demanding that each individual in the audience test his moral hypotheses against his experience in the theater. Thus the skeptical doubt's encroachment upon the foundations of moral judgment is a necessary prerequisite for the proper effect of the play: given a moral order firmly shared by audience and playwright, its form could only give the appearance of chaos.

Since Büchner's time, the doubt has performed more of its corrosive work. Toward the end of *The Golden Notebook* Anna, writing about herself, remarks:

She [Anna] concluded that any act she might make would be without faith, that is, without faith in "good" and "bad," but simply a sort of provisional act.

With her earlier commitment to socialism still intact, Anna might have seen Woyzeck as the victim of an unjust capitalism. But what is she to do with her present moral emptiness, her lack of faith in the notion of morals itself? Is she to take the play as an expression of a destructive nihilism? Some of her contemporaries clearly would. Transforming *Woyzeck* into one of our lesser dramas of the absurd, they would amuse themselves with an unearned sneer at the very idea of a moral order. To consider life, indeed the world, as an appropriate object of morally undirected experiments — the attitude, I suppose, provides the most titillating of all possible roads to disaster. The experiment becomes its own end; the price to be paid by humanity irrelevant. "This quality," Anna writes in one of her notebooks,

this intellectual "I wanted to see what was going to happen," "I want to see what will happen next," it is something loose in the air, it is in so many people one meets, it is in me. It is part of what we all are. It is the other face of: It doesn't matter.

And so we continue with our experiments, with this bullying quest for order which, oddly enough, expresses itself as destructive chaos. We continue regardless of the consequences: whether these be the immolation of Hiroshima, the destruction of Chinese family life, permanent damage to the upper atmosphere, or the defoliation of Vietnam. All, to be sure, are fun experiments. Similarly in the arts: The nature of the artistic experiment itself — not the order such an experiment might lead to — becomes the sole objective of any work. Büchner's clear insight into the possibility of these dangers makes him the only playwright of his time who strikes us as our contemporary. But why not go further? His understanding of the Enlightenment's possibilities and dangers made him the nineteenth century's only indispensable playwright before Ibsen. That *Woyzeck* resists the temptation to be an experiment for its own sake — this, surely, is a measure of Büchner's stature, of his dedication to the artist's concern for order.

A nna's intuition that modern lives are necessarily char-
acterized by compulsive, and random, experimentation — Has
this not been the private nightmare of men of intellect since
the Enlightenment? Feeling this, the passion to impose
order, whatever its nature, becomes the unavoidable occupation of the life of mind. Consider that unintentional (and,
therefore, highly instructive) modern, Lewis Carroll. His
modernity is located in his doubts concerning the foundations of human order. Our unrequited passion for making
connections, Carroll saw, may lead to the imposition of arbitrary rules on the external world; an imposition which may
fill life with absurdities. At the conclusion of both *Alice's
Adventures in Wonderland* and *Through the Looking-
Glass*,[7] Alice rejects imaginary worlds made capricious, and
threatening, by their use of arbitrary rules. At journey's end,
she has quit her argument with these worlds, for they have
their own incontestable logic; common sense simply leads her
to brush them aside. Yet what she has rejected quite clearly
includes a recognizable part of the real world; in fact, some
of the most absurd rules carry the weight of social authority.
And here lies the source of Alice's confusion: To grow up is
to learn the way of the world, to accept the authority of one's
elders; yet which of the world's rules are meaningful, which
simply arbitrary nonsense?

Near the end of *Through the Looking-Glass*, Alice, having
just been awakened, attempts to discover whether her kitten
is identical to the Red Queen of her dream. Carroll describes
her unsuccessful efforts:

[7] Lewis Carroll, *Alice's Adventures in Wonderland* and *Through the
Looking-Glass*, Signet Classics (New York, 1960).

It is a very inconvenient habit of kittens (Alice had once made the remark) that, whatever you say to them, they *always* purr. "If they would only purr for 'yes,' and mew for 'no,' or any rule of that sort," she had said, "so that one could keep up a conversation! But how *can* you talk with a person if they *always* say the same thing?"

On this occasion the kitten only purred; and it was impossible to guess whether it meant "yes" or "no."

Alice's binary logic is arbitrary — even for humans. Its irrelevance to the formal interpretation of meaning has been attested to by the failures of machine translation and the inadequacy of various behavioral models for the learning of language. Yet the lesson of Alice's many attempts to communicate with the strange creatures of her adventures is clear: Worlds, to have meaning, must be governed by rules, by a logic of some sort. In his *Symbolic Logic*, Carroll makes some remarks which are to the point:

The writers . . . of the Logical text-books . . . take . . . a more humble position than is at all necessary. They speak of the Copula of a Proposition . . . as if it were a living, conscious Entity, capable of declaring for itself what it chose to mean. . . . In opposition to this view, I maintain that any writer of a book is fully authorised in attaching any meaning he likes to any word or phrase he intends to use. If I find an author saying, at the beginning of his book, "Let it be understood that by the word '*black*' I shall always mean '*white*', and that by the word '*white*' I shall always mean '*black*'," I meekly accept his ruling, however injudicious I may think it.

And so, with regard to the question whether a Proposition is or is not to be understood as asserting the Existence of its Subject, I maintain that every writer may adopt his own rule, provided of course that it is consistent with itself and with the accepted facts of Logic.[8]

Carroll's formalism may do service for a textbook; something of the sort is, no doubt, a necessity for constructing a logical

---

[8] Quoted in *The Annotated Alice*, ed. M. Gardner (Cleveland and New York, 1960).

calculus; but when applied to actual communication, its use may prove to be somewhat confusing. Humpty Dumpty illustrates Carroll's maxims in action:

"When *I* use a word," Humpty Dumpty said, in rather a scornful tone, "it means just what I choose it to mean — neither more nor less."

"The question is," said Alice, "whether you *can* make words mean so many different things."

"The question is," said Humpty Dumpty, "which is to be master — that's all."

Everyone is his own master, of course. The result is chaos; but chaos which poses an important question. We are asked whether life will allow the imposition of any formal calculus it pleases us to choose; and if the answer be affirmative, whether this calculus will accomplish anything more than an internal ordering of relationships. Consider this exchange between the Red Queen and Alice:

"We had *such* a thunderstorm last Tuesday — I mean one of the last set of Tuesdays, you know."

Alice was puzzled. "In *our* country," she remarked, "there's only one day at a time."

The Red Queen said, "That's a poor thin way of doing things. Now *here*, we mostly have days and nights two or three at a time, and sometimes in the winter we take as many as five nights together — for warmth, you know."

"Are five nights warmer than one night, then?" Alice ventured to ask.

"Five times as warm, of course."

The Red Queen knows her set theory as well as any bright child versed in the New Mathematics: But there appears to be a problem concerning the existential status of her sets.

Logic has released a host of absurdities. The irrelevant application of arbitrary mental constructs to experience may create occasions for comedy, but the resulting confusions, inevitably followed by a sense of frustration, will most likely elicit reactions of anger. In both Alice books, the threat of violence is the inseparable companion of logic-chopping; their intimacy leads to those final anarchic eruptions which lend Alice's fanciful dreams the quality of nightmare. Carroll's point is not, modern absurdists should be warned, that all rules deserve to be tossed aside; rather, since they are arbitrary, those rules needed to keep society in good order must rely, ultimately, on the strong backing of convention and authority; only these have the power to relate logic to the world — unless it be common sense; and, as Alice's encounters have amply illustrated, there is preciously little of the latter in any world.

Yet allowing Carroll's assumptions, the absurdists may, after all, have a point. How much life is there left in those conventions which, according to Carroll, offer the only firm foundation for morals? Very little, I should think. The very possibility of the Alice books marks an advanced point in their decline. Then why not a random happening? Why not absurdist games? Would they not be preferable to the violent reactions elicited by the imposition of arbitrary rules? But recall the differences concerning human possibilities which separate *The Connection* from a happening. Human beings, we know, do create rules ordering their actions: Are they as arbitrary as both Carroll and the absurdists would have them? At one point in *Alice in Wonderland*, the Gryphon and the Mock Turtle try to give Alice a description of a Lobster-Quadrille. What results is a torrent of puns, word distortions, and paradoxes; the strange creatures create their own logic, though it seems to have some relation to ordinary human discourse. By its violation of our ordinary expectations, the scene generates a wildly funny Marx Brothers atmosphere. But the comic effect owes its power to our sure knowledge that the rules being momentarily upended have a real foundation, that they have a permanence which will withstand the onslaught of the most violent logical games. Our uncertainties concerning their foundations, even our skepticism, hardly give us the right to deny the reality of the rules. When the Pigeon, in *Alice in Wonderland*, accuses Alice of being a serpent, this exchange follows:

"I *have* tasted eggs, certainly," said Alice, who was a very truthful child; "but little girls eat eggs quite as much as serpents do, you know."

"I don't believe it," said the Pigeon; "but if they do, why, then they're a kind of serpent: that's all I can say."

Now we *know* that some very fundamental principle in the logic of classification (a notoriously slippery subject) is being violated; indeed, we know this with a convincing degree of certainty, though we are unsure of just what is wrong. Unless our doubts have progressed to the point of pathology, turning us into characters from a Beckett play, unless we wish to give up our humanity, turning ourselves into snakes, we shall have to assume that the capacity for meaning and order is somehow grounded in our biological and social natures.

And Carroll does, after all, make the assumption. The moves in *Through the Looking Glass* may be ordered by the arbitrary rules of chess; but human action, as Carroll makes abundantly clear, is not. And so, to repeat a point: Carroll is not simply playing absurdist games. The effect of *Through the Looking Glass* — the serious consideration which it finally commands — derives not from the rules of chess themselves but from what they suppress. The order imposed by the game of chess is tenuous, for the book's abundant life is always at the point of bursting out of the game's restrictions and scrambling the rules. Both Alice books are about the very real pains of growing up. In *Through the Looking Glass*, Alice must put up with the rules in order to become a

Queen. To grow up, Carroll believes, is to be burdened with the necessity of hiding more and more, of often having to ignore the dictates of common sense. How else is one to keep to the rules? Faced with the necessity of imposing order, the rules we are forced to invent separate us from reality and thereby create the threat of violence and chaos; which threat, in turn, calls for the imposition of more rules. Thus, to grow up is to be forced into an awareness, and acceptance, of the disjunction between logic and reality; it is to be forced into the endless task of fighting chaos. Carroll was incapable of accepting this violation of wholeness: therefore, to follow William Empson's brilliant speculations,[9] his fascination with the world of childhood, with the image of the child as swain, not yet deprived of pastoral wholeness.

Carroll's literary method is made possible by the historical necessity for Kant's famous question, "How is pure mathematics possible?" Kant's magisterial effort to discover and formalize the foundations of knowledge was meant to still, once and for all, the skeptical doubt. About the possibility of knowledge, including mathematics, Kant expressed little, if any, anxiety. What of us? About mathematics, we are not so sure, for Carroll's formalism still provides only one of several equally doubtful answers. Kant's question, as we all know, has had important implications for mathematical physics. Is a mathematical physical theory really possible? The scandal of modern physics — and, ironically, the reason for its success — lies in its abandonment of the notion of a theory as a representation of physical reality; an abandonment made necessary by the desire for a unified theory, that is, the quest for total order. Some of the deeper thinkers in the modern arts have attempted to use this development in physics as a justification for their own games, for their arbitrary construc-

[9] See *Some Versions of Pastoral*.

tion of rules unrelated to the world of feeling or experience. Pure formalism, the notion that a work of art's sole reality is located in its internal relationships, has found its advocates, propagandists, and practitioners in all the arts. But the analogy is dangerous. Surely one ought to recognize that the failure of physical theory to be a representation of reality, its exclusive concern with the consistency of its equations, might indicate that there is something seriously wrong with physics. Experimental physics' current obsession with experiments which will either undermine the unifying hypotheses of the past decades or save them by the creation of new, and more ghostly, particles hardly strikes me as a sign of robust health.

I take the almost exclusive concern for formal consistency, shown by some of our arts, to be no more than the reverse side of chaos. If we take the imposed relationships of a closed system to be the only measure of order, then, who knows, the world as a whole might indeed be totally disordered; and, to complete the vicious circle, if there is nothing but chaos, any arbitrary order we impose will do. The point is illustrated, almost comically, by the current situation in musical composition. The two most vocal groups on the scene — and their talent for propaganda seems at least as brilliant as that for music — are the proponents of aleatory (random) and serial (totally organized) composition. Now the major struggle of music throughout the nineteenth century was both to attain more freedom and to organize the expression of that freedom in a manner more wholly organic than had previously been possible. The example of Wagner, his work being so wholly inclusive of the century's concerns, is of some use. The purpose of his revolutionary, and freeing, experiments was not only to unify all the elements of opera into a *Gesamtkunstwerk* but to make the latter relevant to the needs of the national consciousness, indeed to effect the transformation of men and of society. Music drama, the audience, society, myth, and history — all were to be as one. In its way, the grand effort was Wagner's attempt to rectify the failures of 1848. Thus the derivation of the entire *Ring* from its first few chords reflects a great deal more than Wagner's astounding talent for organization; the cohesion of inner relationships is not its own end but a means of eliciting a specific human response. Wagner's freeing effect eventually led to the much advertised dissolution of tonality early in our century. Schönberg's consequent attempt to order tones in a radically new way is well known, though rarely understood. His methods of organization, further developed by his followers, have, more or less innocently, fathered the serialists' campaign, headed by chief strategist Milton Babbitt, to develop mathematical procedures which will totally organize — indeed predict — the sounds of any musical composition. If this were indeed possible, it would of course destroy music's capacity for surprise — an esthetic quality which I formerly assumed to be of some importance. But then, I had not yet learned that esthetic qualities are an illusion. Babbitt, using an impenetrable jargon, has tried to justify serial procedures on the basis of his somewhat naïve version of logical positivism. We begin with the assumption that esthetic judgments (the words "good" and "bad," "pleasing" or "displeasing") are meaningless. As a consequence, if music is to become a subject of rational — that is, scientific — discourse, its methods of organization must correspond to those used by science. The serialists' notion of a valid scientific theory, it comes as no great surprise, is that of an internally consistent model expressed in the language of mathematics. Having accomplished this much, the serialists are now ready for the ultimate in serial composition: a work generated by the mathematics fed into a computer. Owing to the current feverish pace of scientific research, we have already had the good fortune, at so early a date, to witness the composition of a *Computer Cantata*.

These procedures have the (perhaps not incidental) effect of making the listener's experience irrelevant: an unexpected boon for the criterion of simplicity, for it eliminates the bothersome necessity for dealing with the composition's cultural and historical contexts. But if we require that the modern work of art create the conditions for transference, what are we to make of all this? The question is irrelevant, for the serialists are not concerned with the affective uncertainties which surround a work of art. The mathematical procedures become their own end; the composer, in turn, becomes an expert in the theory of groups, a builder of models. Since we cannot meaningfully say that a model is either good or bad, only that it is consistent or inconsistent, the formal analysis of the work replaces the acts of listening and judging. The ear, in short, is irrelevant. The predictable result is that we lose any sense of what music *is*, of what we expect it to do. At a concert, we may hear beeps or electronic gurgles or, the frequencies being too high for the human ear, nothing. In the face of this, the only function available to criticism may be the act of discovering just what the damned hubbub is.

Such are the ways of creativity and the search for order! Considering the drift of the serialists' efforts, one can only conclude that their practices are based on the assumption that music lacks innate principles of order; for clearly they have not provided us with a mathematical theory of musical creativity but with a few trivial procedures for organizing — not music but sounds. But to say that music has no immanent structure — or at least a structure which relates to the act of hearing — leads, inevitably, to the conclusion that it is random. Thus aleatory music. Cage, Stockhausen, and their less articulate disciples justify their sporting activities by invoking the indeterminacy principle of modern physics: If all those particles do not know where they are going, then it becomes nothing less than the duty of music to do the same. Thus musical performance (composition?) becomes the occasion for free creativity — no, for free play. Since men seem to be incurably committed to the search for meaning, these activities want interpretation, of course. This need is usually provided for, in the writings of both Cage and Stockhausen, by the obscurantist assumption that there exists a secret connection, unknowable to men, between all the random events in the universe; that everything, therefore, has meaning, though we cannot say just what it is. I pointed to the dangers of this notion while discussing Baudelaire's search for correspondences. The difference was that Baudelaire's mystical ideas were part of a purposeful search for order; an order which, he assumed, the stringent practice of his art was capable of elucidating. By simply allowing things to happen, aleatory music seriously distorts human reality; indeed, it falsifies the impulse which underlies all art and creativity. The notion of randomness is, after all, a denial of the existence of human will.

ALL THIS BEING SAID, have we not had our fill of pious pronouncements, of pompous admonitions, concerning the necessity of order in the arts? I am, as I said at the outset, a modern — as, indeed, anyone who pretends to be intellectually and emotionally alive must be. The portion of modernity is the certain knowledge that doubts about order are an inescapable part of our lives. We cannot rid ourselves of these

doubts without falsifying the past, without mindlessly un-
burdening ourselves of all historical knowledge. In themselves, laments about our disorders seem as relevant to the
needs of the moment — that is, to the task of criticism — as
the nostalgia of a sixteenth-century Christian for the
Ptolemaic system. Our disease will not be moralized away,
for our skepticism has put us beyond the blandishments of the
preacher. We must ask the difficult questions, rather than
turning on them. What use are we to make, both in life and
in art, of our present disorders? And how are these to be related to what is left of our traditional artistic objectives?
Surely, these are the real questions to be asked by those con-
fronting, with any degree of honesty, the discouraging confusions of our time.

Having placed these burdens upon the work of art, how
are they to be borne? *The Connection,* as I have said, cannot
wholly perform so difficult a task. I intended to suggest, by
my earlier references to *The Golden Notebook,* that Doris
Lessing's massive novel makes a significant, and exemplary,
attempt to deal with the questions just posed. We begin
with Anna's basic assumption that her capacity to create
order in the writing of fiction is dependent on — indeed
equivalent to — her capacity to order not only her own life
but also the context in which that life is lived: society,
history — in short, everything. The tasks of life and fiction
are thus irrevocably entwined; they are, in fact, the same.
Thus literature is no longer an imitation of reality but a component of reality itself. To bear up under all this will, of necessity, take a fiction of both psychological depth and universal scope; it will need to plunge us into apparent chaos
and allow us to discover if not order at least the meaning of
that chaos. The attempt to create such a supernovel is an act
of supreme arrogance. Yet the artist's desire to become

superman has played an important role in the history of the
novel; a role to which the works of Sterne, Balzac, Proust,
and Joyce bear eloquent witness.

With *The Golden Notebook*, Doris Lessing attempts
nothing less than to match the achievement of this company;
that is, to create a work which, by its very manner, will provide the definitive image of its time. *The Golden Notebook*
goes about its task by alternating a series of narrative chapters entitled *Free Women*, written by an omniscient observer, with entries from the various notebooks kept by
Anna, the main character of *Free Women*. Each of Anna's
notebooks is exclusively devoted to one aspect of her life —
politics, writing, and so forth, for she feels her life to be in
pieces, its various functions split beyond any hope of reconciliation. Well on in *The Golden Notebook*, we make the
discovery that the *Free Women* chapters are, in fact, an
autobiographical novel written by Anna, based on, yet differ-
ing in detail from, her notebooks. The notebooks themselves
are an apparent patchwork which includes some of everything: reportage, clippings from newspapers, political and
philosophical reflections, literary criticism, parodies of many
styles, automatic writing, a novel within a novel — why go
on? Anna's novel, *Free Women*, is an attempt, for one thing,
to objectify, to give narrative flow and substance, to her personal obsessions; for another, to prove that her life is ordered
by more than either the private concerns of her neuroses or
the unyielding enormities of public life — both being certain
instruments of chaos. But the rather neat, almost genteel,
ordering of *Free Women* cannot bear the weight of its subject matter. By itself, it is unreal, thin; indeed, almost fit for
the pages of the more sophisticated women's magazines. And
so the chaos of the notebooks must always intrude if we are
not to falsify reality; for *Free Women* represents no more

than a provisional ordering, an hypothesis which does not quite account for the messy facts.

It is then the measure of *The Golden Notebook*'s fidelity to contemporary experience that it does not, finally, reconcile our sense of chaos with our yearning for order. The book forces us to the awareness — though hardly the acceptance — that one burden of freedom, both in life and in art, is that chaos and order must share a less than happy existence: We are irrevocably split. There is a point, recorded in one of the notebooks, where Anna, about to quit the Communist Party, finds herself in a discussion with Jack, a fellow Party member. She tells him:

Humanism stands for the whole person, the whole individual, striving to become as conscious and responsible as possible about everything in the universe. But now you sit there, quite calmly, and as a humanist you say that due to the complexity of scientific achievement the human being must never expect to be whole, he must always be fragmented.

In joining the Party, Anna, had hoped to unify ideology with action, her private life with politics. Yet, as Jack tells her, consciousness and history do not necessarily travel in parallel lines. We have yet to absorb the consequences of the Cartesian doubt into the ordinary routine of our lives. The consequences of this fragmentation, we are shown by *The Golden Notebook*, strike at our most basic concerns. "What is terrible," Anna writes in one of the notebooks,

is that after every one of the phases of my life is finished, I am left with no more than some banal commonplace that everyone knows: in this case, that woman's emotions are all still fitted for a kind of society that no longer exists. My deep emotions, my real ones, are to do with my relationship with a man. One man. But I don't live that kind of life, and I know few women who do. So what I feel is irrelevant and silly. . . . I am always coming to the conclusion that my real emotions are foolish, I am always having, as it were, to cancel myself out. I ought to be like a man, caring more for my work than for people; I ought to put my work first, and take men as they come, or find an ordinary comfortable man for bread and butter reasons — but I won't do it, I can't be like that. . . .

The freedom of choice allowed Anna by her consciousness is, in fact, forbidden her by the dictates of the historical situation.

Recall one of the lessons of *The Connection:* The freedom characteristic of our modernity is likely to become the cross we must bear. Yet who would want to do without it? Who is ready to give up the possibilities of the present, as well as its horrors? Anna's exchange with her psychoanalyst, recorded in one of the notebooks, is to the point:

"And I don't want to be told when I suddenly have a vision (though God knows it's hard enough to come by) of a life that isn't full of hatred and fear and envy and competition every minute of the night and the day that this is simply the old dream of the golden age brought up to date. . . ."

"Isn't it?" she said smiling.

"No, because the dream of the golden age is a million times more powerful because it's possible, just as total destruction is possible. Probably *because* both are possible."

We are led to ask whether the arts, whether intellectuals, are capable of dealing with these possibilities. Perhaps not. Surely not with any real degree of consistency, nor with any sense of continuity: Our creations and our social ideas, though often brilliant or powerful, no longer turn into traditions; like the latest fad in painting, they merely become the fashion of a year, or a month; our artists are incapable of dealing with the immediate past, either becoming its captives or wiping it away. The Anna of *Free Women* stops writing, gives up the role of intellectual, and devotes her life to social work. Her act is a quiet attempt — after the intensity of her Communist involvement — to attain a measure of pastoral union, to create the semblance of order in her own life. On the other hand, the Anna of the notebooks writes *Free Women,* which, not having the potentiality of affect, is little more, in its neat ordering of events, than an act of self-assurance. Thus both in life and in art there are no resolutions, but, instead, a multitude — or a total absence — of possibilities. In placing these disparate (perhaps irreconcilable) elements alongside each other, Doris Lessing has allowed herself the opportunity of creating a very true — and very great — work of art. *The Golden Notebook,* it should be clear, is singular; its method, like *The Connection's,* cannot be effectively repeated; it is incapable of creating a tradition, nor can it, finally, guide other writers in their search for order: Yet this, precisely, is the nature of its exemplary character.

What, then, is to be the fate of order in the arts? How presumptuous of me to even ask. Both art and life thrive on surprises. After all, freedom — that erratic child of the skeptical doubt — is our dominant idea. Generations of artists and intellectuals have seen to that. Rousseau has taught us that without freedom we are less than human: Then allowing for our humanity, we cannot know what the future holds, for our actions must be free. This I welcome, notwithstanding the real possibility of chaos, or even of extinction. Of one thing I am fairly sure — or at least not uncertain: Any meaningful attempt to create order will need to rise from the deepest wellsprings of its creator's personal commitment; in spite of its subjective origins, it will also need to concern itself with the generality of human experience; and, if we are to survive, hopefully devote itself to our ultimate — no, our present — well-being.

INDEX

[327]